Pricing, Valuation and Systems

To
Lillian R. Tool
and
Paul D. Bush

Pricing, Valuation and Systems

Essays in Neoinstitutional Economics

Marc R. Tool

Professor Emeritus of Economics
California State University, Sacramento

Edward Elgar

Published by
Edward Elgar Publishing Limited
Gower House
Croft Road
Aldershot
Hants GU11 3HR
England

Edward Elgar Publishing Company
Old Post Road
Brookfield
Vermont 05036
USA

British Library Cataloguing in Publication Data
Tool, Marc R.
    Pricing, Valuation and Systems: Essays in
    Neoinstitutional Economics
    I. Title
    330.155

Library of Congress Cataloguing in Publication Data
Tool, Marc R.
        Pricing, valuation and systems : essays in neoinstitutional
    economics / Marc R. Tool.
            p.   cm.
        Includes index.
        1. Institutional economics.   I. Title.
    HB99.5.T67   1995
    330.1—dc20   94–37306
                                                                    CIP

ISBN 1 85278 976 X

Printed and bound in Great Britain by
Biddles Ltd, Guildford and King's Lynn

Contents

Preface

The essays and papers collected in this volume were written over the last four years or so in response to what are for me profound and disturbing trends and developments in the application of standard neoclassical theory to real problems of non- or malperformance in the provisioning processes here and abroad.

First, I have a compelling realization that this orthodox economic theory in general, because of its steadily diminishing relevance in explaining behaviour and offering solutions to continuing problems, has increasing difficulty in sustaining its claims to mainstream dominion. The need seems urgent to reintroduce, as an alternative approach, sources and attributes of neoinstitutionalism (an American heterodox perspective in economics), and provisionally to compare and contrast its methods of inquiry and analytical constructs with those of orthodox neoclassicists. In Part I, two chapters address these concerns.

Second, I have become increasingly persuaded that, in particular, the neoclassical core theory of pricing, as the standard analysis of allocation in the provisioning process, has itself become the major barrier to credible and pertinent analysis of real problems and their solution. Since poor theory is replaced only by better theory, it seems important to me to bring heterodox neoinstitutionalist inquiry to bear in the search for an alternative, and more cogent, theory of pricing and costing. Other heterodox scholars – Post Keynesians, Social Economists, Radical Institutionalists – express similar reservations and ambitions. In Part II, five chapters address this concern.

Third, I have watched with others in dismay as, in response to requests for economic guidance, this same neoclassical orthodoxy has been used to address the economic chaos that has accompanied the dissolution of historic political systems in Eastern Europe and the former Soviet Union. The proffered 'market shock' approach has generated and/or aggravated extraordinary dislocations in the provisioning processes. The predictable consequences of inflation, unemployment, increasing inequalities, industrial disintegration and political instability are thought to be only transitional shortfalls. 'Stay the course' with the market model, it is alleged, and a modern productive European-type economy will emerge. I argue, as do others, that the recipe of orthodoxy is not generating a digestible product. In Part III, three chapters address these concerns.

The collective purpose of these papers, however, is not primarily to offer yet another comprehensive critique of orthodoxy, although evaluative comments on neoclassicism are included in several chapters. Neither do I presume to generate *the* alternative approach to that of neoclassicists. Rather my intent is to contribute to the development of a newly invigorated research agenda especially for younger scholars. Their collective efforts might, after a time, refine and expand neoinstitutionalism into a more persuasive approach to inquiry in political economy and hopefully fashion more pragmatic theories of pricing and costing. I wish to lend support to inquiries into these new and promising directions that are already being pursued by many whose work is cited in the papers comprising this volume. I raise questions, offer observations and propose some grounded tenets that may help encourage an acceleration of neoinstitutionalist inquiry into pricing, costing, valuation and systems.

There is one characteristic of these papers that is for the most part atypical: for some readers it will be unfamiliar; for some readers it may even be uncomfortable. It is the insistence on my part that all social inquiry is and must be normative as well as positive. I contend repeatedly that if inquiry is purposive, it is and must be value-laden. Social inquiry is addressed to problem solving as its *raison d'être*. No one can conceive of a problem except as one distinguishes between what is and what ought to be. What is going on here? What ought to go on here? What can be done about it? Any perception of 'oughtness' must include some conception of social value. Those conceptions of social value, to be credible, must be cognitively formulated, evidentially grounded and analytically assessed. I argue that *normative* premises and principles must be addressed directly and continuously in pricing decisions, costing decisions and all other decisions involving discretion over the institutional fabric of any economy. All of the papers included herein confront the social value aspects directly. Instrumental value theory, as developed by neoinstitutionalists, is reintroduced and explored in several different contexts and settings.

Of the ten papers included, six were originally published elsewhere (as noted in the following acknowledgments); four are published here for the first time. They were written at different times for somewhat different audiences. In consequence, a few redundancies will be found. I have left these intact as reinforcements of certain constructs in the expectation that some readers, not already familiar with the neoinstitutionalist literature, may find their brief reiteration to be instructive. In addition, I have used the opportunity to make some minor revisions in manuscripts as originally presented or as published elsewhere.

Turning now happily to a recognition of those to whom I am heavily indebted in the preparation of this volume, I wish to acknowledge the extraordinary contribution of my friend and colleague, Paul D. Bush, to this collection of papers. He has read and commented at length on every paper. I am deeply grateful for his theoretical insights, incisive critiques and continuing intellectual encouragement. I am most pleased to dedicate this volume to him in warm appreciation of two decades of professional and personal support.

In addition I wish most sincerely to thank James L. Dietz, F. Gregory Hayden, John F. Henry, Philip A. Klein, Frederic S. Lee, Edythe S. Miller, Jerry L. Petr, Yngve Ramstad, James A. Swaney, Harry M. Trebing and L. Randall Wray for most helpful comments and suggestions (many of which have been incorporated) or other assistance on one or more of the included papers. Of course, none of the above mentioned scholars is accountable for any remaining deficiencies.

I wish also most sincerely to thank Edward Elgar for encouraging the preparation of the volume and supporting its development at every stage. I am most appreciative as well of the continuing assistance and technical guidance provided by Julie Leppard and other editors at Edward Elgar Publishing Ltd.

I also wish gratefully to acknowledge the publishers who have kindly given permission to reprint material they originally published:

To Kluwer Academic Publishers (Boston) for permission to republish 'An Institutionalist Mode of Inquiry: Limitations of Orthodoxy' from Philip A. Klein (ed.), *The Role of Economic Theory* (copyright 1994) as Chapter 2 in this volume.

To Edward Elgar Publishing Ltd (Aldershot UK) for permission to republish 'Contributions to an Institutional Theory of Price Determination' from Geoffrey M Hodgson and Ernesto Screpanti (eds), *Rethinking Economics: Markets, Technology and Economic Evolution* (copyright 1991) as Chapter 3 in this volume.

To the *Journal of Economic Issues* (University of Nebraska, Lincoln) for permission to republish (1) 'Pricing and Valuation' from Vol. 27 (copyright June 1993) as Chapter 4 in this volume; (2) 'Reflections on Social Value Theory and Regulation' from Vol. 24 (copyright June 1990) as Chapter 7 in this volume; and (3) a lengthy quote from Vol. 15 (copyright December 1981) in Chapter 9.

To St. Martin's Press, Incorporated (New York) for permission to republish *in* the US, 'An Institutionalist View of the Evolution of Economic Systems' from Kurt Dopfer and Karl-F. Raible (eds), *The Evolution of Economic Systems* (copyright 1990); and to The Macmillan Press, Ltd (Basingstoke UK) for permission to republish *outside* the US, 'An Institutionalist View of the Evolution of Economic Systems' from Kurt Dopfer and Karl-F. Raible (eds), *The Evolution of Economic Systems* (copyright 1990) as Chapter 8 in this volume.

To the *Review of International Political Economy* (Department of Politics, The University, Newcastle upon Tyne UK) for permission to republish 'Institutional Adjustment and Instrumental Value' from Vol. 1 (copyright November 1994) as Chapter 9 in this volume.

Finally, I most affectionately dedicate this volume also to my wife, Lillian, who for over half a century has provided loving and continuing personal support and unfailing professional encouragement.

PART I

Introduction

1. A neoinstitutionalist perspective

No thoughtful student of public affairs can be complacent in a world where one worker in three is jobless or in poverty,[1] where economic systems in the developed world under- or mis-perform, where those in the underdeveloped world founder from internal struggles and flawed Western advice. How ought one to address the shortfall in aggregate provisioning of real income between what our social knowledge and technological capabilities suggest is possible and feasible and what our present institutional structures provide? To what theories, models or systems can one turn for guidance in understanding the actual determinants of economic well-being? What analytical approach(es) will provide pertinent constructs to help guide the formulation of policies to restore and enhance the productive process?

This volume invites fresh consideration of basic attributes of *neoinstitutional* political economy – an integration of the American scholarly traditions of the pragmatic instrumentalism of John Dewey and of the heterodox institutionalism of Thorstein Veblen.[2] Neoinstitutionalism, as a mode of inquiry and policy determination, is, in my view, a candidate to provide some of the above mentioned guidance. These papers are intended to demonstrate, in particular, that in fundamental areas of inquiry, neoinstitutionalism offers a theoretically more credible, and experientially more applicable, approach to the amelioration or resolution of systemic economic problems than does mainstream neoclassicism.

This introductory chapter is addressed especially to those unfamiliar with the American institutionalist contributions. It briefly reintroduces this neoinstitutional perspective by canvassing many of its major intellectual sources for fundamental and applicable analytical principles and constructs.

My task, then, is to present a theoretical sketch encompassing major contributions from pivotal scholars that contribute to and/or undergird the subject matter of the succeeding chapters. In so doing I provide elements of an encompassing framework in which the following more particular neoinstitutionalist considerations of methodology, price theory, cost theory, value theory and system analysis may be placed. Since elements of knowledge take on meaning only when placed in the continuum or context of which they are a part, this chapter is intended to provide a relevant universe of discourse for the subsequent more detailed analyses.

3

Implicit throughout are my perception and contention that the present circumstances call, with some urgency, for heterodox scholars and theorists to continue to build, extend and refine a comprehensive alternative analytical approach to that of neoclassicism. I do not see this effort to extend and refine neoinstitutionalism as providing a revision of or an addition to mainstream theory and practice. When systematically compared, indeed, most of the philosophic underpinnings, governing tenets and principles of neoinstitutionalism are quite incompatible with neoclassical assumptions and dictums. Problem identifications and resolutions are therefore also substantively divergent. There is perhaps no more significant agenda for neoinstitutionalist scholars to pursue than directly to confront neoclassical formulations with their own alternative analyses and policies wherever and whenever, in pursuit of problem resolutions, such opportunities occur or can be created. The material in this volume reflects the spirit and intent of this necessarily rival juxtaposing of construct and policy.[3]

CONTRIBUTORS TO NEOINSTITUTIONALISM

The following is a brief review of the institutional theoretical formulations of Thorstein B. Veblen, John Dewey, John R. Commons, from the pre-World War II period, and those of Clarence E. Ayres and J. Fagg Foster from the post-World War II period.

Thorstein B. Veblen (1857–1929)

By common consent, Veblen was the founder of institutional economics, although he did not name it.[4] Four aspects of his work are of particular significance here.[5]

First, his critique of the prevailing orthodoxy early in this century was and remains devastating. Veblen's view that the scientific mode of inquiry was of necessity post-Darwinian[6] cast doubt on the explanatory adequacies of all pre-Darwinian epistemologies, including the methodology of neoclassicism. He rejected orthodoxy for its pre-Darwinian underpinnings in natural law and characterized its major theoretical contributions as teleological, hedonistic, taxonomic and tautological.[7] He observed that human nature was culturally emergent and reflected identifiable contrasting proclivities (he called them 'instincts').[8] On the one hand there are the parental bent (solicitude), workmanship (taking pains) and idle curiosity (seeking knowledge) that support the social process; on the other hand there are predation (exploitation) and emulation (invidious display) that are destructive 'contaminants' of the social process.[9]

Second, Veblen fashioned a dichotomy that contrasted two different kinds of behaviour and valuation in institutions, distinguishing between those aspects of behaviour which support the provisioning process and those that 'sabotage' it. He pursued this dichotomy in a variety of applications. Examples are business versus industry, ceremony versus technology, ownership versus production, salesmanship versus workmanship and vested interests versus the common man.[10] Veblen disclaimed any normative intent or characterization, but subsequent scholars have used his categorization of proclivities and his basic dichotomy as an initial formulation of an empirically-grounded social value theory. Its further development has been a major focus of neoinstitutional scholarship.

Third, Veblen understood clearly the continuing use of achieved power in the economy. Business as he observed it was a system of power. Reflecting upon the history of trusts, corporate giants, and 'coalition[s] of business concerns', he contended that the pecuniary goals and predatory behaviour of businessmen constituted a 'conscientious withdrawal of efficiency' in quest of 'free income'.[11] He recognized that achieved power could be and was used to set prices 'on the basis of what the traffic will bear'.[12]

Finally, in all of his writings, Veblen identified the growth of knowledge and its application in the form of technology as the primary source of change and growth in an economy. He believed that the growth of post-Darwinian science would make technological expansion feasible. Such technologies held out great promise of enhancing the economic welfare of the community at large. The business system and its 'captains of industry' held such productive potential captive and permitted only those levels and forms of production that did not threaten the continuity of their own control.

John Dewey (1859–1952)

Commonly acknowledged as the dean of 20th-century American philosophers, Dewey's contribution to neoinstitutionalism consists principally of a theory of warranted knowledge, a theory of social value and a theory of democracy.[13]

In his most mature and sophisticated characterization of social inquiry,[14] Dewey provides a model of scientific social inquiry that is processual, pragmatic and instrumental (see Chapter 2 below). He perceives inquiry to be a continuing exploration of conceptual and factual elements.[15] Inductive, deductive and abductive procedures jointly lead to evidentially grounded explanatory propositions. Hypotheses are a particularly creative facet of inquiry. Once fashioned, they guide inquiry in the quest for conjugate correlation between concept and observed conduct, between theory and established fact. These correlative efforts almost always lead to continuing recasting and reshaping of the hypotheses being considered in search of those that provide the most defensible explanations of the causal phenomena under review. Outcomes of inquiry are tentative truths – in Dewey's words, 'warranted assertions'. Dewey's model renders irrelevant, for problem-solving purposes, ways of 'knowing' rooted in mystic intuition, private knowledge or other non-evidential sources of premises and constructs. In his critique of 'abstract rationalism', Dewey contends that deductive reasoning (as in neoclassical orthodoxy), that depends upon logical forms, a priori constructs and given ends, is analytically deficient. In his critique of 'sensationalist empiricism', Dewey contends that inductive reasoning that denies the need for logical forms and theory guidance is also deficient.[16] Instrumental reasoning continuously juxtaposes conceptual and evidential elements in search of generalities that actually explain in causal terms what they purport to explain. In quest of processual means-consequence linkages, the *process* of instrumental inquiry disallows the admission of either means or consequences from any non-experiential realm outside of the inquiry process itself.

Dewey's contribution to the formulation of an instrumental theory of social value is unique in social and philosophical inquiry. What Dewey demonstrated is that the conventional normative-positive dichotomy – fact versus value, science versus ethics, means versus ends – is inadmissible in modern scientific inquiry. All instrumental reasoning incorporates valuational aspects. In this sense, social inquiry is and must be normative as well as positive. This 'instrumentalness' is demonstrated in his treatment of the means-ends or means-consequence continuum. Means and ends (or consequences) are each inescapable facets of inquiry.[17] As the means are chosen, so are the ends defined. Since inquiry is purposive, 'what ought' is inherently involved in determining 'what is'. For Dewey, the source of determining what is 'better' or 'worse' is not subjective feeling states or introspective or intuitive utilities,[18] but what warranted knowledge indicates will most probably restore congruity, continuity and efficiency to the social process and its individual members. Dewey spent much of his professional life seeking reforms in educational institutions that would transform educational experience into a problem-solving process involving instrumental reasoning.

Dewey's theory of democracy is one of his most important contributions, revolutionary in its implications. He saw democracy as the community's principal vehicle of institutional adjustment and reform. As people experience problems with existing rules and practices, they turn to governments as the major communal source with power to change the rules. Dewey explains how 'publics' emerge and request 'oversight and regulation'.[19] According to the democratic principle, those who receive the incidence of policy must themselves be in a position to seek revisions of structure. 'Democratic political forms,' he observed, 'rest back upon the idea that no man or limited set of men is wise enough or good enough to rule others without their consent.'[20]

In sum, I argue, following Dewey, that 'the democratic mode of policy determination subsumes the belief that people generally are educable; governance is by consent of the governed; restraints are self-imposed; non-discriminatory participation is provided for; those exercising discretion are held accountable; and power held is insecure'.[21] When, in the following chapters, accountability is called for on pricing power, costing power or system transformation, the basic democratic rationale implied is a Deweyian derivative.

John R. Commons (1862–1945)

John R. Commons arguably had more direct influence on shaping the structural character of the American economy in this century than any other professional scholar.[22] He and his cohorts and students generated much of the labour, social welfare and regulatory legislation in the period from the 1920s through the 1960s, initially at the state level (Wisconsin), then at the national level.

That contribution reflected the development of theoretical insights based on pragmatic knowledge, much of which was gained through case-study analyses of actual problematic breakdowns in the provisioning process. His theory of political economy 'centers in a distinctive way around the issues presented by social control, ... collective action, the reality of economic power, conflicts of interest and social valuation'.[23] These theoretical insights continue to serve neoinstitutionalists.[24] Ramstad has characterized the perspective as 'holistic'.[25] Of particular significance here are his views on inquiry as processual and interdisciplinary, and on institutional adjustment.

Commons conceived the economy to be a processual continuum providing the means of life and experience. It is comprised of an ever-changing fabric of 'going concerns' guided by discretionary agents. The mode of inquiry itself, then, must also be processually conceived, constituted and pursued. For him, inquiry must be multi-disciplinary; it must encompass not only the provisioning economy, but also the sociological aspects of work, the legal rules that order economic behaviour, and the political and judicial processes of changing economic rules.

Commons conceived institutions to be 'collective action in control of individual action'.[26] Institutional adjustment, he believed, involved changing the working rules that ordered the provisioning process. What the rules specified were the terms and patterns of rights, duties and options in the actual exchange of ownership. Such exchanges were termed *transactions*. Transactions specify the terms of interaction between and among individuals (see Chapter 6 below).

Three basic forms of transactions were bargaining, managerial and ration-ing.[27] 'Bargaining transactions occur between persons who are legal equals.' Each is equal before the law but, if economically unequal, one may coerce the other. Managerial transactions occur between persons who are formally in an inferior-superior or command-obedience relationship. Rationing transac-tions are also legally specified inferior-superior relationships but exchange is accomplished through negotiation, usually by authorized third parties. The fundamental insight embedded in this formulation is that transactions occur as stipulated decisions of empowered persons proceeding according to estab-lished rules. And these rules that correlate exchange behaviour are the pri-mary object of economic and social reform. Atomistic, unfettered market exchange as postulated by neoclassical orthodoxy is rare. Commons posits a discretionary economy in which political and legal processes permit the continuous rewriting of the rules of transactions.

Commons offered a theory of 'reasonable' as opposed to 'instrumental' value (the latter appears below in several chapters).[28] He operated with a negotiational psychology, believing that conflicts could be resolved among and between individuals in a spirit of 'give and take' or agreed compromise. He evidently made little analytical or normative use of Veblen's dichotomy. He seems not to have probed extensively into the subjective sentiments of negotiators. But if one examines the character of the legislative reforms which he and his colleagues advocated over the years – for example, empow-ering workers through union organizations and collective bargaining, work-men's safety and compensation programmes, income protection against un-employment, regulation of public utilities – their *implicit* reflection of instru-mental warrant seems evident.

Finally, Commons, following Dewey, was a strong advocate of democratic rule making. He held that governmental bodies must regularly be the vehicle for social and economic reform. More perhaps than Dewey, he attributed a constructive role to the court system for rewriting the working rules govern-ing 'going concerns' so as to serve the collective public purpose.

Clarence E. Ayres (1891–1972)

Of the post-World War II institutionalists, Ayres was among the most prolific writers and certainly one of the most influential instructors of his generation. As founder of the 'Cactus school' of institutional economics (University of Texas, Austin), Ayres, with his students, revitalized the institutionalist tradi-tion of scholarship, especially in the American West.[29] My concern here is with his philosophical contributions and his theory of economic develop-ment.[30]

Ayres was one of the first to note the similarities in the contributions of Dewey and Veblen. He integrated their philosophical contributions by blending, I have suggested, 'their epistemological approaches encompassing the application of scientific modes of reasoning to social analysis'; by incorporating 'their recognition that human nature is not given but emergent, and a product of the interaction of individual and culture'; by adopting 'their processual perspective of the social order as evolutionary, development and amenable' to human direction; and by accepting 'their implicit (with Veblen) or explicit (with Dewey) recognition that inquiry is inherently normative as well as positive'.[31]

Given this philosophic mind set, Ayres generated a 'master analytical construct that is at once definitive and incisive for his subsequent analyses'. For Ayres, 'two forces seem to be present in all human behaviour in all ages: one progressive, dynamic, productive of cumulative change; the other counter-progressive, static, inhibitory of change'.[32] One force is technological behaviour; the other force is ceremonial behaviour.

In this recasting of the Veblenian dichotomy, Ayres gives technology an enlarged referential content. It includes 'all human activities involving the use of tools – all sorts of tools' together with the acquisition of skills and their employment. Growth in technology is cumulative and processual; it emerges from the invention and discovery of new ways of combining and integrating tools, ideas, instruments, materials, and the like.[33]

Technological growth and development are impaired by ceremonial behaviour. Ceremonialism includes, in addition to myth and ritual, a wide range of cultural rigidities that tended to preserve the status quo including hierarchies, mores, ideologies, indoctrination and ceremonial adequacy, all of which are 'past-binding'.[34] Accordingly, he believed that the growth of cultures and economies is enhanced by instrumental behaviour and retarded by ceremonial behaviour.

A significant application and incorporation of these ideas appear in Ayres's theory of economic development. His characterization of the determinants of development included the following four continuing principles: (1) '[T]he process of economic development is indivisible and irresistible'; both technological and institutional innovations were significant. (2) '[T]he technological revolution spreads in inverse proportion to institutional resistance.' Europeans took their tools and know-how to all parts of the world. Where cultural resistance was minimal, development 'spurted', as in North America. (3) '[T]he creation of human capital' is critical; 'the most important factor in the economic life of any people is the educational level … of the community'. '[A]n ignorant and unskilled community cannot advance except by acquiring knowledge and skills.' (4) The 'technological revolution brings its own values to fruition, to the detriment of all local and tribal value systems'.

'[V]alues engendered in technological process are universal values.' Scientific truth 'is a processual, or operational, or instrumental – tool-defined – conception of truth'.[35]

J. Fagg Foster (1907–1985)

J. Fagg Foster was a major figure in the 'oral tradition' of institutional economics and one of the more prominent graduates of the 'Cactus school'. He was an exceptionally able and provocative instructor but not a widely-published writer.[36] His creative achievements (for example, a debt-creation theory of capital formation; his view of Keynes as an institutionalist) were presented as definitive lectures. He absorbed the philosophic and analytic contributions of Veblen, Dewey, Ayres and, to some extent, Commons to good effect. My consideration here is limited to four other foci of his scholarly work: his conception of institutional economics as the 'American contribution'; his recasting of instrumental value theory; his theory of institutional adjustment; and his theory of mixed economies. As will doubtless become evident, the present writer was one of Foster's students.

Foster saw the emergence of heterodox institutional economics in part as a product of Veblen's singular intellectual vision and personality and of a small group of intellectual dissidents. He saw it also as a cultural product of the pragmatic and practical habits of mind stimulated by the peculiar American experience in settling a relatively unoccupied continent.[37] The frontier experience, over a 300-year period, was a survivalist context in which pressures instrumentally to generate and apply new practical knowledge were constant. As Edythe Miller characterizes his position, 'the patina of use and wont with which particular work practices were imbued in established civilizations was inapplicable. Much of the ceremonial baggage was left behind or jettisoned after arrival in the new territory.'[38] Pressures to try new options and benefit from error, to experiment and innovate, were continuing. Miller adds: 'the frontier experience nurtured a skeptical attitude towards institutional continuity, and a receptive one about the ability of institutional adjustment to improve economic performance'.[39] The 'cake of custom' was unleavened; adaptability, circumventing custom, was the key to survival.[40] According to Foster, institutional economics, as Veblen began to articulate it, was the 'American contribution' to economic analysis.

Foster drank deeply from the Veblen-Dewey-Ayres well of insights on social value theory. He identified the value principle as 'the continuity and instrumental efficiency' of the social process.[41] Perhaps his most important contribution to this emerging value theory was his demonstration that virtually all institutions have elements of *both* instrumental (or technological) and ceremonial (or invidious) behaviour and valuation. The continuing task then is to induce institutional change that increases instrumental aspects and diminishes ceremonial or invidious ones. The early Ayres had dichotomized technology and institutions. Foster recognized that institutional correlation and coordination of behaviour were instrumentally essential and that institutions, though habit-ridden, could be modified to increase instrumental performance of economic activities.

Foster's theory of institutional adjustment (explored more fully in Chapter 9 below) was a distillation, partly from other theorists, of the conditions determining whether or not structural change in the political economy could achieve the outcomes sought.[42] Three constraints are operative in proposing institutional adjustments: (1) 'social problems can be solved only by adjusting the institutional structures ... to bring them into instrumentally efficient correlation with technological aspects of the problem';[43] the prevailing state of warranted knowledge determines what is feasible and desirable; (2) new institutional forms must be specified; existing interdependencies can be successfully revised only with the concurrence of those affected; (3) the rate, degree and extent of change must impinge as little as possible on those areas not deemed to be problematic.

Finally, Foster demonstrated that all operating economies are and must continue to be mixed economies. Their inevitable confrontation with problems – impairments in and obstructions to effectual provisioning – forces modification of existing patterns of correlated behaviour. The structural fabric is continuously revised and revamped. No 'pure' systems exist anywhere. All utopian designs, including the free enterprise model, are irrelevant as recipes to define what ought to be done. At issue, at any point then, is what changes in the existing mixed system may now be warranted by new knowledge about actual economic performance.

Out of the rich and insightful legacy sampled above, I attempt to reinvigorate a pragmatic and pertinent perspective, gather up conceptual tools of inquiry and address compelling theoretical issues and policy problems of the day.

Before moving directly to the topics of pricing, costing and system revisions as such, however, it will be instructive if I explicitly address, in the next chapter, the mode of inquiry of heterodox neoinstitutionalism, in specific contrast to that of orthodox neoclassicism. While methodological analyses may be less dramatic than, say, policy conflicts, their significance can hardly be overstated. *As the methodological model is chosen, so is the subsequent inquiry directed!* These contrasting frames of reference and modes of inquiry may suggest why and how it happens in policy explorations that those reflecting these divergent approaches sometimes have difficulty in communicating and often find little commonality in fashioning 'proper' policy initiatives.

NOTES

1. International Labor Organization (1994), p. A9.
2. Tool (1953), p. 4. I introduced the term 'neoinstitutionalism' to identify those institutional economists who, drawing on Thorstein Veblen, John Dewey, Clarence Ayres and Fagg Foster and their intellectual progeny, tend to utilize pragmatic instrumental analysis to explain economic behaviour and instrumental social value theory to appraise economic behaviour. This referential meaning of neoinstitutionalism has been widely accepted by neoinstitutionalists over the last four decades. However, evidently unaware of its established usage, some latter-day neoclassicists (Eggertsson 1990, p. 6) now use the term 'neoinstitutionalism' to refer to a modified neoclassical approach encompassing information and transaction costs and property rights constraints as a modest erosion of the 'protective belt of neoclassical economics'.
3. An addendum to the foregoing comment is that, given the dominion of neoclassicists over most US graduate schools in economics (curriculums, degree programmes), economic journals and support grants, neoinstitutionalists, in their professional graduate training, are compelled to become intimately familiar with neoclassicism. But the reverse is not the case. Formal graduate studies in institutional economics are exceptional, not commonplace. Moreover, with the gradual abandonment of history of thought courses in graduate programmes (often in response to demands for more extensive and sophisticated mathematical training), graduate degree candidates are rarely introduced to alternative perspectives, historical or contemporary. Indeed, given the rigidities and 'rigours' of neoclassical training and dominion, neoinstitutionalists must expect to continue to wage an uphill struggle, not only to generate a viable and credible alternative perspective, but also to get reasoned exposure and an even-handed hearing for their analyses and policy recommendations.
4. Evidently, Walton H. Hamilton (1919), in an address before the American Economic Association in 1918 entitled 'The Institutional Approach to Economic Theory', was the first to caption the inquiry approach of Veblen and his cohorts as *institutional economics* and to suggest its defining characterizations.
5. For additional material on Veblen, see Simich and Tilman (1985) and Ramstad (1994).
6. Veblen (1961), pp. 1–55.
7. Ibid, pp. 82–179.
8. Veblen (1946), pp. 25–47.
9. Ibid, pp. 38–52.
10. Tool (1986), pp. 36–7.
11. Veblen (1965), chs 1 and 2.
12. Veblen (1932), p. 261.
13. Tilman (1988), pp. 427–49; Tool (1994b).
14. Dewey (1938).
15. A particularly helpful summary is ibid, pp. 487–512.
16. Dewey (1938), pp. 419–41 and 513–35.
17. Dewey (1939a), pp. 40–50.
18. Ibid, pp. 6–33.
19. Dewey (1946).
20. Dewey (1939b), p. 401.
21. Tool (1994b), p. 157.
22. Rutherford (1994).
23. Parsons (1950), p. 342.
24. Ramstad (1986), pp. 1067–105; Schmid (1978), ch. 10.
25. Ramstad (1986).
26. Quoted in Ramstad (1986), p. 1074.
27. Parsons (1950), pp. 352–3.
28. Ramstad (1989).
29. Phillips (1994).

30. This segment draws directly on Tool (1994a), pp. 16–22.
31. Ibid, p. 17.
32. Ayres (1978), p. xiv.
33. Tool (1994a), p. 17.
34. Ibid, p. 18.
35. Ayres (1978), pp. xxvi–xxxiii.
36. Miller (1994).
37. For a somewhat divergent view, see Mayhew (1988), pp. 21–48.
38. Miller (1994), p. 257.
39. Ibid.
40. Brogan (1944), pp. 6–7.
41. Foster (1981a), pp. 899–905.
42. Foster (1981b), pp. 929–35.
43. Ibid, p. 932.

REFERENCES

Ayres, Clarence E. [1944] (1978), 'Foreword-1962', *The Theory of Economic Progress*, 3rd ed., Kalamazoo: New Issues Press, Western Michigan University.

Brogan, Dennis W. (1944), *The American Character*, New York: Alfred A. Knopf, Inc.

Commons, John R. (1950), *Economics of Collective Action*, New York: The Macmillan Co.

Dewey, John (1938), *Logic: The Theory of Inquiry*, New York: Holt, Rinehart and Winston.

Dewey, John (1939a), *Theory of Valuation*, Chicago: University of Chicago Press.

Dewey, John (1939b), 'The Democratic Form', in Joseph Ratner (ed.), *Intelligence in the Modern World: John Dewey's Philosophy*, New York: The Modern Library.

Dewey, John [1927] (1946), *The Public and Its Problems*, Chicago: Gateway Books.

Eggertsson, Thráinn (1990), *Economic Behaviour and Institutions*, Cambridge: Cambridge University Press.

Foster, J. Fagg (1981a), 'The relation between the theory of value and economic analysis', *Journal of Economic Issues*, **15**, December.

Foster, J. Fagg (1981b), 'The theory of institutional adjustment', *Journal of Economic Issues*, **15**, December.

Hamilton, Walton H. (1919), 'The institutional approach to economic theory', *American Economic Review*, **9**, March.

International Labor Organization (1994), 'Job crisis grips globe, U.N. says', *The Sacramento Bee*, 7 March.

Mayhew, Anne (1988), 'The Beginnings of Institutionalism', in Marc R. Tool (ed.), *Evolutionary Economics I: Foundations of Institutional Thought*, Armonk, N.Y.: M.E. Sharpe.

Miller, Edythe S. (1994), 'Foster, J. Fagg', in Geoffrey M. Hodgson, Warren J. Samuels and Marc R. Tool (eds), *The Elgar Companion to Institutional and Evolutionary Economics*, Aldershot: Edward Elgar. Hereafter cited as *The Elgar Companion*.

Parsons, Kenneth H. (1950), 'John R. Commons' Point of View', in John R. Commons, *The Economics of Collective Action*, New York: The Macmillan Co.

Phillips, Ronnie J. (1994), 'Institutional Economics, Texas School of', in *The Elgar Companion*.

Ramstad, Yngve (1986), 'A pragmatist's quest for holistic knowledge: the scientific methodology of John R. Commons', *Journal of Economic Issues*, **20**, December.

Ramstad, Yngve (1989), '"Reasonable value" versus "instrumental value": competing paradigms in institutional economics', *Journal of Economic Issues*, **23**, September.

Ramstad, Yngve (1994), 'Veblen, Thorstein', in *The Elgar Companion*.

Ratner, Joseph (1939) (ed.), *Intelligence in the Modern World: John Dewey's Philosophy*, New York: The Modern Library.

Rutherford, Malcolm (1994), 'Commons, John R.', in *The Elgar Companion*.

Schmid, A. Allan (1978), *Property, Power and Public Choice*, New York: Praeger Publishers.

Simich, Jerry L. and Tilman, Rick (1985), *Thorstein Veblen: A Reference Guide*, Boston: G.K. Hall & Co.

Tilman, Rick (1988), 'The Neoinstitutional Theory of Democracy', in Marc R. Tool (ed.), *Evolutionary Economics I: Foundations of Institutional Thought*, Armonk, N.Y.: M.E. Sharpe.

Tool, Marc R. (1953), *The Philosophy of Neo-institutionalism: Veblen. Dewey, Ayres* (PhD dissertation), Boulder: University of Colorado, (unpublished).

Tool, Marc R. (1986), *Essays in Social Value Theory*, Armonk, N.Y.: M.E. Sharpe.

Tool, Marc R. (1994a), 'Ayres, Clarence E.', in *The Elgar Companion*.

Tool, Marc R. (1994b), 'Dewey, John', in *The Elgar Companion*.

Veblen, Thorstein B. [1904] (1932), *The Theory of Business Enterprise*, New York: Charles Scribner's Sons.

Veblen, Thorstein B. [1914] (1946), *The Instinct of Workmanship*, New York: The Viking Press.

Veblen, Thorstein B. [1919] (1961), *The Place of Science in Modern Civilization*, New York: Russell and Russell.

Veblen, Thorstein B. [1921] (1965), *The Engineers and the Price System*, New York: Augustus M. Kelley.

2.   A neoinstitutionalist mode of inquiry*

Who can deny that the discipline of economics is in vigorous ferment? Scholars both within and outside the mainstream tradition recognize that the fundamental neoclassical methodology and its theoretical applications are in important respects inadequate and inappropriate.

Scholars within the orthodox tradition seek more pertinent explanations and greater relevance: Arthur Okun analyses an economy of price setters, not price takers, in labour and commodity markets;[1] Herbert Simon addresses 'bounded rationality' as a behavioural approach to economic choice making;[2] Douglass North wishes to imbed a theory of institutions, combining behavioural and transaction cost analyses, in neoclassical theory;[3] Oliver Williamson joins law, economics and organization theory to enhance understanding of corporate decision making;[4] and Frank Hahn expects to see more historical and evolutionary elements in conventional analysis.[5]

Heterodox scholars outside the orthodox tradition offer alternative approaches to neoclassical scholarship: Philip Klein explains why institutionalists insist that power as discretion must be a part of economic inquiry;[6] Harry Trebing explores the impact of orthodoxy on regulatory theory and offers institutionalist alternatives on pricing and control;[7] Thomas DeGregori rejects the endowment theory of resources and instead includes technological determination of resources in analyses of development;[8] Randall Wray offers a Post Keynesian theoretical explanation of an endogenous money supply[9] and Alfred Eichner provides a pertinent theory of administered pricing in oligopolies,[10] among others.

Horrendous problems of malperformance and restructuring in both rich and poor countries stimulate further agonizing reappraisals of how scholars and policy framers 'do' economics.[11] A remark of Paul Homan's concerning institutionalists, made more than half a century ago, has contemporary relevance: 'They caused the whole structure of economic theory to be subjected to searching and critical scrutiny'.[12] Challengers now extend well beyond institutionalists. Contemporary economists, when called upon by governments to frame policy on such questions as accelerating growth, alternative pricing systems, resource creation, technological development, macroeco-

*Originally published in Philip A. Klein (ed.) (1994), *The Role of Economic Theory*, Dordrecht: Kluwer Academic Publishers. Reprinted with permission.

nomic stability, budgetary management, investment strategies, environmental impacts and the like, must also give contemporary orthodoxy 'searching and critical scrutiny', must self-consciously redefine and assess its relevance for policy guidance if problem amelioration or resolution is to occur.

At issue here is the character of the process of inquiry that will generate applicable theory. What model or approach to inquiry should be employed? How do and how should economists generate causal explanations as relevant theory? How does one distinguish good theory from bad theory? What are the tests of relevance? It is my purpose here to explore such questions.

This chapter consists of three sections. In the first, I present a neoinstitutionalist view of an instrumentally warranted theory-building process. In particular, I examine and in the main accept John Dewey's theory of inquiry (developed primarily in his *Logic: The Theory of Inquiry*) as the most credible and functionally useful mode of inquiry available for economists and social scientists. In the second section, I use this model as a standard with which to appraise orthodox constructs that contrast with and depart from warranted instrumental inquiry. Given present constraints, these considerations are limited to examples drawn from neoclassical economics, although a similar exercise could be undertaken for other paradigmatic formulations in political economy. In the final section, I address briefly the significance of impaired and obstructive theorizing in the process of inquiry. I suggest that flawed neoclassical theorizing leads to irrelevant definitions of economic problems, to inadequate explanations of phenomena examined, and to a denial of creative institutional options for problem resolutions. The fundamental purpose of this discussion, of course, is not to formulate ultimate solutions. Rather, it is to help keep inquiry into inquiry as a topic of high priority in the continuing quest for more pertinent and sophisticated economic theory.

I   DEWEY'S THEORY OF PRAGMATIC INSTRUMENTAL INQUIRY

In presenting this characterization of Dewey's theory of pragmatic instrumentalism,[13] I consider in turn the purposes, context, scope, character and outcomes of instrumental logic as a model of inquiry.[14] What Dewey contributes regarding social inquiry applies generally and directly to economic inquiry.

Purposes of Inquiry

For Dewey, the purposes of social inquiry derive directly from the continuum of human experience. Inquiry is invoked to remove doubts that arise about how to think and behave in particular settings. More specifically, inquiry is 'the controlled or directed transformation of an indeterminate situation [uncertain, unsettled, disturbed] into one that is so determinate in its constituent distinctions and relations as to convert the elements of the original situation into a unified whole'.[15] Doubt prompts questions. Inquiry is set in motion by the effort to answer such questions as 'why?' and 'how come?'

For Dewey, the logical attributes of inquiry emerge in the course of its conduct. '[L]ogical forms accrue to subject-matter when the latter is subject to controlled inquiry.'[16] Social inquiry is a quest to create or restore coherence and order, to recorrelate and reintegrate concept and conduct. Successful inquiry reduces or removes doubt, although in the process new doubts and questions most often arise.

Social inquiry, for Dewey, is addressed to problem solving. 'The indeterminate situation becomes problematic in the very process of being subjected to inquiry.'[17] It is a continuing effort to gain understanding of causally related phenomena in order to perceive the origin and nature of problems. It is a quest for comprehension of the determinants of problems as breakdowns, impairments, terminations, disorders, conflicts, and disrapport in and among the functions and structures comprising the social process. These include in particular the production and distribution of real income in the economy and the determination and administration of public policy in the polity. 'Inquiry is a progressive determination of a problem and its possible solution.'[18] Inquiry is purposive; its relevance is derived from its applicability to real problems affecting real people.

Context of Inquiry

Dewey attempted to formulate a model of social inquiry that would generate levels of causal explanation and understanding comparable to those achieved in the physical sciences. But he did not seek to develop a physics-mimicking, mechanistic approach,[19] as has evolved in neoclassical thought in the last century or so.[20] His mode of inquiry shows none of these attributes. Because the subject matter of social inquiry is human beliefs and conduct, with all their complexities, motivations and judgmental dimensions, Dewey thought that social inquiry was more difficult than physical inquiry. His drawing of parallels with physics is not fuelled by concerns of status or dominion; he is simply seeking comparable explanatory capacity in his quest for problem-solving capabilities for social theory.

Dewey's central concern was to generate philosophic undergirdings for a *social* science. The subject matter is person-person relations – behavioural patterns and reflections thereon. Individuals are both products and creators of culture. The object of social inquiry is the social process, the universe of person-culture interdependencies. Inquiry is addressed to this universe of emergent organisms and their cultural conditioning. Accordingly, it is concerned with cognitive and analytical perceptions of persons in these human relationships. Such inquiry encompasses theoretical constructs, existential materials, demonstrable connections, evidential grounding and reflective assessments. Conspicuously absent from this contextual frame of inquiry is any deference to extra-sensory, extra-experiential or teleological sources or relations of conduct. It is inquiry into real world problematic relations among persons.

Dewey believed that people generally have the inherent developmental capacity to perceive means-consequence connections. The institutionalist meaning of rationality is rooted in this generalized capacity. But such capacity develops and is enhanced only through the interaction of persons and culture. Cognitive, linguistic, motivational and behavioural capabilities are acquired through this interaction. People are both creatures of habit and discretionary agents. They are educable. They are tool-designing and tool-using organisms. They create conceptual and material tools as instruments with which to facilitate and expand both understanding and participation in a problem-solving context. All wants, tastes and preferences are acquired – unconsciously through conditioning and adaptation, and consciously as chosen and learned attributes. Many, if not most, become habitual.

People in their daily lives routinely engage in problem-solving reflections and actions: they convert doubts and concerns into questions; they explore the factual context in which questions arise; they review their own experience for clues and ideas about what is going on and how to proceed; they create modest conceptual and manipulative tools with which to extend their understanding and control; they consider alternative 'scenarios' to account for what they experience and expect; they focus on what seems to be the most plausible explanation among competing accounts; they select a course of action or response that attempts to answer the question raised and adjust conduct as seems necessary or desirable. Such activity is not an unfamiliar experience; it is commonplace. For Dewey, scientific social inquiry is mainly an effort to deal with more intricate and complex realms of causal connections than can be addressed through commonplace levels of understanding. As he put it: 'Scientific subject-matter and procedures grow out of the direct problems and methods of common sense, of practical uses and enjoyments, and ... react into the latter in a way that enormously refines, expands and liberates the contents and the agencies at the disposal of common sense'.[21]

Scope of Inquiry

The scope of scientific social inquiry for Dewey is broad and open-ended. Boundaries are not set a priori; dimensions are not predefined. The scope is not set by forces or determinants anterior or external to the inquiry process itself. On the contrary, the scope of pragmatic instrumental inquiry is set and reset in the context of conducting the inquiry process itself. Inquiry must encompass whatever is found, through inquiry, to be pertinent as significantly determining the conditions or problems brought under critical scrutiny. Inquiry is delimited by the identification and tracing out of causal determinants of problematic conditions, not by disciplinary boundaries.

By implication then, social science for Dewey is not compatible with or accommodative to nihilism, fatalism or any of a variety of determinisms which generate a priori monocausal accounts (such as psychological, environmental, geographical, historical, cultural and racial deterministic formulations). Neither does it include special, intuitive and private knowledge which is beyond the reach of communication or demonstration.[22] With Dewey, 'logical theory is liberated from the unobservable, transcendental and "intuitional"' ways of knowing.[23]

Character of Inquiry

The foregoing, of course, is only a prologue to comments on the character of Dewey's mode of inquiry, a pragmatic instrumental theory of knowledge. Dewey saw inquiry as a collective endeavour, a discretionary continuum, into which individual inquirers move and from which they emerge. Inquiry is a conjoint process of truth seeking. It is evolutionary, incremental, cumulative, instrumental and, indeed, even self-corrective in considerable measure. Dewey characterized the process as he perceived it to be actually engaged in by inquirers. He sought to characterize how thinkers actually respond to reflective doubts and behavioural questions that become matters of conscious and substantive concern.

Inquiry is a quest for causal comprehension. Observable linkages and regularities of experience, exhibiting complexities of causal relations – these are the object of the search. One may well begin with conceptual material, relate it to evidential material and emerge with revised conceptual material. However, the central concern is not the sequential ordering of conceptual and evidential material; it is the disclosure of their interdependence that has explanatory significance. Inquiry is a search for conjugate correlation between concept and conduct, between theory and fact, between explanatory constructs and evidence.

Dewey was not constrained by the conventional distinction between inductive and deductive constructs and materials. He did not impose a reductionistic deductive-inductive construct as a template. In social inquiry there is a necessary, continuing and interdependent moving of the mind between theoretical formulations and observed evidence in the search for increased understanding. Does the theory explain what it purports to explain? To elevate either the rational (deductive) or the empirical (inductive) aspect into a pre-eminent role is to abort the inquiry process. Inquiry demands operations of data acquisition and of conceptual analysis. The control of the process of inquiry requires that each of these operations be undertaken with reference to the other. Dewey argues that 'the distinction between induction and deduction does not lie [then] in the processes of inquiry but in the direction which the processes take – according as the objective is determination of relevant and effective existential data or relevant and effective interrelated conceptions'.[24]

Dewey's model of inquiry, moreover, encompasses substantial and continuing creativity. His particular, but by no means exclusive, locus of creativity in the inquiry process, reflecting the influence of Charles Sanders Peirce, is in the formulation of hypotheses – an abductive exercise. As Peirce explains: 'Abduction is the process of forming an explanatory hypothesis. It is the only logical operation which introduces any new idea; for induction does nothing but determine a value, and deduction merely evolves the necessary consequences of a pure hypothesis.'[25] Hypotheses are tentative, usually preliminary, formulations in ideational form of what a plausible, possible, even probable, causal accounting of observable relations could be. The creation of hypotheses calls for the most imaginative and perceptive recasting of prior knowledge and experience, analytical capabilities and anticipatory insights that can be marshalled. What is required is an evocative and judicious distillation of insight and understanding – an abductive creation – applied in a novel but demanding context.

Illustratively, consider the role and function of a medical diagnostician confronting a complex and difficult array of symptoms in a patient.[26] The habitual diagnostic characterization appears not to apply; it does not fit or serve; the condition of physical impairment continues. Inquiry is invoked. New tools of disclosure may be employed. These new tests may themselves alter conditions and modify the causal complexities. Possible alternative explanations are conceptually reviewed. New diagnostic insights generate the need for a fresh selection and ordering of evidences. The process of juxtaposing hypotheses and observed reality continues. Each recasting is tested for its explanatory capacity. The diagnostic responsibility is concurrently to create and sensitively to explore more definitive explanations and more confirming factual information. Ultimately, but provisionally, the diagnostician selects the hypothetical explanation which most completely accounts for the observed impairment and treats the condition so diagnosed. Creativity is thus invoked internal to the inquiry process; it also leavens that process. It is reflective of the continuously evolving experiential and ideational acquisitions in the diagnostician's mind.

Finally, Dewey saw that the creation of hypotheses was of special significance in inquiry. 'An hypothesis, once suggested and entertained, is developed in relation to other conceptual structures until it receives a form in which it can instigate and direct an experiment that will disclose precisely those conditions which have the maximum possible force in determining whether the hypothesis should be accepted or rejected.'[27] While the opportunity to conduct a controlled 'experiment' of the kind implied here may not be all that frequent in social and economic inquiry, the more general insight is crucial. For Dewey, hypotheses guide and direct inquiry; they set and revise the questions invoking inquiry. They contribute directly to the identification of relevant evidence, help arrange it for analysis, and offer implications of correspondence and significance. They must often be modified to establish and retain their applicability and suitability 'to interpret and organize the facts of the case'.[28] 'As a broad statement, no important scientific hypothesis has ever been verified in the form in which it was originally presented nor without very considerable revisions and modifications. The justification of such hypotheses has lain in their power to direct new orders of experimental observation and to open up new problems and new fields of subject-matter.'[29]

But the character of Dewey's theory of inquiry does not, as the foregoing might mistakenly imply, dismiss traditional and formal logics as being irrelevant or of no consequence. He did correctly challenge the claims of these logics to superiority and sufficiency. He did dispute their often accorded status as creators of eternal truths. For Dewey, logical forms and models were tools of inquiry; they were conceptual constructs to be used, as is any tool, in the operational tasks appropriate to their design and function. As conceptual tools, they are products of human invention in various times and places. Their usefulness is a function of their capacity to contribute to the coherent ordering and causal comprehension of phenomena under review. Dewey was not unmindful of, nor insensitive to, such formal logical concerns as internal consistency, dichotomous or dualistic relations, and the warrantability of deductive and inductive inferences. But the question of the relevance and significance of these logical constructions relates to their instrumental role in the conduct of inquiry. Relevance of logical forms does not derive from or relate to their ancestry, authorship, longevity, elegance, simplicity, aesthetic appeal or rigour. Neither does it relate to the numbers who concur in support, or the status of originators of such defining constructs. When perceived as potential instruments for the ordering and relating of subject matter to enhance understanding of causal connections, formal logics may have an important instrumental contribution to make. Dewey used conventional logical forms when the circumstances of characterization and analysis made their use appropriate.

Outcomes of Inquiry

In Dewey's view, the outcomes of inquiry reflect the character of inquiry from which they emerge. All truths, for Dewey, are tentative in the sense that subsequent inquiry may require their modification or abandonment. In social science inquiry, there are no absolute truths – truths that have standing and credibility apart from the process from which they emerge and of which they are determined to be a part. Truth status requires the placement of the item in the continuum of which it is determined to be a part, as J. Fagg Foster often insisted in his lectures.[30] References to anterior truths, a priori truths, revealed truths, deductively derived truths, intuitive truths and the like, because they exhibit a detached, out-of-process status, are not admissible as definitive subject matter in the continuum of social inquiry.

Following Dewey's theory of the generation of knowledge, outcomes of inquiry are captioned in his own words as generalizations having 'warranted assertibility'. That is, one can demonstrate warrant for asserting that the causal determinants of the observed phenomena are as hypothetically formulated. Such knowledge is reliable even though tentative. The capacity to assert with evidential warrant means that sufficient confidence has been generated, in establishing conjugate correlation between theory and fact, to permit and justify the incorporation of such warranted assertions into subsequent research. It constitutes knowledge reliable enough to be used analytically in further inquiry, even though subsequent experience and theoretical investigation may invalidate a part or even the whole of what earlier was warrantably assertable.

Finally, Dewey's theory of inquiry incorporates a running recognition that normative assessments and judgments are an inherent and continuing part of the process of inquiry.[31] This demonstration is reflected in part in Dewey's rejection of the normative-positive dualism. This dualism posits an allegedly necessary and given excluded middle (mutually exclusive) relationship between, for example: ends and means, ethics and economics, ought and is, value and fact, ideal and real, and art and science. Dewey rejects this dualism on the grounds that it blocks the path of inquiry. But a dichotomy is not a dualism. To invoke inquiry with the emergence of doubt or the perception of a problem (especially about social relations or institutions) compels the use of a dichotomous distinction between 'what ought to be' and 'what is'. Both the 'is' and the 'ought' are an integral part of the inquiry process. To conceive of a social problem is inescapably to apply social value criteria. If inquiry is purposive in its application to problem solving, it is and must be value-laden. For Dewey, the relevant criteria are embedded in and derive from the inquiry process itself and what is required to keep it viable and pertinent.

Dewey's rejection of the normative-positive dualism and the inclusion of value tenets in inquiry evidently originates with his recognition of the processual, developmental character of inquiry.[32] This recognition takes cognizance of the fact that means determine consequences; the latter in turn become means to further consequences. Processual inquiry is an evolutionary continuum. As the means are chosen, so are the outcomes determined. But the captioning of what are 'means' and what are 'consequences' is a judgmental act of the inquirer. No item is per se either a cause or an effect, a means or a consequence; its placement in inquiry defines its role and consequences. Means and consequences have the standing in inquiry of relational, temporal and causal connections. Consequences do not have the standing of ends antecedently given from outside the inquiry process. As integral elements within the inquiry process, Dewey called them 'ends-in-view'. They are consequences sought as outcomes of a kind or character that permit further inquiry about, and continuity in, the social process itself.[33] Those ends-in-view (consequences) that enhance the capacity for further inquiry and/or that provide for the continuity of the social process are termed 'instrumental'; they are essential as means in generating further consequences. The continuing development and application knowledge, identified here as that which is 'warrantably assertible', is required for the identification and resolution of economic problems.

The use of reliable knowledge reflects the employment of the pragmatic instrumental theory of social value. Such knowledge is used to restore and enhance the provision of the material means of life; that is, to improve efficiency and rapport among institutions coordinating production, to ensure noninvidious economic participation, to restore adequacy and continuity in flows of real income, to provide for the fullest intellectual and social development of individuals, and the like. The social value principle embedded in instrumental value theory as formulated by J. Fagg Foster is 'the continuity and instrumental efficiency of the social process' or, more simply, 'instrumental efficiency'.[34] I have revised and elaborated on Foster's value principle in my own work as follows: do or choose that which provides for 'the continuity of human life and the noninvidious re-creation of community through the instrumental use of knowledge'.[35] When neoinstitutionalists, following Dewey, attribute purposiveness to economic inquiry as making a contribution to problem solving, it is my observation that, implicitly or explicitly, they are employing instrumental social value theory and the criteria embedded therein.

Accordingly, for neoinstitutionalists, criteria for choosing among alternative institutional options in problem solving cannot be drawn from antecedently given idealistic ends, ideological utopias, absolute truths or other nonevidential sources. Such inquiry outcomes may be characterized as ethically absolute; as criteria, they are anterior, given, matters of faith and unexaminable. Neither can neoinstitutionalists accept the ethical relativism embedded in utility-based criteria such as consumer equilibrium or the Paretian optimum: these are criteria based on personal tastes and preferences and are presumed to be unexaminable. As an inherent part of the Deweyian mode of social inquiry, instrumental criteria function to facilitate inquiry, and to identify and resolve economic problems.

II   COMPETING VIEWS OF ECONOMIC INQUIRY

I now contrast a neoinstitutionalist view of inquiry with that of aspects, elements or applications of neoclassical approaches to inquiry. In so doing, I will use attributes of Dewey's theory of pragmatic instrumental inquiry, as introduced in Part I, as ordering topics.

At the outset, a caveat may help clarify matters: I am fully aware that the materials offered and views attributed will not apply to some or all orthodox neoclassical scholars. The spread of orthodox positions on some issues addressed may well be quite broad. Whether I have chosen 'representative' positions to address is certainly arguable and is an important concern, but it cannot be pursued here. Since my purpose is to stimulate inquiry, not finally to settle methodological debates, the pertinent question is: do the examples chosen illuminate the issues addressed? And although it is my intent to view the character of economic theory inclusively, as through a wide-angle lens, a definitive or comprehensive treatment is not attempted.

Purposes of Inquiry

Neoinstitutionalists engage in inquiry to extend the substance and range of warrantable economic knowledge, to facilitate social and economic problem solving, and to aid and abet the initiation or restoration of instrumental functions in the institutional fabric of the economy.

Neoclassical theorists, particularly in the tradition of Milton Friedman, purport to be concerned primarily with predicting economic behaviour. Given a covey of conjectural assumptions, they seem less concerned to generate a causal understanding or explanation of observed behaviour than to make economic predictions. In Friedman's words: the 'ultimate goal of a positive science is the development of a "theory" or "hypothesis" that yields valid and meaningful (i.e., not truistic) predictions about phenomena not yet observed'.[36]

This neoclassical presumption suggests that deductive inferences will generate behavioural predictions. Their basic assumptions include the following: first, that tastes and preferences, technology and capitalistic institutional structure are given; second, that the singular motivation of individual participants is to maximize utility (in cardinal utility theory), or to prefer more to less (in ordinal utility theory); third, that entrepreneurs will seek to maximize profits; and fourth, that workers will seek real wages to offset the also assumed disutility of work (in cardinal theory) or loss of leisure (in ordinal theory). Given these assumptions, one can predict that an inverse relation between price and quantity will obtain for the demand function, and that a direct relation between price and quantity will obtain for the supply function. One might additionally predict that the alleged contending market forces would generate movement towards an equilibrium position which, in the absence of disturbing influences, would remain stable. Employing the technique of deductive inference, the predictive purpose appears to be served: if A and B and C obtain, then one can predict D; given such elaborate assumptions, price-quantity relationships can be predicted.[37]

All of this provides nothing more than the logical foundation for the primacy of certain types of prediction. There is no derivation of an explanation in complex interactive causal terms, of how the economic process correlates behaviour, how motivations are acquired, how institutions evolve, how relevant knowledge is generated and applied to economic experience as technology. Predictive inferences, even if rigorous, do not constitute explanation.

But other purposes are also served by the economic theory of many neoclassicists. Their theory raises few questions about institutional malfunction, technological inadequacy, or the presence and use of economic power. Historically, they have had no history-based theory of institutional adjustment, although Douglass North now seeks to provide one.[38] The growth of warranted knowledge and its application as technology is mostly outside their scope of inquiry; manifestations of economic power and its use are treated as aberrational and pathological. Even their consideration of 'market failures' is typically couched in the deductivistic language of 'barriers to entry', 'externalities' and 'internalities'.[39] One implication is that, with rare exceptions, little serious threat is posed by their theory to existent concentrations of power by megacorps, privately organized interest groups or international consortia. Purposively or tacitly, theoretical contributions of neoclassicists do not point to restructuring and institutional reform. They appear, rather, to support the status quo – the existing structure and power systems of the political economy.

Contemporary rational expectations theory, for example, generates a modern defence of laissez faire; Say's Law is resurrected. Doing nothing about instability is superior to using governmental interventionist policy – fiscal, monetary or incomes – to cope with instability. Rational economic agents with full information (expectations) act predictably and promptly enough to modify their behaviour to thwart and defeat any such interventionist strategy.

'There is an implicit, and often explicit, belief that the market economy, left to its own devices, would perform more adequately than when intruded upon.' 'Inappropriate' fiscal and monetary policies 'will be discounted *ex ante*'.[40]

Contestable market theory, as another example, argues that even in highly concentrated markets, in the absence of sunk costs, the simple elimination of entry and exit barriers will bring monopolist or oligopolist behaviour into conformity with competitive standards. The absence of barriers to entry will intimidate incumbent providers and lead them to forego supra-normal profits in order to avoid the attraction of new entrants. The presence of this 'potential competition' leads monopolists to act 'as if' actual competitive conditions prevailed. The elimination of legal barriers to entry through deregulation is all that is required. The theory is blind to the presence and use of economic power. In the words of its advocates:

> A wide difference in appearance between a particular market and the form of perfect competition need not deprive the invisible hand of its power to protect the public interest ... we can no longer accept as *per se* indicators of poor market performance evidence such as a concentration, price discrimination, conglomerate mergers, nor vertical or horizontal integration ... [such] phenomena ... can be desirable and should indeed be presumed so.[41]

What is good for megacorps (for example, the telecommunications industry) is good for the country. Interventionist antitrust or other regulatory action is viewed as counterproductive. Regulation is, in such circumstances, unnecessary and pernicious. In effect, an ideological apologia is employed to defend an existing power system. Is the public interest thereby served?[42]

There is another and related implication of neoclassical theory relating to the purposiveness of inquiry. The capitalist model, undergirded and validated by neoclassical theory, as the standard with which to judge existing economies or to define the route of restructuring from socialism, shapes the purpose of inquiry. It is the road map; it identifies which direction is forward. Here inquiry becomes a tunnel-vision exploration of the extent to which an economy is moving towards or away from the competitive market model. Inquiry is pursued in order to demonstrate the a priori contention that a capitalist system is a superior ordering and coordinating arrangement for economic activity.

This affirmation of superiority derives from the natural law tradition of the 17th and 18th centuries. As Veblen put it, 'natural law is felt to exercise some sort of a coercive surveillance over the sequence of events, and to give a spiritual stability and consistence to the causal relation at any given juncture. ... [A] sequence ... must be apprehended in terms of a consistent propensity tending to some spiritually legitimate end.'[43] This teleological rootedness underpins the conviction that capitalism is the natural system and that what is natural is good. In a world devoid of interdictions to natural impulse and arrangement, this natural system autogenetically appears; its inherent law-like propensities function; it automatically generates allocative efficiency. Departures from the capitalist model are 'unnatural' and 'inefficient'. Problems are then defined as departures from or shortfalls in the emergence of that system; they are 'disturbing factors'. The search for routes to the achievement of the closest approximation to the competitive model defines the purposes of inquiry and policy. Its realization, presumably, would constitute a 'solution' for problems and a vindication of neoclassicists' theoretical purpose.

This normative use of the competitive model – extolling the price system as the only efficient allocative instrument – truncates inquiry, seals off other plausible options, and constrains inquiry to the reaffirmation of prior orthodox truths.[44] For neoclassicists, problem solving through institutional adjustment does not drive the process of economic inquiry, whereas for neoinstitutionalists, this is its fundamental motivation.

Human Focus and Context of Inquiry

For neoinstitutionalists, economic inquiry is pursued as a social science. The object of inquiry is the social process in which institutional structures organize and implement continuing functions of the provisioning process. In the social sciences generally, with the exception of mainstream economics, there is now common agreement that people in this social process are at once creators of culture and conditioned products of it. Although most patterns of their reflection and behaviour are or become habitual, they are rational, discretionary agents engaged in transforming themselves coincident with the transformation of their cultural fabric. They perceive causal-effect or means-consequence relations; they understand if-then propositions. They are rational in this sense. All of their tastes, preferences, motivations and behaviour are culturally acquired, although basic drives may prompt their formation.

For neoclassicists, the singular human agent has two facets; as with sides of a coin, each is an expression of the other. Man is rational; man is a maximizer. And each defines the other. In their view, an economic agent who determines the net benefits of every act, and then elects the one that best maximizes his/her satisfactions, is rational. To exhibit inherent rationality means to maximize utility in any form. This characterization is a given psychological attribution, not a distilled product of reflective inquiry. It is acultural and asocial. I will argue that it is reductionistic and without demonstrable evidential grounding.[45]

Their model of man is acultural because it encompasses no concern with the evolutionary emergence of individuals who are both contributors to and conditioned products of their respective environmental settings. The rational agent of neoclassical analysis has no history; there is no analytical consideration of acquired habit, custom or behaviour of which account must be taken except as it becomes manifest in market behaviour. There is no analytical account taken of growth in perception, of transformation of choices, of maturation of capacities through cultural interdependencies. He or she is simply a utility maximizing organism. This attribute is given; it is a natural characteristic of people. Bentham's pleasure-pain calculus is converted into a utility based benefit-cost calculation. We are offered an archaic posture of 'metaphysical individualism' as a theory of human behaviour.[46]

The neoclassical premises are asocial in their continuing myopic stress on the individual agent whose character, motivations and behavioural traits, other than as a rational maximizer, are without analytical interest. 'Greed is enough.' Neoclassicists do not grant that the whole of human experience is that of interaction with others in consequence of which people reason, articulate, learn, organize, direct, assess and participate. The economic agent is a social agent; his/her individual judgments and actions are an emerging product of interaction with others.

The neoclassical view of human nature is reductionist in its singular focus on maximization, on individual gain, on self-serving motives, on insensitivity to the concerns of others. 'The idea of utility grows out of the attempt to understand all of an individuals' choices in terms of a single thing he is trying to maximize – happiness, pleasure, or something similar. We call this utility.'[47] But the substance of what constitutes 'utility' cannot be explored; it is an asserted feeling-state that is beyond inquiry. In consequence, orthodox theory is unable to accommodate the complexity, the continuing transformation of purpose and motive, of action and appraisal, that is the common character of economic participation at any level.

Finally, claims of utility maximization are nondemonstrable and indefensible. An alleged universal characterization is used to affirm any economic behaviour whatsoever. Whatever the act, whatever the judgment, the presumption is that the individual must have been maximizing utility or he/she would have acted otherwise. It is a universal account that explains nothing. All behaviour – any behaviour – is maximizing behaviour. The circularity is inescapable. It strips the maximization premise of all analytical significance. As a conceptual tool it cannot discriminate; it is analytically sterile. To continue with the utility maximizing premise as the core attribute of the rational economic agent is to distort and misdirect the inquiry process at its very core.

Scope of Inquiry

In neoinstitutional analysis, that which is included in any particular inquiry – its perimeters and content – is set and reset as the course of the inquiry proceeds. Since the purpose of inquiry is to generate causal understanding of what is observed and to utilize such analytical insights to contribute to problem resolution, there can be no given anterior delineation of scope that might constrain or inhibit the inquiry process. Doubt is the stimulus for questions; questions invoke inquiry. The investigator cannot know in advance of inquiry which determinants of an indeterminate situation will be identified as significant, which subject matters will have to be tapped, which theoretical tools and constructs will prove instrumentally useful, which hypotheses may show plausible promise and effectually guide the inquiry process itself. Inquiry is open-ended but directed by initial questions and preliminary hypotheses, focused but amenable to being refocused, creative and interconnected but still evolving. Theory building is demanding, frustrating and untidy; it continues as a search for coherence and causal understanding.

In neoclassical analysis, ironically, the scope of inquiry is both remarkably narrow and exceedingly broad. Its analytical focus is narrow in the sense that its practitioners have generated a remarkably elaborate and sophisticated system of analytical models relating to a very limited facet of the economic provisioning process – 'the price system'. As any orthodox college-level intermediate theory text will confirm, to explain price is purportedly to explain the whole of what is significant in the economic process. The price theory core, supported by the logic of constrained maximization, is set out early on; the remaining chapters extend, refine and apply that core theory.[48] Whatever can be made to fall within that delineation is economics; whatever cannot be accommodated in that model is something else. The model defines the discipline.

This model of inquiry is exceedingly broad in the imperialistic sense. Having conquered economics, its practitioners have moved on supposedly to explain how this rationalistic maximizing model, or derivatives therefrom, can explain, with only minor amendments, the political process,[49] operation of households,[50] governmental operations,[51] economic history,[52] corporate power systems[53] and economic development,[54] among topical areas. This allegedly pan-cultural and pan-temporal model converts reductionistic price theory into a universal mode of social analysis. No one questions the instrumental need for abstraction and selectivity in addressing ideas in inquiry. But with price theory, aspects of the real world are massaged, compressed, selectively ignored and manipulated in order to wrap this conceptual cloak around any chosen subject matter.

Consider more directly what is excluded from consideration in this model, its claims to breadth and relevance notwithstanding. As noted, the 'givens' of orthodoxy – including wants, tastes and preferences, technology, institutions of a capitalist system, character of motivation – are all largely assumed; they are not often themselves objects of analysis in the neoclassical paradigm. Also generally outside the pale of consideration are such areas as the possession and use of economic power (including administered pricing), the nature and significance of corporations, the role of education for economic growth, and the cultural, political, technological and social determinants of economic development.

Even more significantly, in their claims to positivist analysis, neoclassicists eschew any serious consideration of criteria of social value in exercising discretion in the provisioning process. Embracing the normative-positive dualism, they are content to perceive utility as the meaning, and price as the measure, of value. The exercise of discretion in markets is guided by individualistic and unexaminable preferences. The 'ought' is implicitly realized if behaviour follows price theory directives. No value theory to guide choices among or between institutions is required; the facilitating structure for price determination, through which utility choices are made, is not at issue in their inquiry.

There are, to be sure, 'in house' responses to perceived limitations in the foregoing. In order to provide an approach thought to be of greater relevance to the real world, neoclassicists sometimes push back the self-imposed constraints on the scope of economic inquiry. Ramsey pricing (the inverse elasticity rule), for instance, provides regulated utilities with the power to place expansion costs on buyers of basic services whose purchases are inelastic.[55] Transaction cost economics acknowledges the intracorporate need to choose between markets and hierarchies in making judgments on costs.[56] Human capital formation theory acknowledges the significance of the growth of skills and knowledge to provide for more effective market participation.[57] The stages theory of economic growth acknowledges the presence and importance of cultural influences on the capacity to become productive over time.[58]

A case-by-case examination would disclose some limited departures from the neoclassical paradigm in the foregoing, but there is no intention in these departures to challenge the fundamental claims to near universal relevance of neoclassical orthodoxy as defining the scope of economic inquiry. Scholars who accede to neoclassical constraints on the scope of inquiry risk loss of significance for their inquiry generally.

Character of Inquiry

Institutionalists view inquiry as a conjoint process of truth seeking in which deductive, inductive and abductive procedures are interrelated elements of an evolving and processual quest for causal understanding of the experiential phenomena under scrutiny. Its creative dimensions are reflected in the posing of questions for inquiry, in the creation and application of tools of inquiry, in the formulation and continuing assessment of hypotheses that guide inquiry, and in the use of instrumental judgments to direct and pattern the inquiry process in pursuit of theoretically coherent and evidentially grounded comprehension. The inquiry process is purposive, evolutionary, judgmental and provisional. It seeks conjugate correspondence of theoretical and evidential material.

That neoclassical inquiry has, in the last half century, become predominantly formal, particularly in the mathematical sense, needs no elaboration here.[59] A few minutes spent with the most recent issue of the *American Economic Review*, for example, will disclose little else. Complaints of Wassily Leontief,[60] Robert A. Gordon[61] and others about this formalistic refocusing of economics since the Second World War has had little discernible effect on the character of mainstream economic inquiry.[62] In explaining this 'mathematization of economic theory', Gerard Debreu candidly acknowledges that values 'are imprinted on an economist by his study of mathematics'. Indeed 'the very choice of the questions to which he tries to find answers is influenced by his mathematical background. Thus, the danger is ever present that the part of economics will become secondary, if not marginal, in that judgment.'[63]

As Ken Dennis sees it, neoclassicists 'seek above all else a precise, orderly, simple, and rigorous version of economic truth, a version that offers full scope for the exercise of predictive powers, based upon the projection of measured uniformities derived from the recorded past'.[64] To pursue this kind of inquiry, they must assume that, in all matters of economic substance, the basic analytical constructs are all reducible to and can be expressed in mathematical symbolistic terms; moreover, that these constructs can and should be subjected to mathematical deductivistic reasoning.[65] Mathematical symbolism is not just a form of logic, but 'a full-blown and self-contained language by which to "formulate" (i.e., express) the propositions of economic theory'.[66]

This concern is amplified in Philip Mirowski's assessment of how a 'system of obscure symbols' can be responsible for 'the maintenance of orthodoxy'. His explanation draws attention to the following attributes of mathematics, as reflected in neoclassical economics. Mathematics is

> a restricted language ... it possesses a certain ritual efficacy over and above its content; [it is a] discourse where the assertion of the discreteness of intellectual constructs is pushed to its extreme; mathematics fosters the impression that the actors who are the subject of analysis are determined by alien extraneous forces;

the discrete character of mathematics encourages ... 'the norm of closure' ... the
creation of a system restricted in time and in space; the penetration of mathematics induces a particular form of hierarchy within a discipline ... theorists become
separated from a lower class of researchers ... mathematics frees the theorist from
having to create a context of justification.[67]

The problems with this focus are many and can only be summarized here.

(a) While the statistical assembling of pertinent information and the sum-
maries drawn therefrom do sometimes constitute significant data in the evidential grounding of hypotheses of behaviour, their usefulness may be impaired by the conceptual frame that specifies and guides their acquisition.
After all, as Fagg Foster often admonished his students, it is theory that tells
us which facts to gather and how to arrange them for analysis. Mathematical
expression per se indicates nothing about the significance of the acquisition;
that must be determined by theoretical analysis external to the mathematical
reasoning process itself.

(b) The comprehensive effort to translate economic propositions into mathematical formulae denies to inquiry constructs and propositions that cannot
be so translated. Indeed, as noted, the discipline has increasingly been more
narrowly defined to include only material and constructs that are amenable to
mathematical formulation and expression.[68]

(c) The alleged 'explicitness, precision and rigor' claimed for this methodology are illusory. As Dennis observes, 'the deductive validity of any logical
argument that passes from one language or symbolism into another language
or symbolism depends as much upon the adequacy of the translation linking
the two symbolisms together as it does upon the validity of any deductive
inference that is expressed entirely by means of either one of those
symbolisms'.[69] However, the adequacy or appropriateness of those transla-
tions from mathematics to economics, imposing law-like orderings that incorporate simplistic assumptions, is rarely considered. Dennis continues:

[M]ost of the standard assumptions of economic theory are propositions about
human behaviour (actions) or human dispositions (beliefs, preferences and inten-
tions, as well as capabilities), propositions such as 'economic actors possess
perfect knowledge'; and 'economic actors prefer to maximize their utility,' and
yet these receive no formally explicit expression ... their role in assuring deductive validity is totally gratuitous.[70]

(d) The character of neoclassical inquiry, to the extent that its major analytical mode is converted to mathematical formalism, symbolism and
deductivistic reasoning, exhibits a reductionism that leaves most of the major
analytical questions unaddressed. These include the determination and revisions in economic structure, negotiational policy making, motives other than
greed for participation, locus and use of economic power, technological

determinants of production and acquisition of skills, among others. Mathematical models, econometric regressions and the like may at times be pertinent tools or instructive exercises, but their analytical significance and contribution can be identified only through recourse to pragmatic instrumental inquiry. As Kenneth Boulding observes, mathematical reasoning is very useful, but its language structure has so few verbs. 'It is hard to think of more than four: is equal to, is greater than, less than, or is a function of'.[71] That is, such symbolism and reasoning may at times be useful, but they are incidental to – not the defining character of – economic analysis.

The narrowing of scholarly focus in neoclassical economics to what can be conceived, analysed and predicted through mathematical symbolism, deductivistic reasoning and economic regressions constitutes a major impediment to the inquiry process. The pursuit of more pertinent modes of inquiry is left underdeveloped and undersupported.

Outcomes of Inquiry

For neoinstitutionalists, pragmatic instrumental inquiry culminates provisionally in tentative truths, with what Dewey called 'warranted assertions'. With the establishment of conjugate correlation between ideational hypotheses and evidential grounding, sufficient confidence is generated in the outcomes of inquiry to warrant their tentative inclusion in subsequent inquiry and in provisional problem solving. This continuously emerging fund of evidentially warranted knowledge is derived from a deliberative, processual, cumulative and self-corrective inquiry activity. The tentative concluding query in neoinstitutionalist inquiry is this: will the proposed alterations in institutional structure, based on reliable knowledge derived from pragmatic instrumental inquiry, enhance the provisioning process? That is, as noted above, will they improve efficiency and rapport among coordinating institutions, ensure noninvidious participation, maintain flows of real income, provide for full development of individuals, ensure a healthy and sustainable environment and the like?

Neoclassicists, in contrast, generally perceive economic inquiry to culminate with a reaffirmation of their initial position, albeit with modest refinements or addenda. What is reaffirmed is a conceived economic model with ungrounded assumptions about human agency, given structure, market phenomena and naturalistic tendencies that provides movement towards (a) allocative efficiency (identified as Paretian optimality), (b) equilibria and (c) the reaffirmation of the competitive model. Indeed, the outcomes, as perceived by the orthodox, are conjointly realized: given 'competitive markets … every conceivable Pareto condition of economic efficiency would tend to be fulfilled if profit-maximizing firms and utility-maximizing households were to determine the optimum quantities they wished to trade with the help of equilibrium prices established in such markets'.[72]

This approach to inquiry does rest on a priori truths – deductively derived truths – that become constructs which serve as bases for mathematical truths. But nowhere is this inquiry activity genuinely processual, cumulative or self-corrective. Tests of deductivistic inference, cogency, elegance and simplicity are, by themselves, insufficient to establish reliable knowledge. In orthodoxy, the inquiry givens are derived anterior to and outside the inquiry process itself. Although claims are sometimes made that these assumptions are tentative or hypothetical, in both text and classroom they remain remarkably constant and unmodified.

Claims to allocative efficiency appear as conjectural and inhibitive. The outcome of allocative efficiency is presumed to result from the uninhibited functioning of the competitive market system. The attributes of this resultant are that profits are 'normal'; real wages equal the marginal productivity of labour; pricing power is zero; innovative incentives are present; maximal product is generated at minimal cost, and consumers maximize utility. The achievement of allocative efficiency in the private sector constitutes the public's economic interest. Few neoclassical economists believe in the descriptive merits or adequacy of this characterization, but its quest defines the direction and character of much of their inquiry. It is conjectural because of its flawed descriptive capacities; it is inhibitive because it tends to foreclose alternative approaches.

Corollary claims are made that the Paretian optimum serves as a primary criterion of allocative efficiency, a major stipulation of an analytically desired outcome, and an effectual and employable judgmental premise. Such claims, however, are also conjectural and inhibitive.

When compelled to abandon their positivism in judgmental contexts, neoclassicists consider the Paretian optimum a quite acceptable principle of social value. It is a criterion of judgment that allows an 'ought to be' choice to be made without the need for comparative assessment of preferences or their cardinally measured utility. Indeed, it is the only principle of normative assessment that most neoclassicists will acknowledge. (The Kaldor-Hicks extension/revision is cut from the same conceptual cloth.) The Paretian optimum serves as a welfare index in its stipulation of technical marginal conditions of economic efficiency that, if fulfilled simultaneously, indicate that no reallocation could make anyone better off (in their own judgment) without making someone else worse off (in their own judgment). It is not surprising that these Paretian conditions are best met in an unfettered competitive economy.[73] The 'better off-worse off' judgments are referenced back to the given wants, tastes and preferences of individuals. Wants ought to be fully met, but the origin and character of wants are unexamined. An inherent ethical relativism is inescapable. Edythe Miller provides a summary:

> The preoccupation of orthodox economics with Pareto efficiency flaws perspective. ... It portends the existence of a precise set of solutions to any given set of economic problems. But, Pareto efficiency lacks operational content and cannot be measured by independent criteria. It is ambiguous and esoteric and, at bottom, metaphorical. A Pareto optimum turns out at any time to be 'what is', for if what is were not optimal, individuals would not have negotiated in order to achieve it.[74]

Claims to the inherent emergence of equilibriums as a desired outcome are conjectural and inhibitive. As most are aware, the construct of 'equilibrium' lies at the heart of orthodoxy,[75] both as a descriptive characterization of economic phenomena and, notwithstanding vigorous contentions to the contrary,[76] as a normative quest or condition that ought to prevail. Equilibrium plays a linchpin role; withdraw the construct and much of orthodox analysis collapses – a major organizing premise disappears.

The construct of equilibrium presents a stasis view of reality instead of an evolutionary one. Even a limited survey suggests that contemporary inquiry in socio-biology,[77] bio-economics,[78] biopolitics,[79] welfare economics,[80] chaos theory,[81] as well as evolutionary economics,[82] points to a processual reality of continuous, if not necessarily regular, change. Incessant change involves creation, mutation, displacement, abandonment, reconstruction, readjustment; it will reflect cumulative and, at times, circular causation.

However, economic change does not necessarily exhibit cyclical or rhythmic patterns in which previously established conditions are restored. Rates of change do vary, of course, but the fact of change is a constant. Critical here is the recognition that change is not inherently or characteristically a movement towards or away from an equilibrium state – a place or point from which there is no directional movement.

Inquiring whether movements are towards or away from equilibrium in my view misconceives the nature of economic change. In its more rigid form, movement is mistakenly conceived as episodic: (a) an original quiescent state, (b) disturbance of quiescent state, (c) restoration or return to quiescent state – an equilibrium condition; the episode is completed. Whether this essentially static focus is intended merely to provide a conjectural construct for inqui:y or to characterize reality, it ill serves either intent. As a construct, it tempts inquirers to misspecify determinants of change; as a description in social analysis, it is inadequate and misleading.

Observable reality, as noted, is processual, unexceptionally so: causal linkages tie the past and the present; conscious choices shape the character of the future; even approximate replications of previous conditions are exceedingly rare. Perhaps the most obtrusive fact is that all social and economic systems are in a state of flux. Rates of institutional change vary from minimal to rapid; the character of institutional change may be modest or convulsive. But structural change is continuous. Growth in knowledge, meaning and understanding generates capacity for change; emergence and recognition of major impairments in the flow of real income activate interest in change. But all such change is processual; it is neither episodic nor inherently equilibrium-seeking.

Conventional economic instruction, disclaimers notwithstanding, does tend to attribute normative significance to equilibrium outcomes. The workings of alleged free and unfettered markets ought to culminate in consumer equilibrium – a state or condition in which the 'rational greedy economic agent'[83] cannot alter his or her purchasing behaviour in any way to increase his or her total utility. This is the consummate resultant – desired and preferred. Equilibria are normatively better than disequilibria.

What will be obvious on reflection, however, is that the neoclassical construct of equilibrium, as such, is normatively barren; it has no evaluative content. Its claim to relevance – as in consumer equilibrium reflecting maximized utility, producer equilibrium as maximized profits, and general equilibrium (via Walras) as the above with fully cleared markets – is wholly conjectural. Even if equilibrium could be demonstrated in some way, the question of the character and significance of the emergent consequences must be determined by other than ethically relative criteria. (Such criteria, as noted, reflect the insistence that all ethical norms are relative to the individuals and cultures that exhibit them.) No interpersonal comparisons of preferences or cross-cultural assessments of choices are permitted. Criteria of choice may not be subjected to social and ethical inquiry. A frequent outcome, then, is simply to contend that 'what is, is right'; the status quo is reinforced.

The neoclassical outcome of inquiry that emerges as a reaffirmation of the competitive model is, in another sense, an ethical absolute. Not only is there an inherent circularity in the reaffirmation of that with which inquiry began – the virtues and alleged merits of the competitive model – but also there is a continuing insistence on the normative use of this competitive model.[84] Although there have been many refinements and extensions over the years, it is not an exaggeration to contend that the fundamental character of that model has not been significantly modified over the last half-century through the scholarship of orthodox economists. The mathematical revolution in economics, the development of axiomatic theory, rational expectations formulations, cost-benefit analysis and contestable market theory, for example – all have left the main corpus intact. The basic market model has become a Platonic ideal, always to be sought but never to be realized. Its substance, its role as an analytical construct and its normative guidance are given; they are not sufficiently admitted into the inquiry process.

III CONSEQUENCES OF DEPENDENCE ON THE NEOCLASSICAL MODEL OF INQUIRY

In these concluding comments, I note three implications of reliance on this mainstream approach. First, the neoclassical model of inquiry tends to stress predictability rather than causal understanding and, in so doing, truncates inquiry in a manner that leaves the real problems of institutional breakdown largely ignored. The neoclassical conception of an 'economic problem' is specified by its deductivistic mode of inquiry and by its ideological commitment to the institutional structure of free and equilibrating markets. The inquiry constraint delimits by discarding as noneconomic all approaches save those that are derived from or accommodative to the price theory model. The institutional constraint is imposed by the absence of a credible theory of institutional change or adjustment. Neoclassical theory simply does not encompass or address as such the myriad prescriptive and proscriptive patterns of correlated behaviour that organize the provisioning process. Accordingly, it cannot identify a 'problem' of malfunction within that structural fabric.

A neoinstitutionalist asks how and to what degree correlated patterns of behaviour and attitudes, institutional forms and the values upon which they rest operate to impair the provisioning process. Neoinstitutionalists focus their analyses on the institutional malfunctions that generate inefficient production, involuntary unemployment, macro-instability, inequality of income distribution, environmental deterioration, discriminatory denial of participation, deprivation of medical care and the like. Impairments in the provisioning process constitute the universe of 'problems'. A neoinstitutionalist asks where in the structural fabric are invidious or ceremonial patterns of judgment and behaviour impeding or distorting the continuous and adequate provision of real income; these patterns constitute regressive forces. A neoinstitutionalist asks how instrumentally warranted knowledge and value can be brought to bear to guide the restructuring of the institutional fabric in a progressive fashion.[85]

Second, the neoclassical mode of inquiry does not provide an adequate explanation of economic phenomena: its predictive purposes are sometimes pertinent but quite insufficient; its views of human nature, rationality and motivation are truncated and in some measure archaic; its scope of inquiry does not extend to the demonstrable determinants of real breakdowns in the provisioning process; its shift in character in recent decades to mathematical formulations has permitted concern with method to overtake and subvert substance; its answers for institutional breakdowns – recommending free markets, deregulation, etc. – have exacerbated, not resolved, fundamental distortions and obstructions in the flow of real income.

Neoinstitutionalists, building on Dewey, try to implement a mode of analysis that pursues an open-ended, causal accounting of institutional malfunction that neither encompasses nor recommends any prepackaged ideological answers as policy. It continuously attempts to pose significant and answerable questions. The test of the adequacy of its theory is whether or not it explains what it purports to explain; the test of the relevance of its theory is whether or not it is diagnostically significant and creative in identifying and resolving real problems, as identified above.

Third, when neoclassicists use their model of inquiry to generate policy recommendations, they discover that, in their quest for relevance, it deprives them of creative institutional options. As an extension of both the first and second observations above, I note that the creation of new institutions can scarcely be brought on the agenda. The invention, recasting and reinvigoration of correlated patterns of behaviour are foreign to their perspective. Their options are limited to the 'givens' of their model. Consider the following example.

Neoclassical recommendations concerning the provision of medical care would typically call for privatization of services, 'market' allocation by providers of medical care, termination of 'impure' price administration by organized hospitals or other care providers, pecuniary incentives to alter behaviour, minimization of governmental involvement or supervision out of deference to market surveillance and fears of bureaucratic dominion, and rationing of access to care via market constraints. Compliance with this ethically reductionistic market model might well take precedence, for example, over concern about inequitable availability of care. These policy considerations derive from the price theory model.

When a neoinstitutionalist is asked what kind of medical delivery system should be generated, the answer would derive fundamentally from a Dewey-based model calling for meticulous examination of causal phenomena observable in the existing structure, belief systems, health industry power systems, government's role and the like, in an effort to identify where the obstructions and shortfalls lie. Administered prices paid, negotiated costs incurred, conflicts among organized power groups, quality of care actually available, professional and political control over the development and use of new knowledge, adequacy of supply of skilled personnel and the like would all enter the inquiry process as subject matter. But it is their causal interdependencies, linkages and determinants that would be the main object of analysis. What regressive beliefs and behaviours invoke the consequences observed? Hypotheses are created and cast against emerging evidences in search of understanding. Once attained, this understanding can then support a tentative but relevant progressive programme of institutional creation, revamping and adjustment intended to extend and enhance the health care provisioning process. This increasing understanding of actual causal determinants of the malfunctioning of medical institutions undergirds the formulation of credible policy recommendations as institutional adjustments.

In sum, the pragmatic instrumentalist mode of inquiry provides philosophic bases for the creation of neoinstitutional economic theory. This model of inquiry supports and guides policy making. Its normative dimensions serve neither relativistic nor absolutist goals or interests; they promote only the furtherance of inquiry and problem solving. This perspective satisfies no ideological enclave; it invites pluralistic explorations. Its character, use and relevance are under constant scrutiny. It does not generate new forms of impairment; it fosters open inquiry and creative applications.

NOTES

1. Okun (1981).
2. Simon (1979), pp. 493–513.
3. North (1990), p. 27.
4. Williamson (1986), pp. 172–3.
5. Hahn (1991), pp. 47–50. In the future, he says, 'there will be an increasing realization by theorists that rather radical change in questions and methods are required if they are to deliver, not practical, but theoretically useful results' (p. 47). Also, for a brief overview of departures from orthodoxy, see Hodgson (1994).
6. Klein (1980), pp. 871–96 and Klein (1987), pp. 1342–77.
7. Trebing (1984), pp. 353–68; Trebing (1987), pp. 1707–38; Miller (1994).
8. DeGregori (1985); Lower (1988), pp. 197–226.
9. Wray (1990).
10. Eichner (1976).
11. Murrell (1991); Etzioni (1991), pp. 4–10.
12. Homan (1932), p. 15.
13. The caption 'pragmatic instrumentalism' has recently been reintroduced from Dewey's early work by Paul D. Bush to distinguish Dewey's version of instrumentalism from various other contemporary usages, including those of Milton Friedman and Imre Lakatos. See Bush (1993), pp. 59–107.
14. The primary source for this model of inquiry is Dewey (1938).
15. Ibid, p. 105.
16. Ibid, p. 101.
17. Ibid, p. 107.
18. Ibid, p. 110.
19. Ibid, p. 438.
20. Mirowski (1989).
21. Dewey (1938), p. 66.
22. This topic was the subject of an interesting exchange between Dewey and Philip Blair Rice; see Dewey (1946), pp. 250–72. On 'immediate knowledge', see Dewey (1938), pp. 139–58.
23. Dewey (1938), p. 103.
24. Ibid, p. 484.
25. Charles Sanders Peirce, quoted by Mirowski (1988), p. 62.
26. A similar account will be found in Dewey (1938), p. 318.
27. Ibid, p. 112.
28. Ibid.
29. Ibid, p. 519.

30. J. Fagg Foster was Professor of Economics at the University of Denver from the mid-1940s until the mid-1970s.
31. Dewey (1939).
32. Ibid, pp. 40–50.
33. On these and related matters, see Dewey (1938), pp. 496–7 and 502–3.
34. Foster (1981), pp. 899–905.
35. Tool (1985), pp. 291–314.
36. Friedman, M. (1953), p. 7.
37. Comments of Paul D. Bush were incorporated into the preceding paragraph.
38. North (1990), part II.
39. Spulber (1989), pp. 8–10.
40. Klein (1986), pp. 16–17.
41. Baumol, Panzar and Willig (1982), p. 477; cited in Klein (1987), pp. 1351–2.
42. Comments from Edythe Miller were incorporated into the foregoing paragraph.
43. Veblen [1919] (1961), p. 61.
44. Tool (1986), pp. 104–25.
45. For an extensive critique along these lines, see Hodgson (1988), pp. 51–144.
46. Dewey (1939), p. 64.
47. Friedman, D. (1990), p. 68.
48. An example is D. Friedman (1990).
49. Downs (1957).
50. Becker (1976).
51. Buchanan and Tullock (1962).
52. North (1990).
53. Williamson (1986).
54. Bauer and Yamey (1957).
55. Sheehan (1991).
56. Williamson (1986).
57. Schultz (1961).
58. Rostow (1990).
59. Debreu (1991), pp. 1–7.
60. Leontief (1971).
61. Gordon (1976), pp. 1–14.
62. For a somewhat vigorous consideration of this, and related, matters, see Wiles and Routh (1984), pp. 1–77 and 293–325.
63. Debreu (1991), p. 5.
64. Dennis (1994), p. 252.
65. Ibid; Lawson (1994), pp. 179–81.
66. Dennis (1994), p. 252.
67. Mirowski (1986), pp. 192–4.
68. Watkins (1992).
69. Dennis (1994), p. 254.
70. Ibid.
71. Boulding (1986), pp. 5–12; cited in Watkins (1992), p. 3. J. Fagg Foster offered a similar observation in his lectures.
72. Kohler (1990), p. 491.
73. Ibid, pp. 484 ff.
74. Miller (1990), p. 729.
75. Hahn (1973), pp. 4–5 argues that the construct of 'equilibrium' has significance for economic inquiry even if it is not perceived as having normative implications or of describing 'a sequence of actual economic states [that] will terminate in an equilibrium state'. The term is given a role in delineating the meaning and significance of agent rationality in the mainstream abstract model of a market economy. He writes: 'an economy is in equilibrium when it generates messages which do not cause agents to change the theories which they hold or the policies which they pursue'. The sense of quiescence remains.

76. Robbins (1952), p. 143.
77. Wilson (1978).
78. Georgescu-Roegen (1971); Dragan and Demetrescu (1991).
79. Thorson (1970).
80. Hahnel and Albert (1990).
81. Goodwin (1990).
82. Hodgson (1993).
83. Hahn (1973), p. 40.
84. Tool (1986), pp. 104–25.
85. On the distinction between 'progressive' and 'regressive' change, see Bush (1988), pp. 125–66.

REFERENCES

Bauer, P.T. and Yamey, B.S. (1957), *Economics of Under-developed Countries*, Chicago: University of Chicago Press.

Baumol, William J., Panzar, John C., and Willig, Robert D. (1982), *Contestable Markets and the Theory of Industrial Structure*, New York: Harcourt Brace Jovanovich.

Becker, Gary S. (1976), *The Economic Approach to Human Behavior*, Chicago: University of Chicago Press.

Boulding, Kenneth (1986), 'What went wrong with economics?', *The American Economist*, 30, Spring.

Buchanan, James M. and Tullock, Gordon (1962), *The Calculus of Consent*, Ann Arbor: University of Michigan Press.

Bush, Paul D. (1988), 'The Theory of Institutional Change', in M.R. Tool (ed.), *Evolutionary Economics, I: Foundations of Institutional Thought*, Armonk, N.Y.: M.E. Sharpe.

Bush, Paul D. (1993), 'The Methodology of Institutional Economics', in M.R. Tool (ed.), *Institutional Economics: Theory, Method, Policy*, Dordrecht: Kluwer Academic Publishers.

Debreu, Gerard (1991), 'The Mathematization of Economic Theory', *American Economic Review*, **81**, March.

DeGregori, Thomas R. (1985), *A Theory of Technology*, Ames: University of Iowa Press.

Dennis, Ken (1994), 'Formalism in Economics' in Geoffrey M. Hodgson, Warren J. Samuels and Marc R. Tool (eds), *The Elgar Companion to Institutional and Evolutionary Economics*, Aldershot: Edward Elgar Publishing Ltd. Hereafter cited as *The Elgar Companion*.

Dewey, John (1938), *Logic: The Theory of Inquiry*, New York: Henry Holt.

Dewey, John (1939), *Theory of Valuation*, Chicago: University of Chicago Press.

Dewey, John (1946), *The Problems of Men*, New York: Philosophical Library.

Downs, Anthony (1957), *An Economic Theory of Democracy*, New York: Harpers.

Dragan, J.C. and Demetrescu, M.C. (1991), *Entropy and Bioeconomics: The New Paradigm of Nicholas Georgescu-Roegen*, 2nd ed., Rome: Nagard.

Eichner, Alfred S. (1976), *The Megacorp and Oligopoly*, White Plains, N.Y.: M.E. Sharpe Inc.

Etzioni, Amitai (1991), 'Eastern Europe: the wealth of lessons', *Challenge*, **34**, July–August.

Foster, J. Fagg (1981), 'The relation between the theory of value and economic analysis', *Journal of Economic Issues*, **15**, December.

Friedman, David D. (1990), *Price Theory*, Cincinnati: South-Western Publishing Co.

Friedman, Milton (1953), *Essays in Positive Economics*, Chicago: University of Chicago Press.

Georgescu-Roegen, Nicholas (1971), *The Entropy Law and the Economic Process*, Cambridge: Harvard University Press.

Goodwin, Richard M. (1990), *Chaotic Economic Dynamics*, Oxford: Clarendon Press.

Gordon, Robert A. (1976), 'Rigor and relevance in a changing institutional setting', *American Economic Review*, **66**, March.

Hahn, Frank H. (1973), *On the Notion of Equilibrium in Economics*, Cambridge: Cambridge University Press.

Hahn, Frank H. (1991), 'The next 100 years', *The Economic Journal*, **101**, January.

Hahnel, Robin and Albert, Michael (1990), *The Quiet Revolution in Welfare Economics*, Princeton: Princeton University Press.

Hodgson, Geoffrey M. (1988), *Economics and Institutions: A Manifesto for a Modern Institutional Economics*, Cambridge: Polity Press.

Hodgson, Geoffrey M. (1993), *Economics and Evolution: Bringing Life Back into Economics*, Oxford: Polity Press.

Hodgson, Geoffrey M. (1994), 'Critique of Neoclassical Microeconomic Theory', in *The Elgar Companion*.

Homan, Paul T. (1932), 'An appraisal of institutional economics', *American Economic Review*, **22**, March.

Klein, Philip A. (1980), 'Confronting power in economics: a pragmatic evaluation', *Journal of Economic Issues*, **14**, December.

Klein, Philip A. (1986), 'Reinventing the square wheel', in P.A. Klein (ed.), *Handbook on Behavioural Economics*, New York: JAI Press.

Klein, Philip A. (1987), 'Power and economic performance: the institutionalist view', *Journal of Economic Issues*, **21**, September.

Kohler, Heinz (1990), *Intermediate Microeconomics: Theory and Applications*, 3rd ed., Glenview, Ill.: Scott, Foresman & Co.

Lawson, Tony (1994), 'The Limits of Econometrics', in *The Elgar Companion*.

Leontief, Wassily (1971), 'Theoretical assumptions and nonobserved facts', *American Economic Review*, **61**, March.

Lower, Milton D. (1988), 'The Concept of Technology within the Institutionalist Perspective' in M.R. Tool (ed.), *Evolutionary Economics, I: Foundations of Institutional Thought*, Armonk, N.Y.: M.E. Sharpe, Inc.

Miller, Edythe S. (1990), 'Economic efficiency', *Journal of Economic Issues*, **24**, September.

Miller, Edythe S. (1994), 'Theory of Economic Regulation' in *The Elgar Companion*.

Mirowski, Philip (1986), 'Mathematical Formalism and Economic Explanation', in Philip Mirowski (ed.), *The Reconstruction of Economic Theory*, Boston: Kluwer-Nijoff.

Mirowski, Philip (1988), 'The Philosophical Bases of Institutional Economics' in M.R. Tool (ed.), *Evolutionary Economics. I: Foundations of Institutional Thought*, Armonk, N.Y.: M.E. Sharpe.

Mirowski, Philip (1989), *More Heat than Light: Economics as Social Physics: Physics as Nature's Economics*, Cambridge: Cambridge University Press.

Murrell, Peter, *et al.* (1991), 'Symposium on economic transition in the Soviet Union and Eastern Europe', *Journal of Economic Perspectives*, **5**, Fall.

North, Douglass C. (1990), *Institutions, Institutional Change and Economic Performance*, Cambridge: Cambridge University Press.

Okun, Arthur M. (1981), *Prices and Quantities*, Washington D.C.: Brookings Institution.

Robbins, Lionel (1952), *On the Nature and Significance of Economic Science*, 2nd ed., London: Macmillan Co.

Rostow, W.W. [1960] (1990), *The Stages of Economic Growth*, Cambridge: Cambridge University Press.

Schultz, Theodore William (1961), 'Investment in human capital', *American Economic Review*, **51**, March.

Sheehan, Michael (1991), 'Why Ramsey pricing is wrong: the case of telecommunications regulation', *Journal of Economic Issues*, **25**, March.

Simon, Herbert A. (1979), 'Rational decision making in business organizations', *American Economic Review*, **69**, September.

Spulber, Daniel F. (1989), *Regulation and Markets*, Cambridge, Mass.: MIT Press.

Thorson, Thomas Landon (1970), *Biopolitics*, New York: Holt Rinehart Winston.

Tool, Marc R. [1979] (1985), *The Discretionary Economy: A Normative Theory of Political Economy*, Boulder: Westview Press.

Tool, Marc R. (1986), *Essays in Social Value Theory: A Neoinstitutionalist Contribution*, Armonk, N.Y.: M.E. Sharpe.

Trebing, Harry M. (1984), 'Public control of enterprise: neoclassical assault and neoinstitutional reform', *Journal of Economic Issues*, **18**, June.

Trebing, Harry M. (1987), 'Regulation of industry: an institutionalist approach', *Journal of Economic Issues*, **21**, December.

Veblen, Thorstein B. [1919] (1961), *The Place of Science in Modern Civilization*, New York: Russell and Russell.

Watkins, John (1992), 'Neoclassical economics as an exercise in ceremonialism: economics as physics envy', Paper presented at meetings of the Association for Institutional Thought, Denver, Colorado, (April), photocopy.

Wiles, Peter and Routh, Guy (1984) (eds), *Economics in Disarray*, Oxford: Basil Blackwell.

Williamson, Oliver (1986), *Economic Organization: Firms, Markets, and Policy Control*, New York: New York University Press.

Wilson, Edward O. (1978), *On Human Nature*, Cambridge: Harvard University Press.

Wray, L. Randall (1990), *Money and Credit in Capitalist Economies: The Endogenous Money Approach*, Aldershot: Edward Elgar Publishing Ltd.

PART II

Pricing, Costing and Valuation

3.   Contributions to neoinstitutional pricing theory*

Since all modern economies are, and must remain, monetary exchange econo-mies, theoretical explanations of ratios of exchange – prices – and their determination must constitute a major area of inquiry in any encompassing examination of the economic process.

This chapter is part of a more extensive inquiry into the character and explanatory capabilities of a neoinstitutionalist theory of price determination. My general concern is to help formulate a logically coherent and empirically grounded theory of discretionary pricing. 'Discretionary pricing' here refers to the use by individuals of achieved economic power significantly to specify or to influence monetary terms of exchange.

Following Eichner,[1] I distinguish at the outset between prices, which as ratios of exchange refer to numerical values indicating the amount of funds that must be given up for a good or service, and pricing, which refers to the behaviour and judgments that determine prices. This chapter is addressed primarily to pricing, that is, to matters relating to the formulation of prices.

In this chapter, I examine (a) the theoretical context of price determination, (b) the institutional context of price determination, and (c) contributions of institutional economists to a theory of discretionary pricing, especially with regard to the corporate oligopolistic sector. I give particular attention to the views of Thorstein Veblen, Walton Hamilton, Gardiner Means and John Kenneth Galbraith, as well as to contributions of Alfred Eichner and Arthur Okun that are correlative with neoinstitutional economics.

I   THE THEORETICAL CONTEXT

Neoclassical economists have long understood the significance of price de-termination as part of the exchange process. Indeed, their primary interest has been to offer analyses of market pricing in different settings on the assump-

*Paper presented at meetings of the European Association for Evolutionary Political Economy, Florence, November 1990. Published in Geoffrey M. Hodgson and Ernesto Screpanti (1991) (eds), *Rethinking Economics: Markets, Technology and Economic Evolution*, Aldershot: Edward Elgar. Reprinted with permission.

tion that to explain market price determination is tantamount to explaining virtually everything of importance in the economic process. Their universe of inquiry has typically been confined to an analysis of pricing phenomena tending to market equilibria that define economic efficiency. The model of a free competitive market system is advocated as the most efficient allocative mechanism. Unfettered price determination within such markets, as explained by marginal analysis, accomplishes this efficient allocation. Such a perspective reflects 'the intuitive belief', as Professor Kaldor characterizes it,

> that the price mechanism is the key to everything, the key instrument in guiding the operation of an undirected, unplanned, free market economy. The Walrasian model and its most up-to-date successor may both be highly artificial abstractions from the real world but the truth that the theory conveys – that prices provide the guide to all economic action – must be fundamentally true, and its main implication that free markets secure the best results must also be true.[2]

Here 'truth' is a matter of logical and rhetorical affirmation, not of comprehensive evidential demonstration, while 'best', in a typical case, is an approximation of Paretian optimality. The better off-worse off calculations in such Paretian judgments are undergirded by a tacit acceptance of utility as the meaning of social value and utility maximization as the preferred social goal.[3] Prices paid in unfettered markets are the valuation measures.

This a priori focus of neoclassical inquiry has defined the discipline of economics for mainstream scholars for most of this century. Its advocates have generated 'market mentalities' (Polanyi, Kindleberger) as the products of their instruction and dominion. Neoclassical orthodoxy constitutes the 'conventional wisdom' (Galbraith) on all manner of policy options. Vigorous advocacy of shrinking governments, deregulation and enterprise zones are among recent policy reflections of this view. Moreover, positivist claims notwithstanding, such price determination is presumed by these market mentalities to have both practical and moral significance.[4] The neoclassical 'price system' is alleged to be simultaneously a pervasive characterization of how prices tend to be determined in most markets and a stipulation of how prices ought to be determined in virtually all markets. Departures from price-competitive market determinations are examined as pathology. The abstract ideal defines the proper price system. The normative use of this competitive model remains endemic in orthodox neoclassical theory generally.[5]

But within the sometimes contentious house of orthodoxy there is widespread recognition that the postulated theory of automatic, mechanistic price determination in free competitive markets is not necessarily descriptively adequate. Orthodox economists do not contend that free market pricing under conditions of pure or perfect competition actually and comprehensively prevails in any economy. The earlier literature on monopolistic competition[6] and imperfect competition,[7] and the more recent literature on externalities and market failures,[8] are troublesome contributions, among others, that confirm extensive behaviour at variance with the general model.[9] They suggest that neoclassical theory does not provide the general theory of price determination after all.[10] One can hardly claim generality when confronted with substantial nonconforming conduct and events.

As I explore below, managers, at least of large-scale enterprises, are increasingly perceived as price makers rather than price takers. Fixprice models usually come closer to reality than flexprice models. As Arthur Okun observed, 'models that focus on price takers and auctioneers and that assume continuous clearing of the market generate inaccurate microeconomics as well as misleading macroeconomics'.[11] Even so, it appears that neoclassical theorists assume that the general theory is one of free market price determination, from which there are occasional departures. Neoinstitutionalists, in contrast, argue that the more inclusive and descriptively accurate theory is one of discretionary pricing and that instances of free market determination are exceptionally rare.

II THE INSTITUTIONAL CONTEXT

All social orders, of necessity, provide for the function of exchange to occur. Institutional arrangements are everywhere used to facilitate the reciprocal activity of trading money in some form for goods or services. Monetary exchange typically involves the transfer of discretion over the objects of exchange.

'Institutions' are often defined by neoinstitutionalists as 'socially prescribed patterns of correlated behavior'.[12] Institutional arrangements comprising markets both condition and correlate behaviour in the exchange process. Such patterns of correlation clearly include the establishment and publication of prices. Markets are defined by Hodgson as 'a set of social institutions in which a large number of commodity exchanges of a specific type regularly take place, and to some extent are facilitated and structured by those institutions'.[13]

In the neoclassical market model, the primary institutions facilitating exchange are private ownership and legally enforceable contracts. Ownership consists of a legally sanctioned area of discretion over the possession, use and disposition of an item. Ownership is transferred with agreed-upon exchange; contracts stipulate the terms of the exchange; governments ensure compliance with contracts. But in the neoclassical formulation, markets themselves remain largely unspecified, being accorded no other structural character.[14] Neoclassical analyses do not reflect the breadth and complexity of behaviour actually correlated in markets, nor the roles of customs and habits in conditioning market conduct, nor the patterns and varying criteria of choice-making exhibited. Market motivations are simplistically affirmed as profit and/or utility maximization; market participation reflects 'constrained maximization'.

Neoinstitutionalists recognize that modern markets are comprised of a large number of usually complex correlated patterns of behaviour, all of which, though typically habitual, are initially creations of people as discretionary agents. Such correlated patterns organize and structure exchange activity. They specify behaviour not only with reference, at times, to property and contract, but also, for example, to acquisition of information, communication among participants and transportation of items exchanged.[15] Customary, legal, political and economic patterns of behaviour are all present to regularize exchange practices and to provide some measure of predictability or security of expectations for participants. *Customary*: tradition may stipulate who in a family or a corporate firm is (are) the power-wielding and status-bearing market participant(s). *Legal*: laws specify the place, time, character, media and terms of exchange. *Political*: stipulations of governing bodies define where, and to what extent, discretion over market exchange shall reside, and whose economic interests are to be served. *Economic*: organizations of market participants – unions, megacorps, cartels, marketing coops, trade associations, business 'clubs' – impinge on and help shape market conduct. In brief, 'markets are organized and institutionalized exchange'.[16] However, the customary and conventional character of market institutional structures, including prices, requires emphasis. Established exchange arrangements, once created, tend to persist. Habitual patterns of behaviour, as conventions in price setting, are commonplace.[17] G.L.S. Shackle suggests a reason:

> Prices which have stood at particular levels for some time acquire thereby some sanction and authority. They are the 'right' and even the 'just' prices. But also they are the prices to which the society has adapted its ways and habits, they are prices which mutually cohere in an established frame of social life.[18]

This recognition will recur in the contributions of Galbraith and Okun below.

As with other facets of the economic order, the structures of prices, the lists, schedules and patterns of relative prices, and price-setting practices all vary widely among economies and among sectors within economies. The traditional customs and conventions of pricing in the National Health Service in Great Britain, for example, will reflect indigenous judgments somewhat unique to that culture; they will diverge from the pricing of socialized medicine on the Continent and from fee-for-service medicine and private health insurance in the US. Similarly, pricing patterns and practices in agriculture accomplished by subsidies and management of aggregate supplies, or in the learned professions through fee schedules, will differ dramatically from price leadership and mark-up pricing in industry, as well as from regulatory commission control of prices in public utilities. There is thus extensive variation among political economies and among economic sectors within them both in the structure of prices and in the correlating patterns through which the determination of prices is accomplished.

But the generalization that virtually all significant prices are set as discretionary acts of identifiable persons – that existential markets are, in large part, shaped and staffed by price makers rather than price takers – is an argument I make here and throughout the rest of the chapter. As Galbraith observed:

> We are profoundly conditioned by the theology of the market. ... A price that is fixed by the seller to a singular degree does not seem good. Accordingly, it requires a major act of will to think of price-fixing as both normal and having economic function. In fact, it is normal in all advanced industrial societies.[19]

Why, from an institutional perspective, is price fixing 'normal' in all major economies? Why has discretionary price setting become endemic? Market participants seek and acquire control over price setting in order to reduce uncertainty of judgment. The reason one looks virtually in vain for examples of an actual pure or perfect market in the real world is that no market seller, in such a setting, can get sufficient relevant information to make informed economic judgments. The continuing uncertainties are destabilizing. Continuous unfettered competition, where markets actually determine prices, would be traumatic and intolerable. The inability reasonably to predict and control the character and direction of exchange phenomena (most particularly price changes), and the difficulties of influencing price elasticities of demand, make the following exceedingly hard, if not impossible: reflective, means-consequence judgments concerning the level and character of production, the nature and extent of investment, the creation and/or employment of new technology, hiring policies and practices, and the like. The most critically significant variables are unpredictable. Having to adjust to prices determined elsewhere narrows one's own choices; gaining the ability to adjust one's own prices widens choices.

An observation made by Jan Kregel with regard to investment decision making in Keynesian theory, applies, in my view, more generally:

> The information required for rational decision making does not exist; the market mechanism cannot provide it. But, just as nature abhors a vacuum, the economic system abhors uncertainty. The system reacts to the absence of the information the market cannot provide by creating uncertainty-reducing institutions: wage contracts, debt contracts, supply agreements, administered prices, [and] trading agreements.[20]

I would modify this view only by attributing the reaction to the absence of market information, not to the 'system', but to those in the polity and/or economy who have achieved discretionary control over institutional adjustments, and are willing and able to use it. The discretionary agent(s) responsible for any significant economic organization (public or private) must gain and retain some appreciable control over prices charged, and, if possible, over prices paid.

The quest for increasing security of expectation is unending. To seek and acquire as much control as possible over the forces and factions which ultimately determine the extent of discretion, the character of discretion and the duration of the organization, constitute the real 'bottom line'. Among such 'forces and factions' price-setting powers figure prominently. Price fixing is, and must continue to be, 'normal' – meaning typical, habitual and, in some considerable measure, predictable.

Having now considered the institutional character of markets and pricing, and why discretionary control over price determination is sought, I conclude this section with a brief illustrative exploration of institutional configurations in and through which pricing judgments are made.

In most advanced economies, the modern large corporation is the major institutional complex through which industrial goods and major services are produced and distributed. Although its specific form varies, it is usually created only with governmental permission. As a legal person in the eyes of the law, it has legal entity status and standing; it can sue and be sued. Ownership is nominally 'private', but private owners' discretion may or may not be a viable instrument for attaining and retaining control. In most megacorps, through fragmentation and wide dispersion of shares, discretion for ordinary stockholders may well be limited to a passive claim to dividends. Ownership is dispersed, but control is concentrated, as Veblen observed[21] and Berle and Means demonstrated.[22]

The modern large corporation is, in effect, a legally sanctioned private government usually run by a self-perpetuating dynastic management. Its government-like powers include the abilities to impose, deny and manipulate behaviour of persons subject to its hegemonic control. It is subject to constraints of competitive rivalry, but normally not price competition. It defines cultural tastes; it creates demand for its own products; it influentially participates in determining the content of higher education; it significantly shapes the social life of its employees.[23] It also exhibits a continuing participatory role in bringing pressure and influence to bear on political processes at all levels.

The modern oligopolistic corporation is subject, in varying degrees, to public constraints of environmental compliance, labour laws, anti-discrimination and fair employment rules, etc. Firms may confront governmental price constraints (general or industry specific), negative political responses to pricing judgments made, and government macromanagement policies (fiscal and monetary) that help importantly to define the context for price administration. The megacorp may be a recipient of public largess through subsidies (including tax expenditures), trade protections, public education of its employees, and, at times, mandated exemption status to regulations (pollution controls, safety standards) and the like.

In their unique concerns with price determination, price setters in a typically oligopolist organization do not necessarily have an easy time of it.[24] They must, of course, set prices which cover their continuing costs of materials and labour, and a mark-up margin to generate the pecuniary options which residual balances provide. But as well, they must function in a difficult and risk-filled, institutional environment that may well include the following: intraindustry concerns over retaliatory pricing responses from rivals at home; accommodation to or adjustment of pricing judgments of material suppliers; negotiation of wage agreements under collective bargaining rules and regulations; market sharing agreements, etc. In addition, they may face interindustry pressures from aggressive, state-subsidized and supported contenders from abroad and negotiation of pricing accords (cartel or otherwise) with international firms.

Given the foregoing and the significance and complexities of price making, it comes as no surprise that corporations have developed highly trained specialists as price setters who work in specific and sophisticated agencies (bureaus or divisions) within the corporate or conglomerate complex and are responsible solely for price determination.[25]

Similarly, there are multiple loci of pricing powers scattered through the various branches and levels of government. These are considered in Chapter 5 below.

When one asks, then, where are discretionary prices determined, the answer must be sought among the complexities and intricacies of the institutional fabric through which pricing power has been achieved, retained and exercised. In any problematic context where access to such information is crucial, only inquiry into the complexities of the structural fabric involved can disclose the particular pricing power centres, who the price-setting agents are, the criteria reflected in their decisions, and the consequences that flow therefrom.

At this point, the focus of the chapter narrows, given space constraints, to the consideration by institutionalists of price determination, mainly in oligopolistic enterprises. It is in this realm that disarming apologias for price-setting power, rooted in neoclassical price theory, are most persistent; it is also in this area that many of the major price-fixing decisions are initiated, with wide repercussions through the economy.

III   INSTITUTIONALIST CONTRIBUTIONS TO A THEORY OF DISCRETIONARY PRICING

Institutionalists in the US have been contributing to a theory of discretionary pricing for nearly a century. That contribution began with Thorstein Veblen and involves two largely complementary and converging approaches. The older tradition encompasses a literature on administered pricing, to which Walton H. Hamilton, Gardiner C. Means and John Kenneth Galbraith, among others, contributed. The more recent and more technical tradition is reflected in writings on mark-up or cost-plus pricing by Alfred Eichner, Frederic S. Lee[26] and other such heterodox-leaning and empirically-oriented scholars as Arthur Okun. After touching base with Veblen, I canvass selected examples of work of some of these contributors in search of conceptual tools, analytical formulations and synthetic characterizations for a neoinstitutional theory of discretionary pricing.

Thorstein B. Veblen

Although Veblen certainly was among the first American scholars to observe and explain the nature and significance of the corporate revolution in the organization of the economy,[27] he did not dwell at length on the pricing power of the then newly-emerging giant corporations. He did, however, see a general trend towards the development of 'business coalitions' that had an important bearing on price setting:

> 'Cutthroat' competition ... can be done away by 'pooling the interests' of the competitors, so soon as all or an effective majority of the business concerns which are rivals in the market combine and place their business management under one directive head. When this is done, by whatever method, selling of goods or services at competitively varying prices is replaced by collective selling ... at prices fixed on the basis of 'what the traffic will bear'.[28]

Moreover,

> [W]hen the coalition comes effectually to cover its special field of operations, it is able not only to fix the prices which it will accept ... but also in a considerable measure to fix the prices or rates which it will pay for materials, labor, and other services (such as transportation) on a similar basis.[29]

For Veblen, the drive to create monopolies – what he called 'business coalitions' – is motivated by the quest for pecuniary gain, is prompted by the need to employ and control newly-emerging technologies, and is necessary to provide 'the only refuge from chronic depression'. The incorporation of newer machine technology 'makes competitive business impracticable ... but it makes coalition practicable'.[30] At the time he wrote, the trend to concentration was already well-advanced: 'it is doubtful if there are any successful business ventures within the range of the modern industries from which the monopoly element is wholly absent'.[31]

With Veblen, then, we get an early characterization of a corporate dominated, administered price, industrial economy.

Walton Hale Hamilton

In the more than 40-year publishing career of the distinguished lawyer and economist, Walton Hamilton, are to be found some of the most penetrating and significant analyses of the emergent corporate economy. Less sardonic and somewhat more empirically grounded than Veblen, Hamilton explores the evolutionary transformation of the locus and use of economic power by corporations in labour relations and wage setting,[32] in the use of patents and their protection,[33] and in administered pricing judgments and practices,[34] among others. Attention here is necessarily confined to his concern with administered pricing.

Heading a small research staff for the Cabinet Committee on Price Policy appointed by President Roosevelt in 1934, Hamilton guided an inquiry into the actual pricing practices of a number of basic American industries. At issue was consideration of industrial policy which he defined as 'an aggregate of the measures contrived for the guidance of industry by all the agencies which operate upon it'.[35] Of the completed studies, those on the automobile, tire, gasoline, cottonseed, dress, whiskey and milk industries were published in Hamilton (ed.), *Price and Price Policies*.[36] In the Preface to that work he observed that

> the literature of industry was inadequate to the demands of price policy. Accounts of how in general industry is organized and how in the abstract prices are made were available in abundance. Yet, with notable exceptions, little was at hand upon the structures of particular industries, their distinctive habits, their unique patterns of control, and the multiplex of arrangements – stretching away from technology to market practice – which give magnitude to their prices.[37]

Hamilton and his fellow researchers sought to fill that gap in knowledge and thereby to contribute to policy deliberations.

In his concluding chapter,[38] Hamilton did not presume to draw general principles from this sampling of industrial practice. He distilled no synthetic summary of price determination. What he found in these empirical studies, rather, was an extraordinary complexity of institutional structure bearing on pricing practices. Each industrial area studied revealed an idiosyncratic fabric of diverse interrelations and interdependencies. Each had a different history of emergence; each exhibited a somewhat unique pattern of customary behaviours; each had its own way of arriving at pricing decisions and of implementing pricing judgments. Although cost considerations were of some significance in virtually all pricing judgments, nowhere were they an exclusive concern. Loci of discretion over price varied widely among the industries studied, but nowhere could one presume or show that atomistic, automatic, freely competitive market forces were determining prices in auction markets. Hamilton recognized the cultural origins of demand: tastes are acquired; preferences are learned; industries must lead in creating markets for their goods. They must also adapt to changes induced by the growth of knowledge and new technology. Custom influenced the cost structure as well. He was aware of the differing habits and practices which impinge on workers' wages and salaries; acknowledging the complexity of production programmes, he recognized the difficulties of assigning cost in joint-product firms.

In sum, 'a touch of the motley rests upon the ways of price making. ... Price bears the marks of the process from which it emerges.'[39] 'The business unit is not content to leave its affairs ... and its survival to the arbitration of an impersonal market. It must bestir itself to hold its own.'[40] 'Price, quality, service, blarney, guile, and the creative touch are alike weapons of promotion and devices of accommodation.'[41] But the manipulation of price, in quest of market control or shares, may be 'too dangerous a mechanism to be employed'. That is, discretion over prices is held, but prevailing circumstances in the industry may discourage its use. Industrial leaders will then seek a formal or informal understanding to shift to non-price forms of rivalry.[42] 'Thus price – and the costs which attend it – are a pecuniary reflection of the usages which impinge upon the making and marketing of a good. These usages run through the whole industrial process. ... They are embedded in the ways of an industry just as the folkways are embedded in the culture of a primitive or a civilized people.'[43]

Hamilton's contribution to an institutionalist theory of discretionary pricing, then, consists of: (a) his recognition and demonstration of overt and pervasive pricing power in industry, (b) his uncovering of the role of convention and custom in actual industrial pricing practice, (c) his revelation of the remarkable variability and complexity in pricing practices, (d) and, in recognizing the probable need for an industrial policy to impinge on industrial leaders' discretion over pricing, his implication that the criteria of pricing judgments be examined and appraised.

Gardiner C. Means

For much of Gardiner Means's professional life, his research ambition was to provide a 'new paradigm for macrotheory' – a 'new macrotheory based on the realities of our modern economy',[44] differing fundamentally from the neoclassical and Keynesian approaches. Early in his career, he had 'laid down basic postulates for the new theory', two being of special significance here. One is that 'a large part of production is carried on by a few great corporations in which final ownership is widely dispersed, ownership and control are largely separated, and management is largely a self-perpetuating body'. A second is that 'most prices are administered privately (or by agencies of government) and behave in a fashion quite different from that indicated by traditional theory'.[45] While the 'new paradigm' was evidently never completed, Means's contribution to a theory of discretionary pricing is revealed principally in his empirical demonstration of these two postulates.

Means was not academically trained as an institutional economist; his early empirical research into corporate structure and agricultural pricing drove him, as a fledgling scientist, to seek theory that would better explain the factual realities he observed. Heterodoxy was fuelled by his experience as a scholar.[46] His research (with Adolf Berle) that culminated in *The Modern Corporation and Private Property* (1932) generated the first postulate; a series of papers, incorporating his empirical research and prepared as testimony for Congressional hearings, provided the second.[47]

Means was the principle formulator of 'the theory of administered pricing'. The following is one of his more illuminating presentations of this idea:

> An administered price has been defined as a price which is set, usually by a seller, and held constant for a period of time and a series of transactions. Such a price does not imply the existence of monopoly or of collusion. However, it can occur only where a particular market is dominated by one or relatively few sellers (or buyers). It is the normal method of selling in most markets today. Its significance ... rests, first on the fact that it lies entirely outside traditional economic theory and, second, that where the area of discretion in price administration is large, administered prices produce economic results and problems of economic policy quite different from those dealt with by traditional theory.[48]

The theory of administered pricing was the basis for some partially successful federal policies.[49] Though the object of considerable professional controversy,[50] its credibility has survived.[51] Price administration is accomplished in large corporations through various techniques, including target pricing. As perceived by Means[52] and John Blair,[53] price determination is customarily accomplished by the calculation of a 'target rate of return on capital'. What is sought is the highest rate of return on capital 'consistent with a healthy growth of the business'. Calculations of such target rates require decisions on the level of operation, estimates of the costs of production at various operating levels, determination of prices which will yield the desired target rates, and, given costs and operating rates, the setting of discretionary prices in view of actual market conditions.[54] Recourse to this pricing technique was confirmed in the Brookings study on *Pricing in Big Business*[55] and later by John Blair.[56]

Finally, it is interesting to note that, although Means did not make explicit use of social value theory, he did recognize that judgments of appropriateness or propriety must be made concerning prices administratively set. In this particular context, he argues that target rate prices which yield returns on capital no greater than 'the competitive cost of capital' may be considered as consistent with the public interest. A rough approximation of such a rate is that allowed public utilities by effective regulatory commissions.[57] '[Any] form of regulation should ... bring about the same type of economic behavior that would prevail if the industry were competitive.'[58] In this latter deference to the normative use of the competitive model, Means's break with orthodoxy was clearly incomplete.

Means, however, did not believe that market forces would provide a sufficient constraint on the power to administer prices. Although his specific policy recommendations shifted over the years as the problems to which he addressed himself changed, he consistently advocated public government supervision sufficient to ensure that the public interest was served. He argued, for example, that 'inflation in the concentrated industries can be restrained only by the imposition of direct price and wage controls', and that 'restraints should be imposed on sudden and substantial increases in the target rate of return'.[59]

In sum, Means repeatedly demonstrated, to his own satisfaction if not to that of his neoclassical critics, the continuing fact and practice of administered pricing in American industry. He posed, but did not adequately answer, the question of how to decide when judgments reflected in private price determination are in the public interest.

John Kenneth Galbraith

Perhaps no American economist in this century has been confronted with a more dramatic or significant challenge of applying institutional analysis to an area of critical public policy than was John Kenneth Galbraith upon his appointment, in 1941, as head of what later would be called the Office of Price Administration (OPA). This 'Price Czar Novitiate'[60] had the task of introducing and managing a comprehensive programme of price control and rationing for the wartime American economy. As preparation for that task, the long tradition of market-deferential, neoclassical analysis was, in his view, largely irrelevant. Orthodox economists thought it was unwise for him to undertake such a responsibility and impossible for him to achieve the goal sought.[61] In an important, if small and unfortunately neglected, book reflecting on this experience entitled *A Theory of Price Control*,[62] Galbraith explained how his original understanding of corporate pricing behaviour was comprehensively expanded and empirically reconfirmed by his experience as head of the OPA. In brief, he could generate his own tautology and assert that 'it is relatively easy to fix prices that are already fixed'.[63]

Here he distinguished between markets that were imperfectly or monopolistically competitive (oligopolies) and those that still resembled price competitive markets. This developed into a distinction between the 'planning' sector and the 'market' sector in his later work.[64] Imperfect markets could be controlled directly and with greater ease than was anticipated. Price competitive markets could also be controlled, but with more difficulty and only if rationing was also employed.

In imperfect markets, OPA administered price control was easier because a comparatively smaller number of firms were involved, enforcement was facilitated, and prices – having become institutionalized – were already relatively inflexible.[65] Supply-price conditions were also relatively stable at the time. Given unused capacity, production (except for agriculture and the extractive industries) could generally be expanded for war purposes without increasing fixed costs and thus without creating major pressures for increasing prices. In a few instances, subsidies were used to 'offset higher "marginal" costs in increasing-cost industries'.[66]

But even in efforts to control prices at the retail level, Galbraith came to realize that customary and conventional pricing was the rule. The price charged for the product or service is strictly a conventional markup. Profit maximization is not an operational option. The small seller 'has neither the information nor the capacity to adjust his margins commodity by commodity, week by week, or season by season, in such manner as might maximize his returns'; he 'relies on rule-of thumb'. 'The effect of a well-designed system of price control in markets of this kind is merely to continue accepted rules'.[67]

In sum, price control in imperfect markets is comparatively easy and can be quite successful; price control in price competitive markets – where market shares are small and pricing power is more limited than in oligopolistic firms – can also succeed, but is more difficult. What is confirmed for our purposes, however, is the pervasiveness of administered pricing in the so-called private sector, and the fact that comprehensive public control of privately administered prices, in this instance at least, was demonstrated to be both feasible and successful.

For Galbraith, the 'technostructure becomes the commanding power' in the modern giant corporation. As organized management, it is the locus of discretion over pricing decisions and much else that affects the corporation's character and continuity. Its decisions are collegial, but authoritarian.[68] The technostructure consists of the technical specialists who exercise de facto power and are placed hierarchically just below the pro forma executives and directors. These specialists generate and pool the specialized and technical knowledge that is required to fashion the productive process, creating and updating technological innovations and product improvements. 'For the exercise of this power – for product planning, to devise price and market strategies, for sales and advertising management, procurement planning, public relations and governmental relations – specialists are also needed.'[69] Governance of a megacorp is necessarily conjoint; members of the technostructure contribute their respective expertise and insights in reaching judgments. 'Collective intelligence' guides managerial decision making; the positions of hierarchical 'heads' – president, chairman, director – are often status-conferring, anachronistic relics of an older order from which power is eroding. But if they are aggressive, members of the board can sometimes influence the power of the technostructure and the direction in which it moves by eliciting sufficient support to change leadership officers (for example, chief executive officers), 'directing the decision-making process into new areas', and/or by calling in outside experts to appraise the performance of the directive cadre.[70]

The purposive goals which drive the technostructure – the uses to which its de facto power are put – are twofold: to protect 'the autonomy of its decision-making primarily by seeking to secure a minimum level of earnings', and to reward 'itself affirmatively with growth' of the firm. Incident to these quests, technological innovation and increasing earnings may also be pursued. Profits will be sought; they are not typically maximized, orthodoxy notwithstanding.[71]

If these 'protective and affirmative purposes of the technostructure' are to be realized, prices must be set and must remain under the tightest possible control.[72] Productive technology is specialized, complex, time-consuming to create and expensive. Corporate planning of price setting must be able to ensure that the necessary materials and equipment can be acquired. Prices must be firmly under discretionary control so that they can be revised, as necessary, to cover costs not wholly under control of the technostructure – as with the wage bill. Increased wages can be (and are) readily covered with increased prices. Prices must be firmly controlled to permit management and manipulation of demand.

Discretionary agents in megacorps must control prices to maintain their position vis-à-vis other firms. They must participate in a communal effort to preclude unplanned or preemptive price cutting. 'Oligopolistic cooperation'[73] with others is required to avoid losing control over their own enterprise. They must maintain a necessary level of earnings through adequate sales promotion. Prices must be set low enough to ensure adequate expanding sales. Unless they accommodate to existing price elasticities, growth and its benefits for the technostructure cannot be realized. Roughly uniform prices will be commonplace in an industry. If there is a dominant firm, its technostructure will serve as price leader and its affirmative purposes and protective patterns as the model for the industry. Given the complexity and interdependencies of the pricing patterns set, the intent is to leave most prices unchanged for an extended period of time. Each participant gains from predictability and is more adequately able to sustain control.

In sum, Galbraith reconfirmed the pervasiveness of discretionary pricing in the industrial sector, identified the dominant price setting group or cadre, and explained 'the protective and affirmative' criteria that guide its pricing choices.

Alfred S. Eichner

Although Alfred Eichner generally described himself as a Post Keynesian, there is a great deal of overlap between his critique of neoclassical orthodoxy and his recommended alternative approach, and those of neoinstitutionalists. Indeed, he sought to bring the two approaches into closer analytical congruity with his edited volume on *Why Economics is Not Yet a Science* (1983). He considered the neoclassical tradition, and especially its price theory, as 'intellectually bankrupt'; its claims to generality and scientific status were without foundation; moreover, because of its vacuousness, it was an unreliable guide to policy making[74] – judgments with which neoinstitutionalists concur.

Eichner set the familiar institutional context: 'commodity markets have been largely superseded by industrial markets and the family business by the megacorp as the representative firm within those markets'.[75] Megacorps, by 'virtue of their size and dominant market position, have considerable discretion in setting prices'. These firms, 'with their administered pricing policies for financing growth and expansion, have become the locus of decisionmaking within the decentralized system of private planning that operates within the US economy'.[76]

It was Eichner's central purpose to explain 'how prices are determined in the oligopolistic sector of the American economy, and how those prices, so determined, affect the growth and stability of the economy as a whole'.[77] He sought to provide a new micro foundation for Keynesian macroeconomic theory. The explanation offered may be characterized as a dynamic, extended cost-plus model in which the 'plus', as it varies over time and among industries, is also explained.[78] Two attributes in particular distinguish this pricing model from orthodox approaches. First, 'it is predicated upon realistic assumptions'. Second, it yields determinate solutions: empirically demonstrable accounts of pricing can be derived.[79]

The 'realistic assumptions' are rooted in institutionalist contributions: megacorps are characterized by a separation of ownership and managerial control. 'Production occurs within multiple plants or plant segments' in which factor coefficients are fixed by both 'technological and institutional constraints'. 'The firm's output is sold under conditions of recognized inter-dependence'; oligopolistic cooperation prevails.[80] Indeed, Eichner's 'operational definition of an industry' is 'that group of firms which share a day-to-day interest in the same set of price quotations for a class of goods they are each capable of producing'.[81]

The 'deterministic solutions', as explanations, become evident 'only from the long-run perspective of the industry as a whole, with one megacorp, the price leader, acting as a surrogate for all members of that industry'. The long run view does not explain the 'absolute price level but rather the change in that price level from one period to the next ... the marginal adjustment'. The megacorp price leader 'will vary the industry price so as to cover (1) any change in per unit average variable and fixed costs, and (2) any increased need for internally generated funds'.[82] What is demonstrated is that the pricing decision for a price leader megacorp 'is ultimately linked to the investment decision; ... prices are likely to be set so as to assure the internally generated funds necessary to finance a firm's desired rate of capital expansion'.[83] The substantial convergence of this view with the 'target return' arguments of Means and Blair (above) is now apparent.

Eichner summarized his discretionary pricing theory as follows:

> Thus, once the institutional context in which firms find themselves has been correctly identified, it is possible to explain the price observed in any industry ... according to the change in cost ... or the change in markup ... from the preceding time period. The prices actually observed are therefore the outcome of a historical process, with the change in cost ... reflecting the changing input-output relationships that define the reigning technology, and the change in markup ... reflecting the need for investment funds relative to the pricing power of firms.[84]

To pursue his broader goals of inquiry, Eichner extended his analysis to the corollary microeconomic consideration of factor pricing, in the course of which he found the neoclassical marginal productivity theory to be largely irrelevant. His own reformulation, in addressing the cost structure confronting megacorps, drew variously on the institutionalist literature on economic power, the sociological focus on social norms, the Marxian interest in surplus value, and the Keynesian stress on aggregate demand factors.[85] Beyond observing that factor prices are also largely administered, we need not, for present purposes, follow Eichner on this conceptual path.

In addition, Eichner explored the significance of his revised microeconomic theory for macroeconomic analysis. Here, given the megacorp's concern with price setting and investment to assure growth, and consequent concern with aggregate demand, Eichner's analysis 'lends theoretical support to the accelerator model of investment', and also to the recognition of the significance for the economy generally of the megacorp's investment spending from retained earnings. Megacorps thus play a central role in determining the secular growth rate of the economy.[86] Economic power, reflected in discretionary pricing, does matter.

Finally, in exploring policy implications, Eichner must, like other scholars, address the character and consequences of price judgments made by megacorps. He concluded that 'effective social control over the individual megacorp can be achieved by no more and no less than regulating both the rate of growth and the composition of aggregate investment'. The economic welfare of both individuals and the economy generally cannot otherwise be served. His major recommendation, then, was 'that a system of national indicative planning be established'.[87]

Arthur M. Okun

I have found nothing to suggest that Arthur Okun ever characterized himself as an institutionalist. Yet he, like institutionalists, was a theorist and a realist. I construe his analysis of pricing, with minor exceptions, to be both compatible with, and an extension of, earlier institutionalist contributions to a theory of discretionary pricing. More specifically, his work may be viewed as a plausible explanation of the conventional and customary markup pricing which Galbraith found in administering comprehensive price controls in non-oligopolistic markets during the days of OPA.

Okun appears to have been committed to the premise that theory ought actually to explain what it purports to explain. For him, mainstream orthodoxy had long since ceased to offer an adequate explanation of the pricing process; it did not provide a general theory of market behaviour.

As noted in Part I above, Okun distinguished between the realm of price makers and that of price takers in the modern economy. The portion of the economy exhibiting price takers in 'auction markets' is

> a small and shrinking sector of the U.S. economy. ... Most of our economy is dominated by cost-oriented prices and equity-oriented wages. Most prices are set by sellers whose principal concern is to maintain customers and market share over the long run. ... Prices are set to exceed costs by a percentage markup that displays only minor variations over the business cycle.[88]

The realm of price makers, then, is not confined to oligopolistic sellers only. It includes most of the economy except for 'active auction markets' reported on the financial pages of daily newspapers – financial assets, agricultural commodities, some primary metals and the like.[89]

In a fairly elaborate analysis of the complexities which price makers must face in determining the markups to be reflected in selling prices, Okun demonstrated, as have earlier institutionalists, that actual markets are institutionally complex. Of particular importance for Okun were the conventions and expectations that develop between sellers and buyers. Sellers offer stable prices, continuing services, access to credit, refund prerogatives, advanced sales notices and the like to secure customer loyalty and repeat purchases.[90] Such 'implicit contract' arrangements 'economize on a variety of information and transaction costs'.[91] Predictability, dependability and fulfilment of expectations through such correlated patterns give the firm some measure of control over its own demand as well as insulation from the competitive rivalry of other firms. Decisions on the size and frequency of price changes are then of critical significance. Alienating or disruptive changes in the continuity of expectations regarding prices are to be avoided. Firms regularly engage in price fixing as a routine effort to maintain their market shares. Their achieved market power is reflected in the degree to which their ambitions in that quest can be implemented.

Discretionary managers, in Okun's view, were more influenced in their pricing decisions by supply-side costs than by changes in demand:

> The setting of prices by marking up costs is a good first approximation to actually observed behavior in most areas of industry, trade, and transportation. Firms not only behave that way, but also condition their customers to expect them to behave that way. ... Price increases that are based on cost increases are 'fair,' while those based on demand increases often are viewed as unfair.[92]

A significant hazard in using 'cost-oriented pricing' as a standard in setting prices, however, is that customers do not, and cannot, observe the price setting deliberation process. They must take on faith any contention that price increases were caused or validated by cost increases.

The conceptual dilemma facing price setters is itself quite complex. The definition and measurement of costs that are to become part of the bases for price determinations require price setters to take account of such standards or constructs as historical costs, replacement costs valuation adjustments, standard volume unit costs, full or direct costs, and material costs.[93] Even so, 'the empirical evidence for the United States suggests that cost-oriented pricing is the dominant mode of behavior'.[94]

Okun has one main reservation concerning the Means-Blair theory of administered pricing. His own customer-market model allows for various causal factors to determine the pricing behavior of an industry, while the administered-prices view focuses on the single explanation of industrial concentration. ... Markup rigidity seems ... [to be] simply too pervasive across the US economy to be attributable to oligopoly. ... The aggregate evidence on pricing in private nonfarm business accords closely with the markup model.[95]

Okun's pricing theory, concerning customer-seller attachments, expectations and conventions, does appear to account for this limitation in the Means-Blair position. Recall, in addition, that Okun reconfirms Galbraith's earlier characterization that smaller, private, nonfarm businesses also employ markup pricing practices and reflect price rigidity. Discretionary price determination is thus not confined to oligopolies.

Finally, although Okun did not confront institutional appraisals directly, he considered his 'customer-market view of inflexible prices' to imply an approvable market structure. It is 'an inherently desirable institutional arrangement' because it 'economizes on the expenses of shopping, trying out products, and otherwise engaging in transactions'. There are significant 'benefits of customer attachments'.[96] Accordingly, these pricing conventions serve what are, for Okun, economically defensible purposes; they are normatively approvable.

CONCLUSION

While no elaborate summary is provided, the following generalities may be noted concerning institutionalist and quasi-institutionalist contributions to a theory of discretionary pricing:

- Exchange occurring in non-auction markets is not simplistic and reducible to maximizing tenets and singular behavioural constants. It is accomplished by complex, and widely divergent, patterns of institutional arrangements that facilitate pricing judgments. In all economies, these arrangements continue to evolve as new problems and their consequences are identified and new pricing judgments and structures are instituted to resolve them.
- To these institutionalists, the mainstream neoclassical theory of pricing does not explain the overwhelmingly dominant phenomenon of discretionary pricing in advanced industrial economies. In their view, the explanatory capabilities and policy relevance of that approach become more and more implausible as empirical inquiry and theoretical critiques undermine its claim to significance.

- At the level both of oligopolistic megacorps and of smaller non-auction market sellers, prices are determined as deliberate decisions by price setters to serve a variety of individual and firm goals. The presumption that a Walrasian-like price mechanism – structure-free, atomistic auction-house – is the vehicle through which prices are determined becomes even more conjectural, in their view.

- Such discretionary pricing typically reflects the use of one or other variant of markup, cost-plus, target or similar pricing rule. Actual pricing rules develop into conventions; pricing judgments are made; markets are institutionally ordered; market behaviour is correlated.

- Price-making decision bodies vary with industry structures, custom and conventions, and extant power centres. The technostructure – an information, organization and/or technology dominating (managerial) elite – appears to be a typical locus of price making power in megacorps. But only extensive inquiry will disclose the particular loci of power, the pricing rules and structures employed, and the character of pricing judgments made.

- All contributors acknowledge, but do not extensively address, the need for external standards or criteria with which to judge the propriety of pricing decisions made. Such standards reflect conditioned views of what is a fair, proper, right, or just price. Public appraisals of private pricing decisions, of course, have long been a common practice. But there is no agreement among these contributors on what standards or criteria should be used for such appraisals or what social value theory they should be based on. An agenda for further inquiry is suggested.

NOTES

1. Eichner (1988), pp. 137–66.
2. Kaldor (1985), pp. 13–14.
3. Tool (1986), pp. 89–101.
4. Ayres (1944), pp. 3–38.
5. Tool (1986), pp. 104–25.
6. Chamberlin [1933] (1948).
7. Robinson [1933] (1969).
8. Spulber (1989).
9. Tool (1986), pp. 104–25.
10. Joskow (1975), pp. 270–79.
11. Okun (1981), p. 23.
12. Bush (1988), p. 126.
13. Hodgson (1988), p. 174.
14. Ibid, pp. 182–3.
15. Ibid, p. 174.
16. Ibid.
17. Ibid, pp. 125–34, 182–7.

18. Shackle (1972), p. 227.
19. Galbraith (1967), p. 190.
20. Kregel (1980), p. 40.
21. Veblen [1904] (1932).
22. Berle and Means (1932).
23. Dugger (1989).
24. Hamilton (1974), essay 3.
25. Kaplan, Dirlam and Lanzillotti (1958), pp. 220–47.
26. Lee (1993) presents an excellent survey of Post Keynesian studies of pricing procedures.
27. Veblen [1904] (1932).
28. Ibid, p. 258.
29. Ibid, p. 261.
30. Ibid, p. 263.
31. Ibid, p. 54.
32. Hamilton and May [1923] (1968).
33. Hamilton (1957), pp. 63–99.
34. Hamilton *et al.* (1938).
35. Ibid, p. 528.
36. Ibid.
37. Ibid, p. vii.
38. Ibid, pp. 525–56.
39. Ibid, p. 530.
40. Ibid, p. 549.
41. Ibid, p. 550.
42. Ibid, p. 542.
43. Ibid.
44. Means (1975), p. 154.
45. Ibid, p. 152.
46. Samuels and Medema (1990); Lee and Samuels (1991).
47. Means (1963), pp. 213–39.
48. Means (1959), p. 4.
49. Means (1975), pp. 14–22.
50. Stigler (1963); Adams and Lanzillotti (1963); Blair (1972); Kahn (1975); Samuels and Medema (1990).
51. Kefauver (1965).
52. Means (1975).
53. Blair (1975), pp. 33–67.
54. Means (1963), pp. 220–21.
55. Kaplan, Dirlam and Lanzillotti (1958).
56. Blair (1976).
57. Means (1963), p. 222.
58. Means (1975), p. 66.
59. Ibid.
60. Galbraith (1981), pp. 124–44.
61. Galbraith [1952] (1980), pp. 2–7.
62. Ibid.
63. Ibid, p. iv.
64. Galbraith (1973).
65. Galbraith [1952] (1980), pp. 10–19.
66. Ibid, pp. 20–25.
67. Ibid, p. 18.
68. Galbraith (1973), pp. 83–6.
69. Ibid, p. 82.
70. Ibid, p. 89.
71. Ibid, p. 107.
72. Ibid, pp. 112–21.

73. Munkirs and Sturgeon (1985).
74. Eichner (1983), pp. 205–6.
75. Eichner (1988), p. 137.
76. Eichner here cites Munkirs (1985).
77. Eichner (1976), p. 1.
78. Ibid, pp. 4–5.
79. Ibid, p. 3.
80. Ibid.
81. Ibid, p. 10.
82. Ibid, p. 4.
83. Ibid, p. x.
84. Ibid, p. 164.
85. Ibid, pp. 5–6.
86. Ibid, pp. 7–8.
87. Ibid, p. 9.
88. Okun (1979), pp. 1–5.
89. Okun (1981), p. 134.
90. Ibid, pp. 138–48.
91. Ibid, p. 154.
92. Ibid, p. 153.
93. Ibid, pp. 154–64.
94. Ibid, p. 165.
95. Ibid, pp. 175–6.
96. Ibid, p. 178.

REFERENCES

Adams, Walter and Lanzillotti, Robert F. (1963), 'The Reality of Administered Prices', in U.S. Senate, Committee on the Judiciary, Subcommittee on Antitrust and Monopoly, *Administered Prices: A Compendium on Public Policy*, 88th Cong., 1st sess. Washington D.C.: U.S. Government Printing Office. (Hereafter cited as *Administered Prices: A Compendium*.)

Ayres, Clarence E. (1944), *The Theory of Economic Progress*, Chapel Hill: University of North Carolina.

Berle, Adolf A. and Means, Gardiner C. (1932), *The Modern Corporation and Private Property*, New York: Macmillan.

Blair, John M. (1972), *Economic Concentration: Structure, Behavior, and Public Policy*, New York: Harcourt Brace Jovanovich.

Blair, John M. (1975), 'Inflation in the United States: A Short-Run Target Return Model', in John M. Blair *et al.*, *The Roots of Inflation*, New York: Burt Franklin.

Blair, John M. (1976), *The Control of Oil*, New York: Pantheon.

Bush, Paul D. (1988), 'The Theory of Institutional Change' in Marc R. Tool (ed.), *Evolutionary Economics, I: Foundations of Institutional Thought*, Armonk, N.Y.: M.E. Sharpe.

Chamberlin, Edward H. [1933] (1948), *The Theory of Monopolistic Competition*, Cambridge: Harvard University.

Dugger, William M. (1989), *Corporate Hegemony*, New York: Greenwood.

Eichner, Alfred S. (1976), *The Megacorp and Oligopoly: Micro Foundations of Macro Dynamics*, White Plains, N.Y.: M.E. Sharpe.

Eichner, Alfred S. (1983), 'Why Economics is Not Yet a Science', in his *Why Economics is Not Yet a Science*, Armonk, N.Y.: M.E. Sharpe.

Eichner, Alfred S. (1988), 'Prices and Pricing' in Marc R. Tool (ed.), *Evolutionary Economics. II: Institutional Theory and Policy*, Armonk, N.Y.: M.E. Sharpe.

Flash, Edward S., Jr. (1965), *Economic Advice and Presidential Leadership*, New York: Columbia University.

Galbraith, John Kenneth (1967), *The New Industrial State*, Boston: Houghton Mifflin.

Galbraith, John Kenneth (1973), *Economics and the Public Purpose*, Boston: Houghton Mifflin.

Galbraith, John Kenneth [1952] (1980), *A Theory of Price Control: The Classic Account*, Cambridge: Harvard University.

Galbraith, John Kenneth (1981), *A Life in Our Times*, Boston: Houghton Mifflin.

Hamilton, Walton *et al.* (1938), *Price and Price Policies*, New York: McGraw-Hill.

Hamilton, Walton (1957), *The Politics of Industry*, New York: Alfred A. Knopf.

Hamilton, Walton H. (1974), 'The Price System and Social Policy', in his *Industrial Policy and Institutionalism*, New York: Augustus M. Kelley.

Hamilton, Walton and May, Stacy [1923] (1968), *The Control of Wages*, New York: Augustus M. Kelley.

Hodgson, Geoffrey M. (1988), *Economics and Institutions: A Manifesto for a Modern Institutional Economics*, Cambridge: Polity Press.

Joskow, Paul L. (1975), 'Firm decision-making processes and oligopoly theory', *American Economic Review*, **65**, May.

Kahn, Alfred E. (1975), 'Market Power Inflation; A Conceptual Overview', in *The Roots of Inflation*, New York: Burt Franklin.

Kaldor, Nicholas (1985), *Economics Without Equilibrium*, Armonk, N.Y.: M.E. Sharpe.

Kaplan, A.D.H., Dirlam, Joel B. and Lanzillotti, Robert F. (1958), *Pricing in Big Business*, Washington, D.C.: Brookings Institution.

Kefauver, Estes (1965), *In a Few Hands: Monopoly Power in America*, New York: Pantheon.

Kregel, Jan E. (1980), 'Markets and institutions as features of a capitalist production system', *Journal of Post Keynesian Economics*, **3**, Fall.

Lee, Frederic S. (1993), *From Post Keynesian to Historical Price Theory: Facts, Theory and Empirically Grounded Pricing Model*, Leicester: De Montfort University.

Lee, Frederic S. and Samuels, Warren J. (1991), *The Heterodox Economics of Gardiner C. Means*, Armonk, N.Y.: M.E. Sharpe.

Means, Gardiner C. (1959), *Administered Inflation and Public Policy*, Washington, D.C.: Anderson Kramer Associates.

Means, Gardiner C. (1963), 'Pricing Power and the Public Interest', in *Administered Prices: A Compendium*.

Means, Gardiner C. (1975), 'Simultaneous inflation and unemployment', in *The Roots of Inflation*, New York: Burt Franklin.

Munkirs, John R. (1985), *The Transformation of American Capitalism*, Armonk, N.Y.: M.E. Sharpe.

Munkirs, John R. and Sturgeon, James I. (1985), 'Oligopolistic cooperation: conceptual and empirical evidence of market structure evolution', *Journal of Economic Issues*, **19**, December.

Okun, Arthur M. (1979), 'An efficient strategy to combat inflation', *Brookings Bulletin*, **15**, Spring.

Okun, Arthur M. (1981), *Prices and Quantities*, Washington, D.C.: Brookings Institution.

Peterson, Wallace C. (1982), *Our Overloaded Economy*, Armonk, N.Y.: M.E. Sharpe.

Peterson, Wallace C. (1988), *Income. Employment and Economic Growth*, New York: W.W. Norton.

Riddell, Tom (1985), 'Concentration and inefficiency in the defense sector; policy options', *Journal of Economic Issues*, **19**, June.

Robinson, Joan [1933] (1969), *The Economics of Imperfect Competition*, London: Macmillan.

Samuels, Warren J. and Medema, Steven G. (1990), *Gardiner C. Means: Institutionalist and Post Keynesian*, Armonk, N.Y.: M.E. Sharpe.

Shackle, G.L.S. (1972), *Epistemics and Economics: A Critique of Economic Doctrines*, Cambridge: Cambridge University Press.

Spulber, Daniel F. (1989), *Regulation and Markets*, Cambridge: MIT Press.

Stigler, George J. (1963), 'Administered Prices and Oligopolistic Inflation', in *Administered Prices: A Compendium*.

Tool, Marc R. (1986), *Essays in Social Value Theory: A Neoinstitutionalist Contribution*, Armonk, N.Y.: M.E. Sharpe.

Veblen, Thorstein [1904] (1932), *The Theory of Business Enterprise*, New York: Charles Scribner's Sons.

4. Pricing and valuation*

At least since the Great Depression of the 1930s, institutional and evolutionary economists have well understood that in modern industrial economies most major prices are set by discretionary agents in mainly large corporate firms.[1] Robert T. Averitt distinguished between firms 'large in size and influence' constituting the 'center' of the economy, and small firms comprising its 'periphery'.[2] He identified administered pricing with the 'center'.[3] John Kenneth Galbraith's distinction between the 'planning sector' and the 'market sector' similarly attributed, in some detail, powers of discretionary pricing to the former.[4] This chapter builds on these characterizations of centre sector and corporate planning but the pricing practices in Averitt's 'periphery' and Galbraith's 'market sector' are not considered here.

Discretionary agents of megacorp enterprises acquire and exercise the power to determine prices to whatever extent is possible. They seek security of expectations and control over the determinants that impinge variously on the continuity of the enterprise, and on market share, profit levels, investment planning, product development, technological innovation and the like. Such power implies the capacity to create options and to choose among them, to exercise discretion and alter outcomes, and to modify the behaviour of others.[5] The character of the contemporary corporate economy is such that pricing power is nearly everywhere acquired in some significant measure and widely utilized to serve the purposes of its possessors. Discretionary agents become price makers rather than price takers, as Arthur Okun observed.[6]

An inclusive purpose of this chapter is to contribute to the formulation of a prolegomenon for a neoinstitutional theory of pricing. The continuing dominance of neoclassical approaches to inquiry and policy derives primarily, in my view, from their continuing claims to having provided *the* paradigmatic theory of price as the definitive explanation of how a market system efficiently does, or should, allocate (not create) resources. That hegemonic dominion will continue until and unless a more pertinent and explanatory theory of pricing becomes available.

A neoinstitutionalist research programme in price determination will attempt to explain, characterize and appraise pricing as an exercise of achieved

*Presidential Address, Association for Evolutionary Economics, Anaheim, January 1993; published in the *Journal of Economic Issues*, June 1993. Reprinted with permission.

power by discretionary agents. A central concern is to add an analytical approach to the normative assessment of the use of pricing power. Pricing judgments will necessarily reflect the application of pricing principles, conventions, rationales or 'folkviews' in the determination and support of pricing policies. Such principles, conventions and rationales are in principle amenable to analysis and appraisal and comprise part of the subject matter considered here.

As price setters choose principles of price setting, and even actual prices, they must, both logically and experientially, make value judgments. They must apply criteria of choice in the construction of pricing decisions. *Choice* means selecting from among two or more options that are or can be made available. A *criterion* is a standard in terms of which selective judgments or choices are made. Such standards are human inventions; they are, at least initially, products of deliberative reflection and in some measure discretionary. In the universe of price determination, they may well be multiple, complex and even contradictory.

Primary concerns in Part I then are (1) to provide theoretical constructs from a neoinstitutionalist perspective that facilitate the analysis of pricing practices, and (2) to provide normative premises from instrumental value theory that permit assessment of the criteria of judgment reflected in such administered pricing decisions. In Part II, with these constructs and premises in mind, the historical price-setting practices of the International Oil Cartel are reviewed and an instrumentalist approach to the appraisal of such practices is suggested. In Part III, a similar review and judgmental approach are suggested for its successor, the Organization of Petroleum Exporting Countries.

I   NEOINSTITUTIONAL CONSTRUCTS OF ANALYSIS

Pricing as Institutionalized Behaviour

As all economists agree, prices are ratios of exchange specifying the terms on which goods and services are exchanged for money. Such ratios are necessarily a consequence of human decisions. But are the activities reflected in the discretionary setting of prices to be thought of as *institutions*? Those following the tradition of Fagg Foster identify institutions as prescribed or proscribed patterns of correlated behaviour and attitudes.[7] Institutions direct and inhibit even as they correlate and coordinate. In the aggregate, they constitute much of the cultural fabric and structure. Price-setting activities qualify as institutions in this sense.

Walter C. Neale reminds us that 'an *institution* is identified by three characteristics. First, there are a number of *people doing*. Second, there are *rules* giving the activities repetition, stability, predictable order. Third, there are *folkviews* ... explaining or justifying the activities and the rules' [emphasis in original].[8] People define the terms of exchange according to rules, schedules or patterns previously accepted, and develop rationales in support of such pricing judgments. Institutions as patterning and coordinating instruments shape and direct behaviour in particular and observable ways. They grant or deny options; they organize behaviour. Price setting is an exercise in institutional creation and implementation. Indeed, the acquisition and exercise of pricing power can occur *only* in an institutional context. It is an integral part of any economic institutional complex, including barter.

Prescriptive and proscriptive patterns of behaviour, as noted, organize and coordinate pricing activity. Corporate managerial pricing directives, formal and informal intraindustry pricing covenants, legal constraints delimiting pricing discretion, intraorganizational price review routines, governmental roles in and rules concerning price setting, trade-group pricing advisories, etc. all guide and direct discretionary agents in the design of price levels and structures. Institutionally constituted outcomes of pricing deliberations are illustrated historically by the following correlating patterns: cost-plus-fixed-fee contracts with 'defence' firms in military procurement,[9] price leadership practices in oligopolistic industries,[10] cost-plus and markup pricing conventions in wholesale and retail firms,[11] interest rate determinations by the Federal Reserve and major banks,[12] price discrimination through basing point systems,[13] wage and salary payment patterns that incorporate significant racial, ethnic, gender and age differentials,[14] and cartel pricing concords,[15] among others.

The practices of pricing by discretionary agents are extraordinarily diverse; actual price-setting procedures and structures are typically idiosyncratic to the particular firm, profession or industry, as Walton Hamilton and his co-authors,[16] and A.D.H. Kaplan and his co-contributors,[17] demonstrated decades ago. Pricing activities, whether individual and collective (in the setting of price lists or schedules), do correlate behaviour. They specify how persons will relate to one another in exchange. In serving agents' ends-in-view, they are purposive. They are initiated as deliberate discretionary acts by identifiable persons.

Accordingly, the introduction or modification of price patterns constitutes an institutional adjustment. The acquisition of control over pricing, which permits discretionary agents to rearrange the structural fabric of price determination, provides substantial prescriptive and proscriptive power over other people's economic behaviour.

Predictably, such practices and patterns of price determination often become habitual; 'rules of thumb' are frequently applied in a routine fashion, as for example, pricing at 20 per cent markup over costs or paying the conventional wage. Patterns of pricing are path-dependent such that past decisions constrain and delimit future choices. A dramatic alteration of costs incurred – say a 50 per cent increase in the price of oil – may prompt or force abandonment of what had been customary pricing patterns. Changing perceptions of purpose over time will force reconsideration of habitual pricing judgments. But all genuine choices of procedures and prices, whether rooted in custom or newly initiated, produce consequences; these consequences are in principle knowable and observable. They are, when assessed, instructive in guiding future choices. An educative, evolutionary process thus develops of selecting and applying criteria of judgment, and of continuously appraising their adequacy as criteria. Discretionary agents, as price makers, are engaged in a running *appraisal* of principles of *appraisal*. Habitual patterns are revised; new pricing judgments are proposed and implemented. Criteria employed are experience based, motivation-driven and consequence-tested in discretionary agents' continuing quest for greater security of expectation. Such security derives from increasing influence on, or control over, the institutional determinants of their own economic environment. Choices made, reflecting such criteria, define the extent and character of intended institutional adjustments.

Instrumental Valuation

The theory of instrumental valuation explains terms, conditions and appraisals of such institutional adjustments. I turn now to a brief reiteration of instrumental value theory which neoinstitutionalists use in the appraisal of pricing practices. Paul D. Bush provides a succinct overview of instrumental valuation for present purposes:

> ... an institution is defined by a set of socially prescribed patterns of correlated behaviour. This 'correlation' of behaviour is prescribed by the value structure of society; that is, values function as criteria for the correlation of behavior within the institutional domain. The value structure in turn derives its social warrant from one of two systems of value formation. Values are either ceremonially warranted or instrumentally warranted. The essence of the 'institutional dichotomy' is contained in this distinction between the two modes of social valuation existing within the society.[18]

Elaborating on this distinction between the 'two systems of value formation', Bush observes that:

> Ceremonial values are warranted by those mores and folkways that incorporate status hierarchies and invidious distinctions as to the relative 'worth' of various individuals or classes in the community. They rationalize power relationships and patterns of authority embedded in the status quo. Instrumental values are warranted through the systematic application of knowledge to the problem-solving

process. They emerge from the processes of inquiry into causal relationships. As criteria for correlating behavior, they ensure causal continuity in the problem-solving process. ... Although the value system is dichotomous, behavior is dialectical. A particular activity or behavior may have either ceremonial or instrumental significance, or it may possess *both* ceremonial and instrumental significance ...[19] [emphasis in original].

Institutional patterns and practices of pricing will predictably contain elements of both instrumentally and ceremonially warranted behaviour or attitudes.[20] One or the other value system may well dominate the whole institutional structure of pricing, however. In addition, what is perceived at one time to be a largely instrumentally warranted behaviour pattern may, with the passing of time and alteration of circumstances, become substantially a ceremonially warranted pattern. The reverse seems less likely. Both the price-determining processes themselves and the assessments of consequences they invoke must therefore be continuously viewed in a processual, evolutionary context.

Constructs to facilitate an instrumentalist's evaluation of pricing behaviour and practices can conveniently be set off diagrammatically as dichotomous pairings reflecting differing but related aspects of instrumental as opposed to ceremonial judgments. These constructs are introduced in a diagrammatic form below and then discussed in order.

INSTRUMENTAL VALUATION

Instrumental Judgments		*Ceremonial Judgments*
knowledge embodied	versus	knowledge encapsulated
instrumental efficiency	versus	ceremonial adequacy
instrumental dominance	versus	ceremonial dominance
instrumental purposes served	versus	invidious purposes served

Instrumental Judgments

Knowledge embodied

In economic analysis generally and in discretionary pricing in particular, instrumental judgments derive from a replication of science-like reasoning in which questions are posed and hypothetical insights formulated that guide the selection of evidence. Hypothetical accounts are themselves continuously reviewed and revised as proves necessary to generate explanatory adequacy. Provisional pricing judgments and their probable consequences are explored. Causal explanation grounded in evidence is sought. Outcomes of warranted inquiry augment the more general fund of reliable knowledge about price determination and become available to guide inquiry and to generate the evidential base with which to pursue the fashioning and assessment of pricing institutions. The knowledge-generating process about pricing is cumulative and evolutionary. New knowledge derives from an imaginative recombination and augmentation of existing knowledge of pricing practices and consequences and is embodied in the cultural heritage of price-managing agents in economic institutions. Instrumental judgments reflect reason grounded in evidence generated as new knowledge. Instruments (hypotheses, tools, constructs and principles), chosen because they serve this instrumental role in inquiry, are also embodied as analytical resources in the agent's and the community's fund of knowledge about the determination of exchange ratios.

Instrumental efficiency
Instrumental judgments are efficient to the extent that they both reflect and contribute to the knowledge-governed process of determining prices and of assessing their impact. Pricing theory is instrumentally efficient to the extent that it explains cogently and coherently how *actual* pricing occurs and what the knowledge-generating and progressive consequences[21] of such pricing decisions are or could be. In instrumental inquiry, reason will dominate ideology. Good theory will explain actual pricing behaviour and the invidious and noninvidious allocations derived therefrom; bad theory will not explain pricing in causal terms nor adequately appraise allocative consequences. Discretionary pricing behaviour contributes to instrumental efficiency in the provisioning process to the extent that it facilitates technologically efficient and environmentally acceptable production and exchange of goods and services noninvidiously identified.

Instrumental dominance
Pricing patterns and practices are instrumentally warranted when they serve restorative, problem-solving processes and override or circumvent ceremonial resistances and defences. To the extent that instrumentally-warranted judgments come to dominate the choice-making process, knowledge-based institutional adjustments of pricing patterns can be fashioned and implemented to serve progressive purposes. The dominion of instrumentally-warranted analyses and judgments hinges critically on the maintenance of vigorous, pertinent and open inquiry. Those concerned to appraise pricing judgments (for example, public utility commissioners) must have continuing access to all reliable knowledge and credible theory pertinent to their judgmental responsibilities. Some degree of dominance of instrumentally-warranted inquiry and pricing patterns over ceremonial patterns is essential for significant inquiry to proceed and for problems to be resolved.

Instrumental (public) purposes served

The instrumental functions of pricing judgments, as perceived by neoinstitutionalists, serve the following public purposes: (a) providing for the continuity and efficiency of the provisioning process (fuller employment, increased environmentally-sensitive growth); (b) nondiscriminatory participation in the social process (comparative absence of invidious impairments or denials grounded in race, gender, age, ancestry, ethnicity and the like); (c) expansion in the growth of warranted knowledge and its application to the economic process (open inquiry, full access to evidence and to financial and institutional support); (d) fullest development and use of individuals' capabilities and skills (universal access to requisite employment income, education and health care); (e) assurance of co-evolutionary development of the biotic and social communities (environmental compatibility, interdependence and sustainability);[22] and (f) enhancement of the mechanisms and integrity of democratic self-governance (unfettered and full noninvidious participatory involvement in deliberative processes). For neoinstitutionalists, the acquisition and use of pricing power, public and private, may be appraised utilizing normative standards reflected in these instrumentally-warranted public purposes.

Ceremonial Judgments

Knowledge encapsulated

The growth of new and reliable knowledge, together with its application in technological innovation and in institutional design and creation (including pricing structures), sometimes come under the aegis of individuals and institutions which can determine whether such knowledge is introduced into the economy and, if so, in what ways and on what terms. New knowledge bearing on pricing decision making may well be encapsulated by private power centres, perhaps with innovative ceremonially-warranted stratagems, pending decisions concerning its release. Such encapsulation may take the form of legal patents. More often, perhaps, encapsulation occurs as simple sequestrations within megacorps as reflected in ownership claims from prior funding, rules that require employee-inventors to sign over rights to new ideas to their firms, protection of internally-generated technological, production and cost-management 'secrets' from industrial espionage, or other constraints that impinge on price determination. In Louis Junker's words: 'Spurious "technological" developments ... are those which are encapsulated by a ceremonial power system whose main concern is to control the use, direction and consequence of that development ... [through] the legal system, the property system, and the information system'.[23]

The power to set prices, for example through the licensing process, can be a vehicle for the withholding of knowledge and its encapsulation, or for its diffusion and expansion. Those Veblen repeatedly alluded to as the 'vested interests' determine whether or not new knowledge is, or may become, a significant threat to their existing interests, roles, status and power;[24] its bearing on the extent and continuity of pricing powers figures prominently in most assessment deliberations. In the petroleum industry, for example, Robert Sherrill has observed that, 'by far the most effective weapon the oil industry has used in frustrating federal regulators and manipulating federal politicians is its total domination of information'.[25] Evidently the petroleum industry is the primary source of data on itself; there appear to be no independent sources of information. This control over the basic information base provides 'open season' and 'cover' for recourse to ceremonially-warranted pricing decisions and behaviour.

Ceremonial adequacy
Ceremonial judgments reflect the quest for 'ceremonial adequacy' (Veblen), not for instrumental efficiency. When a price setter's competence is determined and defined, not by instrumental efficiency, but by power, status and ritual, ceremonial adequacy becomes a compelling criterion in the correlation of behaviour.[26] As Clarence E. Ayres put it: 'tribal beliefs, and the institutional and ceremonial practices in which they are objectified, are simulacra of scientific knowledge and technological skills; ... "ceremonial adequacy" is an imitation of technological adequacy'.[27] But the belief is held and the claim is made that instrumental competence is the source of, and warrant for, status and power. The attribution is inverted; in its crudest and most irrational form, the fact of possession of power is taken as sufficient justification for its exercise. The fact of possession of *pricing* power must be presumed to indicate mastery of the determinants and rationales for price setting, and therewith affirms the right to set price schedules and patterns. More particularly, the power to set prices is a source of ceremonial adequacy. The discretionary dominion of oil price makers, for example, sometimes compels deference and accommodation. Wielding pricing power helps sate quests for recognition and status. Threats to the continuity of ceremonially-warranted pricing power are alleged to constitute threats to the instrumental functioning of the economy. Claims to ceremonial adequacy then undergird the use of power. But they may also delimit or preclude the introduction of new knowledge of pricing options and their implications.

Ceremonial dominance
The presence of continuing and unresolved economic problems, as acknowledged in the unfulfilled public purposes alluded to above, is an exceedingly useful and productive indicator of where to direct inquiry to identify ceremonially- and invidiously-warranted patterns of behaviour which (excluding

'natural' disasters) are primarily responsible for the problematic circumstances perceived. Ceremonially-warranted practices may indeed plague, frustrate and even overwhelm instrumentally-warranted patterns of behaviour in major areas of the political economy. The presence of ceremonial dominance prevents an increase in the fund of knowledge and derivative technological innovations from being fully utilized or realized in instrumental behaviour to resolve problems. Reducing ceremonial dominance and the accompanying degree of ceremonial encapsulation is thus required if more instrumentally-warranted patterns of pricing are to emerge and flourish. Indeed, as Bush has shown, an 'index of ceremonial dominance' can be derived that 'describes the value structure of the institution'.[28] 'The lower the index of ceremonial dominance, the higher a level of technological innovation generated by an increase in the fund of knowledge.'[29]

Whatever can be done, then, to displace ceremonially-warranted with instrumentally-warranted patterns of behaviour (that is, to reduce the levels of ceremonial dominance) augments the community's ability to generate and employ new knowledge and its technological applications in the pursuit of public purposes. For example, the petroleum industry's ceremonially-warranted defence of its monopoly on information concerning its lifting ability, reserves, storage levels, refinery capacity, technological innovations, marketing expectations and pricing practices must be challenged. Independently validated knowledge about the industry needs to become more publicly available.

Moreover, structural change that merely relocates ceremonially-warranted pricing authority from one corporate power system to another with equivalent power may well leave the index of ceremonial dominance unmodified. Similarly, the fact that a price is publicly administered does not necessarily confirm the absence of ceremonial dominance. The only progressive structural change in pricing authority is that which reduces ceremonial patterns and/or adds new instrumental ones 'that will permit the community to enjoy the maximum feasible level of instrumental efficiency from a given technological innovation'.[30] It may well be that, with sufficient forward planning, the assimilation or adding on of instrumental patterns and technological innovations from other cultures can be accomplished without the concurrent assimilation of patterns of ceremonial dominance of the knowledge in the originating culture.[31]

Invidious (non-public) purposes served

The ceremonial encapsulation of knowledge, accomplished by the dominance of ceremonially-warranted patterns of behaviour, mainly serves the purpose of acquiring, using and retaining discretionary control of a major area of the economy by a small fragment of the community. However, given manipulative advertising and culturally conditioned deference to authority, the acceptance of such ceremonial adequacy on behalf of, say, megacorp oil firms may indeed be widely shared and supported in the larger community. Ceremonial dominance may in fact be unattainable, or at least unsustainable, without the provoked and/or manipulated invidious support of a large segment of that community.

Corporate elites will seek to retain de facto control over the structural fabric that, in the main, defines the power, position, status, income and pecuniary prerogatives of their own economic sectors. Continuity of control over pricing is typically at the centre of such quests. Such control may very well be the critical variable whose loss would trigger a more general collapse of ceremonial adequacy and dominance. For example, the particular manifestations of ceremonial dominance may surface as price manipulation in search of a larger market share, or as a price leader to enforce price-setting discipline on cohorts in the industry. To achieve and retain pricing power, then, is critical to the life of the megacorp as perceived by its discretionary managers.

Thus the pricing purposes served are those of the vested interests. Invidious distinctions are developed to define and to differentiate the 'relative worth' of the power-wielding elite by nationality, ethnicity, income, 'good old-boy' networks, historic roles played, cartel affiliations, political influence and contacts, and the like. Continuing and often passionate claims are made that the interests of the ceremonially-warranted fragment are identical to those of the community generally. 'What is good for Exxon is good for the country.' Such presumptive claims need to be examined critically with an instrumentally-warranted analytical and evaluative approach.

From the neoinstitutionalists' position, progress is obtained, the public interest is served, public purposes are achieved and the 'collective ought'[32] is realized when *pricing arrangements and judgments reflect increasing degrees or magnitudes of instrumentally-warranted behaviour and diminishing degrees or magnitudes of ceremonially- or invidiously-warranted behaviour.* The juxtaposed criteria are themselves dichotomous. Through instrumental inquiry, these differently warranted pricing patterns, structures and practices can be analysed and assessed in ways that contribute to a much fuller realization of public purposes as identified here.

II   THE INTERNATIONAL PETROLEUM CARTEL

The institutional fabric through which the administered pricing of petroleum occurs is both complex and highly idiosyncratic to the oil industry, as a neoinstitutionalist would expect. It is an economic sector in which, especially in the 1960s and later, both unilateral actions of countries and bilateral negotiations between oil companies and exporting countries were continuously reshaping the decision structure. Consuming countries entered the deliberations at times, both directly with companies and politically with countries, to register their concerns and to attempt to tilt the deliberations and outcomes in their favour. The locus and use of price-initiating power shifted among the major firms and the exporting countries respectively. Moreover, within each grouping, there was a continuous jockeying for position and discretion.

Even so, for most of the third quarter of this century, as is well known, a cartel dominated the world-wide petroleum industry. Cartels are institutionalized compacts correlating the behaviour of discretionary agents. Their control derives from agreements among a group of usually private megacorps producing similar products and services for the purpose of constraining and managing competitive rivalries. Corwin Edwards's earlier characterization may still apply: 'the typical purpose and effect of cartelization are to set prices higher than would prevail under competition, to reduce them as seldom as possible, and to raise them further whenever the opportunity permits'.[33]

Cartel agreements may be tacit and secret or formal and visible; they may be legal or illegal; they may be negotiated among sellers or among buyers; they may be national or multinational in scope; they may be wholly private or governmentally sponsored; their duration may be comparatively brief or extend over decades. But whatever the scope and wherever the loci of cartel structures, they are instituted to create and exercise substantial economic power over critical decision areas of participating firms. The exercise of this power is reflected in the determination and administration of prices, assignment of market shares, control of quantities marketed, regulation of technological innovation, exchange of knowledge and techniques, distribution of risks and profits, etc. More particularly, the concept of cartel structure connotes 'price-fixing, explicit collusion, and conspiracy'.[34]

The International Oil Cartel (IOC)

The seven sisters

In the quarter century from 1945 to 1970, British and American oil companies, led by the seven major firms,[35] came to dominate the world oil industry with various cartel-type arrangements. Beginning in the late 1920s, international price wars among the then three major companies (Royal Dutch Shell, Standard of New York, Anglo-Persian) generated 'unacceptable' uncertainties and price instabilities.[36] As a consequence, these dominant corporations met and formulated 'The Achnacarry Agreement' (1928), the first of a series of cartel arrangements to stabilize the industry[37] which stipulated the following: accepting and maintaining existing market shares, adding new facilities only as needed, preserving the financial advantage of each producing area, and preventing excess production from upsetting the market.[38] Within a few years, subsequent agreements provided in greater detail for setting production and sales quotas, dealing with over- and under-trading, setting administered prices and conditions of sale, and coping with outsiders.[39] Concession agreements, joint ownerships and contract leasing permitted these companies to secure and retain control over the international supply of oil. Intracartel coordination was mainly accomplished through joint ownership of pipelines and offshore leases, interlocking directorates within the cartel and between cartel members and major banks.[40] Boycotts, governmental pressures, suppression of discoveries, peddling of political influence and attacks on non-price competition successfully excluded outsiders, public and private, from intruding significantly on the domain of the cartel and its multifaceted control.[41] On the other hand, internal power struggles were sometimes intense, with power-wielding manoeuvres for dominion, access to fields and contests for price leadership were not unusual. The 'house' of the 'seven sisters' was not always quiescent.[42] Although cartels are formally illegal in the US, alleged national security concerns successfully sidetracked litigation.[43]

Price control instruments

More particularly, continuing international control was largely accomplished by the conjoint use of two mechanisms: growth rate management through output controls, and price-matching patterns provided by basing point systems. Operating on the 'conviction that oil in excess of what the market would absorb *at the existing price* simply could not be allowed to reach the market',[44] the cartel developed structures 'to govern the individual rates of output of the various producing countries in such a way as to attain (*and not exceed*) a predetermined growth rate of overall supply' [emphasis in original].[45] In the period from 1950–72, the cartel was astonishingly successful (99.9 per cent on target) in achieving the planned growth rate of some 9.55 per cent per year.[46] Utilizing careful forecasts of the expected level of demand, production quotas were set to realize the desired growth rate.

In addition, the cartel was able, over the years, to move beyond overt collusive pricing agreements by developing and modifying as necessary 'complicated [basing point] pricing systems designed to eliminate differences in delivered prices regardless of the location of the sellers'.[47] John Blair explains the rationale:

> Even if overall supply were limited to total demand (at the existing price), the absence of such a price-matching system would lead to uncertainty among the sellers, as no seller could be sure that his failure to secure a buyer's order was not

the result of price cutting by a competitor. Only if each seller abstained from cutting the f.o.b. price and absorbed whatever freight was necessary from a governing basing point to the point of delivery could this concern (and potential source of price competition) be eliminated.[48]

The original basing point was 'Texas Gulf'; under pressure, an additional basing point was established in the Persian Gulf. Further modifications were later made to equalize delivered prices from Texas and the Middle East. The outcome was the establishment of a plateau of price levels for Mideast 'marker crude' (Arabian light, f.o.b. Ras Tanura) in the range from $1.80 to about $2.05 per barrel for over a decade (1949–59).[49] 'The unique value of the production-control and price-matching systems is that they rendered unnecessary most of the cumbersome (and potentially dangerous) meetings involved in day-to-day market control.'[50] For these and related reasons, 'as late as 1972 the seven international majors were still producing ninety-one percent of the Middle East's crude oil and seventy-seven percent of the Free World's supply outside the United States'.[51] They retained effective international control of petroleum pricing until the early 1970s.[52]

An Approach to Appraising IOC Oil Pricing

A research agenda for a neoinstrumentalist appraisal of such price and output controls by the International Oil Cartel (IOC) might include the following illustrative queries, among others.

Regarding supply management
To what extent did the IOC develop and utilize new knowledge and technology in the exploration, lifting and transport of oil? Was such knowledge shared by the IOC internally and/or encapsulated against external use? What bearing did this have on supply management? Was its dominant supply position in the industry 'rationalized' by ceremonially-warranted power retention practices? How was its supply management structure used as an instrument for discretionary pricing?

Regarding basing-point pricing
Did the IOC's private and collaborative administration of prices, in largely eliminating cut-throat pricing, provide price stability and predictability for those dependent upon oil as their major energy source? If so, does this constitute an instrumentally-warranted outcome for petroleum buyers? Is it a sufficient defence for an integrated oligopolistic structure? Profits from sales were comparatively high, but were they excessive? How might the level of profits be assessed with the distinction between instrumental efficiency and

ceremonial adequacy? Can the complexities of motivation and purposes of basing-point pricing be analytically identified and appraised? Given relative price inelasticity, what sectors or buyers were significantly impaired or had their continuity of operation threatened? What sectors or buyers, if any, were advantaged by the IOC's price administration? Does Bush's concept of 'progressive institutional change'[53] give substance to 'impairment' or 'advantage' beyond mere pecuniary tallies? Were the changes introduced in basing-point structures instrumentally or ceremonially warranted? Was pricing power the primary instrument of retaining world-wide dominance over the industry? Were public regulatory instruments available to impinge on the IOC's basing-point pricing?

Regarding public purposes

To what extent was the IOC, in its primary concerns with supply management and price control policies, insensitive to the environmental hazards generated by oil spills, physical waste from competitive lifting practices, air pollution at refineries and the like? Did their extensive acquisition of smaller alternative fuel companies in the 1970s[54] and their diversification into control of coal firms and reserves in the late 1970s and early 1980s[55] constitute significant ceremonial encapsulation? Did these moves increase their discretionary pricing options? Did the IOC use its pricing powers to become a significant participant in international politics in negotiating with and among governments, thereby generating an aura of ceremonial adequacy? To what degree and in what ways did the IOC impose its pricing authority in particular on African and Middle Eastern exporters? Was it invidiously discriminatory in its price negotiations with Third World producer countries?

Throughout the 1960s the IOC dominated the petroleum industry: it controlled prices, created and introduced new oil production technology, allocated market shares among companies, developed and controlled refinery capacity, determined which fields to develop, specified rates of lifting from these fields, etc. Oil exporting countries, especially in North Africa and the Middle East, became increasingly frustrated because the goals of the IOC did not conform with their own emerging nationalistic ambitions. By the early 1970s, an institution originally created in the early 1960s, the Organization of Oil Exporting Countries (OPEC), through unexpected manoeuvres, began to impose its own will on pricing and petroleum supply management. It is to this institutional complex and power system that I now turn.[56]

IV ORGANIZATION OF PETROLEUM EXPORTING COUNTRIES: OPEC

OPEC's Emergence

This organization of (eventually) 13 sovereign governments of oil producing countries, mainly in North Africa and the Middle East, rose to prominence by the late 1960s; in the early 1970s, it enjoyed substantial dominion over the world's petroleum prices, control over half the world's supplies, and management of vast reserves in Third World countries.[57] The creation of OPEC in 1959–60 was precipitated mainly by price cuts instituted by the majors (the IOC) of some 18 per cent on 'marker crude'.[58] These cuts exacerbated a deepening disenchantment of Third World producer countries with what they regarded as low levels of concession payments (50–50 split of 'profits') from the oil companies, and with the IOC's insensitivity to their wishes for increased control over their own resources, specifically over levels of production and disposition of output. They were weary of being whipsawed in rivalrous intercountry negotiations with the majors. Intramural politics and jockeying for position among the producing countries also stimulated an interest in generating a more coordinated approach to the IOC.[59]

Through most of the 1960s, however, OPEC was not a cartel. Generally, the *companies* (IOC) decided on levels of output, markets to be served and prices to be charged. In addition, the companies held near exclusive control over refineries.[60] To characterize power relations then prevailing as a bilateral oligopoly, with a cartel of companies facing a cartel of countries, overstates OPEC's power.[61]

OPEC may have been an 'Exclusive Club', as Shukri Ghanem describes it,[62] but it was one comprised of *governments* that granted only limited responsibilities to the OPEC organization as such. Member governments proposed agendas and policies; member governments decided whether or not OPEC accords would be supported and implemented. Rivalries of various sorts were vigorously pursued among and between member countries. Producing countries came to periodic OPEC conferences with differing purposes and needs. For example, Saudi Arabia – with extensive reserves and low lifting costs – often pressed for low prices or smaller price increases; Venezuela – with less extensive reserves and higher lifting costs (offshore wells) – often pressed for higher prices. Oil ministers of member governments conferred and negotiated at OPEC conferences, but *heads* of governments were the major discretionary agents who held and retained actual power. For member countries, national interests were never made subservient to OPEC. Draft policy statements emanating from OPEC conferences were, in effect, only advisory measures for participating member governments.

The Power Shift

Towards the end of the 1960s, as noted, the majors still retained control over the pricing of petroleum and over actual production levels in OPEC countries.[63] The power shift on pricing began in 1968 with OPEC's Consortium 'Declaratory Statement' in which the producing countries asserted their sovereign rights to an 'ownership share in companies' concessions', and to 'unilaterally determine the price the oil companies paid them'.[64] 'They declared that the oil companies did not have the right to "excessively high net earnings after tax"; accordingly, excess profits, as determined by the government, "shall be paid by the operator to the Government".'[65] Although at the time of the Declaration the majors paid little attention, by the mid-1970s these objectives were in fact realized.

Although Iran was pressing vigorously for price increases in the early 1970s, it was Libya, with the support of OPEC, that made the major breakthrough in pricing power. In response to the Suez closure in 1967, Libya had increased production of its superior low-sulphur oil to meet growing European demand. With Qaddafi's rise to power, accelerated and enhanced demands, backed by curtailment threats, were made on the dominant independent (non-majors) oil companies for dramatic increases in prices.[66] Qaddafi had in mind pro-Arab and anti-Israel political objectives as well. The companies' tax-paid cost per barrel in Libya was increased by the revolutionary government from $1.40 to $1.70, with the tax rate rising from 50 to 55 per cent.[67] The new rules also provided for five automatic increases thereafter. When, in accepting the Libyan government's terms, the independents conceded pricing and production control power, majors interested in Libya followed suit. Steven A. Schneider summarizes the 'breakthrough' as follows:

> Singling out the companies, one by one, enabled Libya to take advantage of corporate disunity. The companies and the consuming countries alike appeared vulnerable to Libya's production cutbacks. Libya had forced the companies to negotiate posted prices with an exporting country, whereas the companies had previously set prices unilaterally. Also it had demonstrated that sovereign states could abrogate agreements with the world's most powerful multinational corporations.[68]

Libya's success encouraged OPEC to launch a comprehensive effort to shift pricing and production control power to exporting countries generally. In 1970, 'OPEC demanded extension of the 55 percent tax rate to all exporting countries, elimination of disparities in payment among countries, and an increase in posted prices'. If a world-wide price increase was thwarted, OPEC threatened 'concerted and simultaneous action by all Member countries'.[69] Anticipating a Libyan-type 'leapfrogging' approach of split rather than joint negotiations, 15 petroleum companies (all of the majors and most of the independents) organized a unified bargaining instrument called the London Policy Group (LPG). Although consumer governments, especially the US, contributed to the deliberations of the LPG from the sidelines, political considerations precluded unequivocal public support. More concerned with threats to supply than with increased prices, the LPG accepted OPEC's demands. Prices, at the behest of OPEC, began increasing in 1970, were quadrupled in 1973 and doubled again in 1979. Average prices of around $28 in 1980 were roughly 16 times those of 1970.[70] Production controls and price increases permitted members of OPEC to generate hundreds of billions of dollars of net revenue. But the purchasing power of that revenue was eroded over the decade by cost-push inflationary pressures to which the oil price revolution itself significantly contributed.

Moreover, the Khomeini revolution in Iran and the war between Iraq and Iran, among other events, made intra-OPEC decision making increasingly difficult.[71] In consumer countries, the shift to alternative fuels, substantial energy conservation efforts and the development of alternate sources of petroleum gradually reduced global dependence upon OPEC oil from around 50 to about 38 per cent by 1990. The use of OPEC's pricing power through the 1970s generated responses which in the 1980s eroded its price-setting and production-control powers. Production control measures were also eroded. Members of OPEC, 'led by Saudi Arabia, have been producing as much oil as they wish, rendering the cartel useless as a price-setting organization'.[72] OPEC's administered price was around $22 per barrel in the early 1990s;[73] actual sale prices were closer to $18.[74] In September 1992, Ecuador formally withdrew from the cartel. By 1994, the OPEC administered price had dropped to $21; actual sale prices were about $14. Clearly, OPEC's control over production levels and sale prices has dramatically declined with members unable to agree on reduced levels of output to increase prices. Also non-OPEC suppliers (Norway, Britain) threaten their market shares.[75]

An Approach to Appraising OPEC Pricing

A research agenda for a neoinstrumentalist's appraisal of OPEC's pricing structure, behaviour and rationale might include the following queries:

Knowledge embodied; knowledge encapsulated

To what extent did the acquisition of pricing power and revenues from oil sales facilitate a borrowing of the knowledge and technology of finding, lifting and distributing oil? Were OPEC countries denied the encapsulated knowledge and expertise to develop and operate their own oil industries? To what extent did OPEC countries use their oil revenues to develop their own respective cadres of geophysicists, petroleum engineers, design technicians, operating cadres, etc. to operate their own industries? Should neoinstitutionalists concede 'comparative advantage' and argue that individual OPEC countries did not need to develop their own technically efficient petroleum infrastructure? Was enhanced knowledge obtained concerning environmentally safe management of oil extraction and delivery? To what extent did OPEC countries share knowledge and expertise among themselves in the management of oil extraction and sale? What fraction of oil revenues, if any, was used to send Middle Eastern and African students to Europe and North America for technical and higher education? Were such students, upon returning, an effective vehicle for applying warranted knowledge in the petroleum industry and more generally?

Instrumental efficiency; ceremonial adequacy

How did OPEC's administered pricing system of negotiated conference agreements among countries impact upon the achievement of technologically efficient production and delivery of oil? Did the price negotiations among OPEC countries, individually or collectively, reflect a concern with ceremonial adequacy? Were judgments in pursuit of ceremonial adequacy of a character and magnitude such as to impair the development and utilization of warranted technical and social knowledge in the respective economies more generally?

Instrumental dominance; ceremonial dominance

Ceremonial dominance confers ceremonial adequacy. To what extent was OPEC's seizure of pricing power a quest for ceremonial dominance to be demonstrated by the management and pricing of their own vital resource? To what degree and in what ways were the clamour, and at times internecine struggle among member states for ceremonial dominance (rooted in nationality, religion, ethnicity and the like), an impediment to price setting and implementation? Was the continuing struggle in OPEC more in pursuit of political influence – sometimes as aggressors, sometimes as resistors of external pressure – than that of discretion over pricing? Were the predictable consequences of dramatic increases in oil prices on consuming countries, rich and poor, given serious consideration and assessment in OPEC deliberations?

Public purposes served: instrumental and ceremonial

To what extent did OPEC countries use oil revenues to promote domestic economic development? Measured by such social and economic indicators as per capita income (money and real), gainful employment, infant mortality, longevity, caloric intake, etc., did the utilization of oil revenues generate increased economic well-being for all or some of the exporting countries? To what extent did OPEC countries direct their oil revenues to promote development in oil-consuming countries in the Third World? Is the 'optimal goal' quoted below instrumentally warranted?: 'The national interest will be optimally met when the resource is depleted at a time when the highest possible level of economic development has been attained. These are the two factors that must be linked: resource depletion and the rate of economic growth.'[76] How extensive and significant were the inadvertent cost-push inflation effects of the oil price revolution both on the developed world and upon OPEC countries themselves? Did these macro effects turn out to be invidiously discriminatory? If so, to whom and in what ways? To what extent were OPEC revenues used ceremonially to arm and sustain undemocratic regimes of both the radical (Libya, Iran, Iraq) and conservative (Saudi Arabia, Kuwait, Emirates) varieties? More broadly, do the instrumentally-warranted standards identified here as public purposes have pan-cultural warrant, or is their use in appraisals of pricing setting and its consequences by OPEC countries merely an ethnocentric expression of 'Western values'?

As a prolegomenon, the intent in this chapter has been: (a) to suggest an approach for the development of a research programme in pricing as an institutional determination; (b) to provide constructs, tenets and questions that may prove to be analytically useful in such an inquiry; (c) to explore the character of administered pricing in illustrative concentrated power centres of the international petroleum industry; and, (d) to propose an instrumentalist's assessment of such pricing structures, behaviour and practices in pursuit of public purposes.

NOTES

1. Hamilton (1938); Galbraith [1952] 1980; Kaplan, Dirlam and Lanzillotti (1958); Means (1963); Galbraith (1967); Blair (1972); Eichner (1976); Okun (1981).
2. Averitt (1968), pp. 6–7.
3. Ibid, p. 27.
4. Galbraith (1973), pp. 110–21.
5. For the impact of corporate power on education, family and community, see Dugger (1989).
6. Okun (1981), p. 138 and passim.
7. Foster (1981), p. 859.
8. Neale (1988), p. 232.
9. Scherer (1964).
10. Burns (1936).
11. Oxenfeldt (1951).
12. Wray (1990).
13. Blair (1972), ch. 14.
14. Thurow (1975).

15. Stocking and Watkins (1946); Stocking and Watkins (1948).
16. Hamilton *et al.* (1938).
17. Kaplan, Dirlam and Lanzillotti (1958).
18. Bush (1983), pp. 36–7.
19. Ibid, p. 37.
20. Bush (1986), pp. 28ff.
21. Bush (1989), pp. 455–64.
22. Tool [1979] (1985), pp. 310–14.
23. Junker (1982), p. 143.
24. Bush (1986), p. 30.
25. Sherrill (1983), p. 507 and passim.
26. Ayres [1944] (1978), pp. 159–60.
27. Ayres (1961), pp. 30–31.
28. Bush (1983), p. 48.
29. Ibid, p. 54.
30. Ibid, p. 59.
31. Ibid, pp. 60–61.
32. Klein (1984), pp. 53–6.
33. Corwin D. Edwards, quoted in Greer (1984), p. 264.
34. Greer (1984), p. 263.
35. Exxon, Mobil, SoCal, Texaco, Gulf, Royal Dutch Shell and British Petroleum (International). For additional groupings of 'Top Eight (US)', 'Lesser Majors (US)' and 'Leading "Independents" (International)', see Blair (1976), p. xi.
36. Blair (1976), p. 54.
37. Ibid, p. 55.
38. Ibid.
39. Ibid, p. 57.
40. Ibid, pp. 136–47.
41. Ibid, pp. 77–97.
42. Ibid, pp. 54–71.
43. Ibid, pp. 71–6.
44. Ibid, p. 99.
45. Ibid.
46. Ibid, p. 101.
47. Ibid, p. 113.
48. Ibid.
49. Ibid, pp. 114–17.
50. Ibid, p. 120.
51. Ibid, p. 52.
52. Space does not permit exploration of how this international oil cartel also controlled oil production, pricing and distribution within the US.
53. Bush (1989).
54. Schneider (1983), p. 419.
55. Sherrill (1983), p. 493.
56. I must note in passing that no attention can be given here to the highly significant and complex *political* tensions and relations that underlie and impinge on much of the institutional analysis of price setting that follows.
57. The founding five were Iraq, Iran, Kuwait, Saudi Arabia and Venezuela; Qatar, Libya, Indonesia, Abu Dhabi (later the United Arab Emirates) and Algeria joined in the 1960s; Nigeria, Ecuador and Gabon in the 1970s, for a total of 13.
58. Ghanem (1986), pp. 13ff.
59. Ibid, pp. 27–33.
60. Ibid, p. 32.
61. Ibid, pp. 31–2.
62. Ibid passim.
63. Schneider (1983), p. 135.

64. Ibid.
65. Ibid.
66. Ibid, pp. 139–48.
67. Ibid, p. 147.
68. Ibid.
69. Ibid, p. 149.
70. Danielson (1982), pp. 160–62.
71. Schneider (1983), pp. 490–507.
72. 'OPEC reels' (1992), pp. D10 and D15.
73. International Energy Agency (1991), pp. 90–91.
74. 'OPEC Reels' (1992), p. D15.
75. 'OPEC to freeze production' (1994), p. A13.
76. Al-Chalabi and al-Janabi (1982), p. 58.

REFERENCES

Al-Chalabi, Fadhil and Al-Janabi, Adnan (1982), 'Optimum Production and Pricing Policies', in Ragaei El Mallakh (ed.), *OPEC: Twenty Years and Beyond*, Boulder: Westview Press.

Averitt, Robert T. (1968), *The Dual Economy*, New York: W.W. Norton.

Ayres, Clarence E. (1961), *Towards a Reasonable Society*, Austin: University of Texas Press.

Ayres, Clarence E. [1944] (1978), *The Theory of Economic Progress*, Kalamazoo: New Issues Press, Western Michigan University.

Blair, John M. (1972), *Economic Concentration: Structure, Behavior and Public Policy*, New York: Harcourt Brace Jovanovich.

Blair, John M. (1976), *The Control of Oil*, New York: Pantheon Books.

Burns, Arthur Robert (1936), *The Decline of Competition*, New York: McGraw-Hill.

Bush, Paul D. (1983), 'An exploration of the structural characteristics of a Veblen-Ayres-Foster defined institutional domain', *Journal of Economic Issues*, **17**, March.

Bush, Paul D. (1986), 'On the concept of ceremonial encapsulation', *Review of Institutional Thought*, **3**, December.

Bush, Paul D. (1989), 'The concept of "progressive" institutional change and its implications for economic policy formation', *Journal of Economic Issues*, **23**, June.

Danielson, Albert L. (1982), *The Evolution of OPEC*, New York: Harcourt Brace Jovanovich.

Dugger, William M. (1989), *Corporate Hegemony*, New York: Greenwood Press.

Eichner, Alfred S. (1976), *The Megacorp and Oligopoly: Micro Foundations of Macro Dynamics*, White Plains, N.Y.: M.E. Sharpe.

Foster, J. Fagg (1981), 'Economics', *Journal of Economic Issues*, **15**, December.

Galbraith, John Kenneth (1967), *The New Industrial State*, Boston: Houghton Mifflin.

Galbraith, John Kenneth (1973), *Economics and the Public Purpose*, Boston: Houghton Mifflin.

Galbraith, John Kenneth [1952] (1980), *A Theory of Price Control*, Cambridge: Harvard University Press.

Ghanem, Shuksri M. (1986), *OPEC: The Rise and Fall of an Exclusive Club*, London: KPI.

Greer, Douglas F. (1984), *Industrial Organizations and Public Policy*, 2nd ed., New York: Macmillan.

Hamilton, Walton *et al.* (1938), *Price and Price Policies*, New York: McGraw-Hill.

International Energy Agency (1991), *Annual Oil Market Report*, Paris: OECD/IEA.

Junker, Louis J. (1982), 'The ceremonial-institutional dichotomy in institutional analysis', *American Journal of Economics and Sociology*, **41**, April.

Kaplan, A.D.H., Dirlam, Joel B. and Lanzillotti, Robert F. (1958), *Pricing in Big Business*, Washington D.C.: Brookings Institution.

Klein, Philip A. (1984), 'Institutionalist Reflections on the Role of the Public Sector' in Marc R. Tool (ed.), *An Institutionalist Guide to Economics and Public Policy*, Armonk, N.Y.: M.E. Sharpe.

Means, Gardiner C. (1963), 'Pricing Power and the Public Interest', in U.S. Congress, Senate, Committee on the Judiciary, *Administered Prices: A Compendium on Public Policy*, 88th Cong., 1st. sess.

Neale, Walter C. (1988), 'Institutions' in Marc R. Tool (ed.), *Evolutionary Economics. I: Foundations of Institutional Thought*, Armonk, N.Y.: M.E. Sharpe.

Okun, Arthur M. (1981), *Prices and Quantities*, Washington, D.C.: Brookings Institution.

'OPEC reels as Ecuador says adios' (1992), *The Sacramento Bee* (reprinted from *The New York Times*), 19 September.

'Opec to freeze production', (1994), *The Sacramento Bee*, 27 March.

Oxenfeldt, Alfred R. (1951), *Industrial Pricing and Market Practices*, New York: Prentice-Hall.

Scherer, Frederic M. (1964), *The Weapons Acquisition Process: Economic Incentives*, Cambridge: Harvard University Press.

Schneider, Steven A. (1983), *The Oil Price Revolution*, Baltimore: Johns Hopkins University Press.

Sherrill, Robert (1983), *The Oil Follies of 1970–1980*, New York: Anchor Press.

Stocking, George W. and Watkins, Myron W. (1946), *Cartels in Action*, New York: Twentieth Century Fund.

Stocking, George W. and Watkins, Myron W. (1948), *Cartels or Competition*, New York: Twentieth Century Fund.

Thurow, Lester C. (1975), *Generating Inequality: Mechanisms of Distribution in the U.S. Economy*, New York: Basic Books.

Tool, Marc R. [1979] (1985), *The Discretionary Economy: A Normative Theory of Political Economy*, Boulder: Westview Press.

Wray, L. Randall (1990), *Money and Credit in Capitalistic Economies*, Aldershot: Edward Elgar.

5. Administered pricing in the public sector[*]

At least since the Canonists' dicta concerning 'just price' and the Physiocrats' interest in the 'bon prix', the questions of how prices are determined, the warrant for their level and their sometime regulation have remained central concerns of inquiry and policy. They are of particular concern now. Where pricing power is held, how it is used, the consequences experienced and an assessment thereof in light of public purposes remain high on inquiry agendas, whether formally or informally perceived. This chapter is addressed to these continuing concerns.

In what follows, *power* refers to the capacity to create alternatives and to choose among them, to exercise discretion over the behaviour of others and to alter outcomes. *Prices* are ratios specifying the terms of exchange between money and goods and services. *Pricing* is the use of power to determine prices. Prices determined by discretionary agents are referred to as *administered prices*.

In the 'private sector', as earlier chapters have suggested, an extensive literature confirms that most significant prices are determined, wholly or substantially, by conglomerate corporations and megacorps, and by more modestly-sized firms as well, through a variety of agencies, measures and instruments.[1] It is manifestly evident that such prices are *not* determined by impersonal, automatic, power-free, price competitive markets, as orthodox textbooks recommend. The latter are exceptional, not typical. Indeed a price competitive market is usually defined as a power-void exchange structure where no participant can affect price by his/her own efforts; all participants are individually and definitively 'price takers' (Okun). No one is in charge; the 'market' adjudicates; the catering to and summing of private choices *constitutes* the public purpose; but the accountability presumably provided by such zero-power markets simply is not supplied. Accountability to 'public purposes' (Galbraith) is alleged, not demonstrated.

In the real world of managed markets, the governing rule for agents of power-possessing firms is aggressive pursuit of control over all identifiable

*Paper presented at meetings of the European Association for Evolutionary Political Economy, Paris, November 1992.

and significant determinants, *including prices*, which bear on the continuity of the firm and its financial health, productive potential, power options, industrial status and market shares. Such firms are engaged in private governance. Holding such achieved power to account must be, and in some measure is, otherwise accomplished.

'Otherwise accomplished' typically but not uniformly means recourse to public governance. The fact of pervasive administration of prices in the *private* sector compels the community to seek accountability through formal governmental bodies; these are the *only* institutions available to them *as a community*. Administered pricing in the public sector, then, is in part a consequence of corporate control over administered pricing in the private sector. Additionally, there are some areas, as with military procurement, where, because of complexities and the character of production, the exchange process simply cannot approach a free market structure. Even 'competitive' bidding on defence contracts is an instrument of administered pricing.

In the 'public sector', governments at all levels are engaged directly in the determination of prices of public goods and services through, for example, legislative acts, executive orders, agency or commission rules and regulations with, perhaps, judicial review. But in addition, governments are also indirect participants in price determination through surveillance and interventions, as well as through modification of prices determined initially and/ or formally in the private sector. The primary purpose of this chapter is to explore examples of the administration of prices, directly and indirectly, in and by the public sector, and to consider criteria for the appraisal of the use of such pricing power. It is intended as a prototypal contribution to an emerging and more inclusive neoinstitutional theory of administered pricing.

Appraising the use of pricing power and holding achieved pricing power to account will in fact have profound implications for both the private and public sectors. To appraise is to judge the worth or significance of actions against standards; it is substantively and procedurally to apply criteria. To hold to account is to ensure that performance conforms with responsibility to the community. Criteria of judgment must be employed in any such conjoint assessment of the use of pricing options. Social value judgments are not and cannot be evaded; choices among allocative consequences must be made. One contention of this analysis is that the competitive market is not and cannot be a positive adjudicator of social value questions in exchange. The intent of the chapter is to raise directly the questions of appraisal of purposes served and consequences invoked by the administration of prices in the public sector.

The chapter consists of three main sections. Part I considers the institutional context of public-private price administration; it is a brief introduction to the sources and complexities of pricing judgments. With the foregoing as underpinning, Part II develops an illustrative characterization of governmental participation in the determination of prices in two selected areas at the micro level of sectoral price formation and impact: (a) pricing in 'natural monopoly' areas through public utility commissions; and (b) pricing of military defence materiel through negotiational contracting. These two were selected for present purposes from a longer list of pricing structures and patterns including interest rate determination, pricing of medical care and pricing of insurance 'products', among others. Consideration of public sector pricing at the macro level of comprehensive price controls and experience must also be left for subsequent inquiry. Passing reference, as appropriate, will be made to neoclassical arguments about public sector pricing. Part III identifies public purposes to be served and suggests an approach for evaluating governmental determination of prices. Although the illustrative material is drawn from the experience of federal institutions and agencies in the US, I believe that the conceptual approach will have pertinence for institutional and evolutionary analyses of discretionary pricing in other economies.

I THE INSTITUTIONAL CONTEXT

Most political economists recognize that, in all contemporary industrial economies, symbiotic relationships exist between the so-called private sector of oligopolistic enterprises and megacorps, and the so-called public sector of government, although the patterns are idiosyncratic. As John Kenneth Galbraith noted a quarter century ago: 'The industrial system, in fact, is inextricably associated with the state. In notable respects the mature corporation is an arm of the state. And the state, in important matters, is an instrument of the industrial system.'[2] This interdependency has progressed to the point where even the captions of 'private' and 'public' sector no longer seem delimiting or adequate. 'In fact, the line between public and private authority in the industrial system is indistinct and in large measure imaginary.'[3] Each sector often acts in anticipation of, or in response to, initiatives of the other. But the fact of symbiosis does not necessarily imply that their normative goals and purposes converge. In these two highly complex, interrelated and interdependent power systems, each is, individually and jointly, a repository of substantial capacity to define norms and to implement policies, including pricing practices, that impinge on the general economic well-being of the community.

Power Prerogatives: Governments

Power prerogatives of governments are usually established by agreed constitutions, formal or customary, that specify the structure and functions of

government and define the loci, character and extent of discretionary authority within and among segments of the public structure. In the United States,
each segment – legislative, executive, judicial – is able, under specified
circumstances, to blunt or interdict initiatives of another. Governments hold
constitutionally designated powers of mandamus and injunction. Elaborate
institutional structures, such as regular elections, term limits, secret ballots
and the like, are customarily provided in the effort to hold those who wield
public power formally to account.

The prerogatives of government to engage in the administration of prices
at all levels are exercised through diverse and complex institutional arrangements. Governmental bodies at the national level, as we shall see, have
primary roles and responsibilities to fulfil in the administration of prices.
State and local governmental bodies are partially replicative of the federal
structure, but each does have a sphere of pricing responsibility somewhat
unique to its own jurisdiction. Indeed, pricing options and responsibilities not
construed to be uniquely national devolve to the states or local jurisdictions.
Attention here is confined to national- or federal-level price administration.

Except for comprehensive controls associated with major inflationary crises,
governmental administration of prices is characteristically particularistic, that
is, specific to one sector or product or service. When setting prices directly
through some of its agencies, the government can act largely unilaterally.
Interest rates on federally-insured veterans' home loans, prices on timber sales
from public lands and charges for government documents are examples.

Administered pricing also occurs through a variety of somewhat indirect
institutional complexes of government. The Congress itself is continuously
involved as a price setting or price influencing body. It can, for example, take
the lead in government: to set ceiling prices on particular items; to fix maximum rates of interest allowable on loans; to impose cost containment measures on the private provision of public services. The Congress can empower
agencies that it creates to engage in administration of prices, as with federal
regulatory commissions and the Federal Reserve System. Quite commonly,
however, and reflecting the symbiotic relationships noted above, much participation by governmental bodies in price administration involves continuing negotiations with one or another segment of the pro-forma private sector.
Actual pricing discretion may well be shared.

In addition, the Congress can undertake extensive investigations into, and
hold hearings on, private sector pricing practices and in consequence recommend and at times impose constraints on such practices. One post World-War
II case involved the examination of administered pricing in the pharmaceutical industry, with one outcome being the mandated sale of generic drugs.[4]

Congress uses its legislative powers to influence pricing in other areas as
well. In its delineation of tax obligations for firms, it sets part of the cost

structure later reflected in their discretionary prices. In its creation of 'tax expenditures', it grants subsidy-like tax relief to favoured firms or sectors which may be reflected in their discretionary pricing.[5] When it offers investment tax credits and accelerated depreciation allowances, it helps firms pay the cost of new purchases of plant and equipment, thereby impinging on their cost-price structure. Similarly in its more formal extensions of subsidies to agriculture for supply management and price-support purposes, to fossil fuel producers as depletion allowances, to firms who train minority labourers, etc., it participates in pricing judgments concerning the respective firms or sector. When Congress passes minimum wage legislation, when it sets cost-control constraints on Medicare, when it provides tariffs or quotas on imported materials and the like, it impinges indirectly on pricing judgments of the corporate bodies engaged in discretionary pricing.

In sum, the character and complexity of much of the emergent structure through which administered pricing in the public sector occurs largely reflect particularistic desires of the public, through their government, to modify pricing practices in the private sector that are perceived, for example, (a) to reflect insufficient cost-price margins for firms to contribute adequately to the broader economy, as in the agriculture sector; (b) to be excessive in the usurious, exorbitant or self-serving sense, as in the financial or pharmaceutical sectors; (c) to be destructive of 'competition' or of public accountability, as in the case of 'natural' monopolies in the transportation and communication sectors; or (d) to contribute directly to environmental hazards or damage, as in the energy generating sector. Indeed, at times it may actually serve the defensive purposes of mature corporations that are opportunistically positioned to *seek* public administration of prices of goods which they themselves produce.

Power Prerogatives: Corporations

Power prerogatives of 'mature corporations', as noted briefly in Chapter 3, are emergent discretionary capabilities derived from the acquisition and differential use of a variety of institutional arrangements (for example, public chartering, fragmented ownership, limited liability), many of which originated in or were supported by federal laws and court judgments. From these, in addition, the corporation gained the status of a legal personality in the eyes of the law. It can buy, sell and hold property; it can claim due process protections. One of the consequences of interest here is that this corporate entity can be interposed as an institutional buffer or barrier between corporate decision makers (for example, on prices) and those who experience the consequences of their judgments. Corporate decision makers acquire power and have the option of anonymity in its use. Persons actually making pricing decisions remain largely unknown; individual accountability may be impossible to establish.

Large and mature corporations typically have financial resources sufficient to influence significantly the composition of legislative bodies, the character of governmental executive appointments, the interpretation of rules and regulations, and the initiation of self-serving legislation concerning, for example, environmental controls and determination of market access. Giant size and interlocking directorates give corporations differential access to credit and repayment terms from the largest financial corporations.[6] In addition, the impact of corporate economic power on cultural, educational, informational and social spheres has expanded dramatically.[7]

Galbraith has provided a penetrating and corollary commentary on corporate decision making:

> In specific terms this [need to control events] means that prices must, if possible, be under control; that decisive costs must also be under control or so managed that adverse movements can be offset by the controlled prices; that effort must be made to ensure that the consumer responds favorably to the product; that if the state is the customer, it will remain committed to the product or its development; that other needed state action is arranged and any adverse governmental action prevented; that other uncertainties external to the firm are minimized and other external needs assured. In other words the firm is required, with increasingly technical products and processes, increasing capital, a lengthened gestation period and an increasingly large and complex organization, to control or seek to control the social environment in which it functions – or any part which impinges upon it. It must plan not only its own operation; it must also, to the extent possible, plan the behavior of people and the state as these affect it. This is a matter not of ambition but of necessity.[8]

Given the absence of illusory price competition, mechanisms for holding these corporate powers accountable are, for the most part, available only through government. When governmental initiatives and constraints are precluded, preempted or co-opted, there are few alternative and effective instruments of accountability available to the community. Even worker participation in firm decision making rarely occurs without governmental mandate. Direct and indirect use of governmental authority to administer prices, if creatively and persistently undertaken, can contribute to the achievement of improved accountability. Through such accountability, public monitoring of price setting is enhanced and opportunities to explore and apply explicit and public criteria of judgment are provided.

II SECTORAL CASE STUDIES OF THE ADMINISTRATION OF PRICES IN THE PUBLIC SECTOR

The following analysis will be confined to a consideration of two quite dissimilar approaches to administered pricing in the so-called public sector: (1) pricing of basic services in and through public utility commissions, (2) pricing through public-private negotiations in military procurement. Common to each is a demonstration that public assessment of pricing power is unavoidable.

Administered Pricing: Public Utilities

Public utility regulation is an example of the public control of pricing in enterprises 'affected with the public interest' that has been a part of the English Common Law tradition since the 17th century.[9] With the creation of the Interstate Commerce Commission in 1887, a distinctively American approach to the regulation of pricing in private enterprise was instituted. At the federal level (a parallel development occurred at state level), Congress creates an independent regulatory commission, defines its structure and functions, and specifies its powers; the executive branch appoints members of the commission for extended terms; the judicial branch may, in most circumstances, review commission judgments on appeal. Once established, the commission is intended to have autonomy from ordinary political processes and pressures, though actual practices depart somewhat from this intent.[10] The commission renders regulatory judgments, including administration of prices, and implements those judgments. But the structure and functions vary somewhat from one area (electric power) to another (transportation).

More particularly, these commissions are instituted to regulate 'natural monopolies', to ensure the

> adequacy and availability of service, consumer protection from exorbitant prices, and protection against price discrimination in inelastic residential markets ... in industries that deal with basic necessities and that are essential. ... [T]he regulator, as a principal representative of government, should serve as a protector of those social values affecting the environment as well as low-income consumers, and act as a shield in neutralizing the negative effects of the use of market power by the regulated utilities.[11]

Concerning service availability, commissions seek to assure nondiscriminatory access to the product or service, uninterrupted provision of the product or service, and the maintenance of its quality. Concerning consumer protection vis-à-vis prices – the main focus here – substantial control of prices and direct control of earnings are sought. In addition, to 'achieve economies of scale and adequacy of service, commissions have authority over the entry and exit of firms in the regulated markets'.[12] The expectation is that, in monopolistic firms, regulatory commissions will force cost savings from economies of scale to be passed along to rate payers.[13]

Historically, the typical approach to price determination utilized by regulatory commissions in the administration of prices is the 'cost of service rate-base regulation [that] depends upon determining the operating expenses for a representative period ... ascertaining the rate base, and fixing a return on investment (rate base) that services equity and debt'. This generates the 'revenue requirement that must be covered by rates set by the commission for various classes of customers'.[14] In general, the price of the product or service must be set high enough to generate aggregate receipts from sales sufficient to cover all operating expenses and provide a 'fair return' on 'fair valuation' of capital funds invested. The 'fair valuation' sets the pecuniary estimate of the cost of physical capital; the 'fair return' is the specified rate of gain deemed sufficient on the valued property.

The regulated enterprise proposes – presents its case for (generally) higher rates and higher returns; the utility commission disposes – analyses proposals and rules on their propriety, employing their assessment procedures and criteria. Historically at issue in deliberations over the level of administered prices are three elements. (1) Concerning property valuation for rate base specification: should property be valued at original or reproductive costs? Commissions tend to favour the former; firms the latter. (2) Concerning the allowable rate of return: what is a 'fair return'? Are rates in some segment of the *private* financial sector to be used as the standard or measure? Commissions seek cost-covering lower rates; firms seek higher rates. (3) Concerning allowable operating expenses: obviously, costs of labour, materials, energy and the like are covered. But should rate payers have to absorb costs of the regulated firm's advertising budget? How about executive 'perks' and bonuses? Commissions try to hold the line; firms inflate as and where they can.

But *actual* discretion remains divided. Historically, in some cases, 'regulation concentrated upon the overall level of earnings. It left to management the question of the design of rates to generate the required revenues; ... the choice of services and technology was made by industry. Regulation merely acquiesced in that choice. Regulatory policy generally discouraged entry on the assumption that competition was antithetical to efficient service.'[15] Regulation would protect against monopoly power while securing the benefits of economies of scale.

In the last quarter century, however, regulation of prices by public utility commissions has fallen on hard times. Beginning in the late 1960s and accelerating through the 1970s, public support eroded. Dramatically rising energy prices, rising interest rates, mounting conservative pressure for de-regulation (among other influences) converged to erode public confidence. Leadership in both political parties agreed to support deregulation of energy sources, transportation and the like.[16] Accordingly, when Reagan's adminis-trators took over in 1980, they immediately accelerated a more conservative counter-revolution in economic policy, for instance, by significantly intensi-fying the ideological clamour for deregulation.

Discourse over public utility regulation was dramatically transformed for at least three reasons.[17] (a) The Chicago School of neoclassical orthodoxy, having achieved (in the US) substantial dominion over the economics profes-sion and several 'prestigious' policy-originating think tanks, provided leader-ship for the academic and professional consultants' assault on regulation in general and price determination by regulatory commissions in particular. (2) The Reagan Administration had no interest in, and provided no leadership for, regulation of enterprises 'affected with the public interest'. 'Leave it to the free market' became the slogan which discouraged interest in regulatory policy initiatives. (3) The coincident increase in the complexity, aggregate size and power of enterprises (through conglomerate diversification, massive buyouts, encompassing mergers, new holding companies and the like) brought new and sustained pressure, with intimidating consequences, on the older rate-setting bodies and their regulatory approaches.

Although the academic and political assault on pricing in public utility regulation has clearly been massive and multifaceted, only two aspects can be considered here: cross subsidization and price discrimination techniques, and the introduction of contestable market theory into regulatory delibera-tions.

Market discrimination
Megacorp utility firms are able aggressively to pursue cross-subsidization and price discrimination policies.[18] Markets are segmented on demand char-acteristics; inelastic segments subsidize elastic ones, and price discrimination follows. As Harry Trebing has observed:

> When the giant corporation serves a diverse range of markets of differing demand elasticities through a production process characterized by significant common and joint costs, there is a strong incentive to shift the burdens of risk, obsolescence, and revenue deficiencies to inelastic markets. In this fashion the firm will shield itself from market pressures while simultaneously acquiring an advantage over potential rivals.[19]

This issue of discriminatory risk and cost shifting is debated in both commission hearings and in the academic literature, particularly in the tele-communications field. For instance, in their desire to fund a massive technological transformation of their systems utilizing fibre optics, the Bell companies wished to 'assign a major share of the multi-billion dollar costs of premature modernization of ... plant and equipment to residential customers where the costs would not be so assigned if the assignment were made on the basis of cost causation'.[20] Such an assignment is called *Ramsey pricing*.[21] This 'inverse elasticity rule' allocates 'common costs to customer classes in proportion to the elasticity of demand of the various classes of service: those classes with inelastic demands would bear the largest share of costs, while those classes with more elastic demands would be assigned a smaller share'.[22] When commissions concur, Ramsey pricing allows the monopolist, *under regulation*, to discriminate in its pricing to maximize its profits and extend its market share.[23]

More particularly in telecommunications, the technique of 'stand alone pricing' provides for the pricing of services in 'demand elastic, noncore markets [e.g., computer services] at or slightly above variable cost, and have services in the basic market pick up all or the bulk of fixed costs'.[24] The expedient justification for this pricing rule is 'that if basic service were the only service provided (thus, "stand alone"), it would bear full responsibility for all fixed and variable costs of that service. The addition of noncore services to an existing core adds, by definition, no fixed costs, only the variable costs of the provision of these services.'[25] The more fundamental justification is an appeal to a Paretian optimality in which both core and noncore customers are presumed to be 'better off'. In either case, the basic buyer, whose demand is inelastic, subsidizes technological innovations. To the extent that commissions accede to this orthodox argument, the power to administer utility prices shifts increasingly to the monopolist supplier, thus compromising the public's interest in constraining Ramsey pricing. The public-private mix of interdependency tilts – giving 'advantage' to the Bell system, in tennis jargon.

Contestable markets

In the theory of contestable markets – a neoclassical contribution mainly of the 1980s – the claim is made that regulation of industries by commissions can be substantially narrowed. Commission discretion over *pricing*, for instance, would no longer be needed. Starting with the premise that the competitive model defines and provides Paretian welfare norms, to the realization of which policy should be directed, contestable market theory purports to explain how monopoly enterprise can achieve price competitive goals without governmental regulation. This formulation has not remained in the realm of esoteric and speculative discourse. The Interstate Commerce Commission is reported to have incorporated elements of contestable market theory into its deliberations concerning the transportation industry.[26]

'The theory of contestable markets states that the threat of entry is equivalent to active competition among incumbents if a market is perfectly contestable.'[27] In the absence of sunk costs, such contestability is achieved if the following conditions are met: no barriers to entry; no barriers to exit; an entrant has time to enter the market, make above normal profits and then exit before retaliation. The recommendation is that regulators 'should act as "a surrogate for competition unimpeded by entry barriers" ... and that the theory of contestable markets provides a "competitive market model" for a regime of partially regulated multiproduct firms operating under scale economies and competing directly with one another at prices in excess of marginal costs'.[28]

Difficulties arise however. 'Pricing above marginal costs requires departures from perfect contestability.'[29] Moreover, applications of the theory are perceived as 'efforts to protect an incumbent's need to be viable via Ramsey pricing from the perceived threat of profitable entry caused by pricing above marginal cost'.[30] Although it cannot be pursued here, a lively debate continues *within* orthodoxy over the logical structure and applicability of this formulation.[31]

What is clear enough, however, is that this theory takes no account of the use and abuse of power outside the narrow frame of orthodox marginalist-based pricing judgments. Constraints consist only of threats to the incumbent's pricing power from new entrants. Oligopolistic cooperation, collusion, market sharing, technology pooling, demand manipulation, political participation, etc., are all outside the pale. No welfare criteria save Paretian are admitted. It is a severely truncated approach.

Consequences

What is implied from this evolution of pricing principles and policies is that, to the extent that there is permeation of neoclassically grounded, Paretian defended, pricing rules into the process of administering prices in commission deliberations, most serious consequences ensue: (a) the locus of pricing authority – de facto pricing power – will increasingly shift from commissions to the megacorp firms of the 'regulated' industry; (b) the willingness of these corporate price makers to invoke price discrimination, using the inverse elasticity rule, to further their own purposes indicates that private goals will be served at the expense of the public interest in fairness and universal access; (c) the accountability of those actually making pricing decisions will become increasingly tenuous.

Administered Pricing: Military Procurement

The end of the Cold War and the dissolution of the former Soviet Union have, of course, dramatically eroded the rationale for the gargantuan, Reagan-supported military establishment, including its love affair with 'Star Wars' missilery, that drained resources and preempted personnel for over a decade. However, the outcome, a 50 per cent increase in the defence budget at President Reagan's direction,[32] evidently did not produce a commensurate increase in materiel or readiness. As Richard Stubbing argues, 'the rapid defense-budget buildup enacted since 1980 must be seen for what it is – a temporary Band-Aid solution to the real issues facing our defense program; ... we have spent more to buy less'.[33] A flurry of Congressional investigations and reform measures in the 1980s, some of which are mentioned below, sought to improve defence output performance and to bring rising, not to say scandalous, costs under control.[34]

Given the easing of tensions between the great powers, pressures and proposals for substantial reductions in overall military expenditures seem destined to continue in the search for 'peace dividends'.[35] Even so, there is every reason to believe that the US will retain and continue to develop a formidable defensive posture, agreements to reduce nuclear weapons notwithstanding. '[D]efense spending is far and away the largest single purchasing component of the federal budget. ... [W]eapons procurement has given politicians new ways to direct federal spending to their constituents.'[36] How pricing decisions are made involving this sector will thus continue to have major significance for the economy generally.

Pricing in the military industrial complex

The symbiotic relationship between private industry and the national government alluded to above has been, for the last half century, nowhere more evident than in the defence sector of the national economy. While much has been written (a) about the converging domestic and overseas interests of megacorps and oligopolies and the determination and implementation of national security policy, on the one hand, and (b) about the heavy two-way traffic of corporate executives and military personnel (mainly retired officers) between corporate hierarchies and governmental positions, on the other,[37] the focus here must be limited to one facet of this symbiotic public-private institutional complex. That aspect is price determination in procurement of military goods and services.

At the outset, it is clear that there are three main institutional constellations of participants and accompanying foci of discretionary power in this conjoint decision-making area. The main players are: (a) the Executive branch: the President, National Security Council and the Department of Defense (DOD) in the Pentagon; (b) the Congressional legislative branch: the Armed Services Committee of the Senate, the Armed Services and the Appropriations Committees of the House of Representatives; and (c) the 'private sector': the megacorp defence industries including their numerous subcontractors.

The structure of the 'private' defence sector requires an additional word. Not surprisingly, it is a highly concentrated industry. In recent years, the largest 100 firms have accounted for about 60 per cent of all defence contracts; the top 25 firms garner about 45 per cent of dollars awarded. Subcontractors of the major firms number in the thousands. The Defense Department itself contracts with some 30,000 firms each year. With the increasing significance of electronic components in weapons systems, electronic firms have moved into the prime contractor category.[38]

Each of the three components of the sector brings some measure of achieved power of initiation and veto to the deliberations. The President and his advisers mainly set foreign policy and its military support requirements in consultation with the Department of Defense (DOD). The DOD in turn is the government's prime contractor and buying agent. The Congress, especially through its Committees, participates at arm's length in foreign policy decisions, oversees military procurement and authorizes the spending of funds. The 'private' industrial defence sector provides the authorized materiel under negotiated contracts with the DOD representing the government. This military-industrial complex is 'a set of integrated institutions that act to maximize their collective power',[39] even as they compete and contend each with the other. Decisions concerning not only what will be produced, but the pricing of such materiel, are accomplished through continuing deliberation and consensus-seeking among the contending and cooperating parties. It is an elaborate planning and implementing process by which negotiated contracts determine prices. Initiatives for new weapons systems and revisions to existing systems may come from any of the participants, but a typical source is from DOD military advisers in consultation with prime contractor representatives.

Significantly, the negotiating market for military materiel is unique; it has almost nothing in common with (textbook) unfettered consumer markets. The following abbreviated summary of characteristics is adapted and updated from earlier work by Harry B. Yoshpe, Charles F. Franke and others:[40]

- The DOD as buyer establishes the requirements for the product; the producer undertakes development. Consultation is continuous.
- Few heterogeneous products are produced.
- Price is only one consideration; quality, availability and technological capabilities are also central.
- The exchange system is personal; buyers' agents work continuously with sellers' agents.
- The buyer finances most of development and may provide equipment or facilities for sellers' use. Periodic payments are meshed with stages of production.

- The sellers' market is essentially one customer; all buying agents are subject to DOD control; selling agents are influential.
- Demand is a function of Presidential goal setting, Congressional funding, and productive capacity and technology offered by sellers; the scientific capability of the megacorp as prime contractor and its subcontractors is a major concern.
- Prices are comprised of evaluative negotiations of profit levels and actual and expected costs, with selected suppliers chosen by the buyer.
- The market is highly sensitive to domestic and international politics and intrigue.
- International tensions can cause requirements to fluctuate rapidly and comprehensively.

As noted, all players have power roles: their leverage shifts in magnitude and significance as the character and timing of the defence production programme evolves. One such characterization is provided by Thomas McNaugher:

> As a project begins, the government has most of the leverage. Competition [as rivalry in pursuit of contracts] early in development is an important component of that leverage, and the buy-in is one of the more notable symptoms. As a project evolves, sunk costs rise, competitors are eliminated, and the winning firm moves into a monopoly position from which it can deal with the government with increasing authority. From this position it seeks to get well or recoup investments borne of earlier optimism. As in most negotiations in which power is shared, this one includes a good deal of gaming, as each of the two parties seeks to maximize its interests. Insofar as the game forms the core of the relationship between risk and reward in defense projects, the game is, for practical purposes, the Defense Department's market mechanism.[41]

The heart or core of the negotiation process, of course, involves reaching agreement on the governing contract. The character and import of differing contractual arrangements have changed over time and will continue to do so. Even so, these deliberations still encompass mainly the often rival and extensive interests of the DOD as buyer and one or more contract suppliers as seller(s).

Historically, two different kinds of contracting have prevailed. One is the 'firm fixed-price' contract (FFP) in which the 'contractor promises to supply certain specified goods or services at a price which, after agreed upon by buyer and seller, is not subject to adjustments reflecting the seller's actual cost experience'.[42] Profits and costs vary inversely; the lower the costs the higher the profit. An incentive for cost reduction is inherent, but the seller's risks are high. Given the uncertainties involved, the FFP is rarely sought by sellers.

The other, now more common, contract form is the cost-plus-a-fixed-fee contract (CPFF), or some variant of it. In this cost reimbursement, or simply cost-plus, arrangement,

> the buyer and seller initially agree upon a fee or profit amount related to an estimate of total costs. [Note here that 'profit' evidently does not refer to a rate of return on invested capital funds but to a fixed fee or mark-up on costs.] The cost estimate is not binding; the buyer agrees to reimburse within limits all allowable costs incurred by the contractor in executing the contract. ... [T]he 'price' in a CPFF relationship is almost completely flexible. The fee, however, is fixed.[43]

Compared with the FFP, then, contractors' risk from rising costs is less and the government's risk of inflated or windfall profits is reduced.[44]

So far as price determination of defence materiel as such is concerned (leaving aside all other considerations, for example of technical capacities of weapons and the strategic roles they are to play), these mainly bilateral negotiations focus primarily (a) on what will be the allowable 'fixed fee' or markup on costs in the contract, and (b) what are, and are not, 'allowable' costs. Given the rapid acceleration of defence expenditures in the 1980s and the continuing complaints of excessive profits and over-charges as costs, the Congress spent inordinate amounts of time and energy in scrutinizing both of these aspects of defence contracting.[45]

Administered profit rates on defence procurement date from 1934 and the Vinson-Trammell Act (VTA) that set profit limits of 12 per cent on contracts over $10,000 for the construction of military aircraft, and 10 per cent on contracts over $10,000 for the manufacture of naval vessels.[46] New legislation superseded these VTA levels in the period from 1951 to 1976, after which a pro forma return to VTA levels was made. But these were not enforced and were finally and officially waived. There was general agreement that the VTA was 'antiquated, unworkable, and ineffective'.

Through the 1960s and 1970s, however, various new measures were enacted to forestall contracting abuses and to avoid excess profits. One law limits profits on CPFF contracts: 'The limits applied to estimated costs are 15 percent for experimental, developmental, or research work; 6 percent for architectural and engineering services; 10 percent for all other products and services'. More generally, a Defense Acquisition Regulation provides that 'a weighted guidelines method for establishing profit objectives' may be used. Different profit percentages may be applied to differing elements of cost.[47] An additional insight into rates of return is provided in a Congressional Report questioning the pricing of spare parts. In an analysis otherwise concerned with prices of spare parts that were unrelated to their original cost, the routine incorporation of a 16 per cent markup on costs seemed unexceptional.[48]

Cost containment on defence contracting has also absorbed Congressional efforts in the last decade. By 1981, there was a new defence acquisition regulation that identified 'procedures for the pricing and cost analysis of contracts', including principles specifying what costs are allowable.[49] In the later Allowable Cost Reform Act, disallowed costs are specifically delineated: costs of entertainment, costs incurred to influence congressional action, costs incurred in defence of any fraud proceeding, fines or penalties from violating regulations, costs of alcoholic beverages, contributions or donations of any kind, costs of advertising, costs of promotional items and memorabilia, and the like. The Bill also provided for penalties where such costs were incorporated in negotiations with DOD buying agents.[50]

In addition, a Truth-in-Negotiations Act 'requires the contractor to provide the government's negotiator with complete, accurate, and current cost and pricing data prior to contract award. ... Government auditors then review these data before the government agrees on the contract price.'[51] Moreover, the Cost Accounting Standards Act 'requires contractors under certain negotiated contracts to comply with 19 detailed standards regarding the allocation of costs to contracts'.[52]

Enough has been said to demonstrate that the trilateral negotiational fabric through which administered pricing of defence materiel is accomplished is under more or last constant review and reformulation. The character and terms of contracting are mainly determined by the Congress as it reviews prior decisions, prior negotiations and their consequences. Defence firms and their trade associations bargain with and petition both Congressional committees and the DOD to have their views incorporated into these negotiational stipulations.[53] Each of the three categories of participants, possessing some discretion, constantly appraises and responds to these transformations in ways that reflect how they conceive their own interests, with each insisting that these are congruent with and best serve the public interest! What has been made clear, I trust, is that defence procurement indeed occurs in an idiosyncratic context of administered pricing.

III EVALUATION OF ADMINISTERED PRICING

What insights, inferences or conclusions can be drawn from the foregoing analysis? The following are grouped as limitations of orthodoxy and contributions of neoinstitutionalists.

Limitations of Orthodoxy

We have fresh reasons for contending, as neoinstitutionalist and evolutionary economists, that the normative use by neoclassical scholars of the competitive model as the all-purpose, all-occasion measure or standard with which allocative decision-making can be appraised is patently unacceptable. In utility regulation and military procurement, the competitive model as a norm is descriptively irrelevant and normatively inapplicable. Neoinstitutionalists are correct in insisting that the market model is *not* an effective or realistic adjudicator of social values.

While we can expect that efforts will continue to be made to reconfigure quasi-public administration of pricing in public utilities so as to enhance already achieved corporate power, the community – through governmental actions – must resist. Its culturally conditioned support for the 'competition' of the free market model provides few insights for understanding 'competitive rivalry' as reflected in the actual use of corporate power in the struggle for market shares and sector dominance.

Similarly, understanding the negotiational structure and process of the pricing of military materiel owes little or nothing to the competitive model. A comparison between the procurement 'market', as noted, and a Friedmanesque 'free-to-choose' competitive market indicates few if any common attributes; indeed they seem mutually exclusive. Clearly, social monitoring of pricing in the quasi-public sector is now mandatory, as indeed it is in other sectors where pricing power is held. However, the constructs of neoclassical market theory that relate to assessment and evaluation – allocative efficiency, Paretian optima, consumer equilibria, contestable markets, and the like – contribute little to the analysis of administered pricing.

Contributions of Neoinstitutionalists

Through enhanced analytical understanding of pricing in the public sector, reinforcement is provided from yet another major sector of the political economy for the general premise that most prices that matter are administered prices set by discretionary agents. Price makers exercise power; they choose among alternative futures.

Whether as members of regulatory commissions or as petitioning lawyers of corporate firms before such commissions, each is charged with and is engaged in administered price setting. Participants will sometimes refer to 'market forces'; they may even attempt mistakenly to create consequences that are presumed to mimic what those 'market forces' would have generated. But for good or ill they are engaged in deliberations over prices and pricing power. Similarly, the DOD as buyer and the munitions firms as sellers are caught up in a complex and continuing process of contract deliberations; they engage in negotiations and renegotiations over what will be produced and the cost-plus price relationships pertaining thereto. A culminating agreement enables the production process to move forward.

In addition, in reaching agreements, there is increased recognition that these discretionary agents necessarily employ criteria to create and choose among alternatives, rationales and, ultimately, prices. Social value theory is inherently part of any credible analysis of the decision-making process determining prices. Similarly, in any external or internal assessment of agents' price setting judgments, criteria of appraisal must be employed.

In order to address both the use and assessment of social value criteria in deliberations on the setting of prices, neoinstitutionalists often draw on evaluative constructs from the theory of instrumental valuation (which proponents have analysed extensively).[54] It is useful here to reintroduce the fundamental dichotomy that lies at the heart of this value theory. This is the distinction, dating back to Veblen, between ceremonial and instrumental values that function as criteria for the correlation of behaviour within the institutional structure of society. As Paul D. Bush frames the distinction: 'ceremonial values are warranted by those mores and folkways that incorporate status hierarchies and invidious distinctions as to the relative "worth" of various individuals or classes in the community. They rationalize power relationships and patterns of authority embedded in the status quo.'[55] In contrast, 'instrumental values are warranted through the systematic application of knowledge to the problem-solving process. They emerge from the processes of inquiry into causal relationships. As criteria for correlating behaviour, they ensure causal continuity in the problem-solving process.'[56]

That observed institutionalized behaviour will often reflect elements of both ceremonial (or invidious) and instrumental warrant (or justification) is readily acknowledged; either may dominate the other.[57] Indeed, what was earlier perceived as an instrumentally-warranted judgment or behaviour may, with the passing of time and further assessment, become an invidious or ceremonial behaviour or judgment. In the social value principle embedded in this pragmatic and operational theory of instrumental valuation, there are criteria of judgment – continuity of human life, non-invidiousness, recreating community, instrumental use of knowledge – that provide guidance for neoinstitutionalists in formulating the following 'public purposes' against which to cast the price setting procedures and judgments considered above.

Among the instrumentally-warranted public purposes to be served by pricing judgments of regulatory commissioners, the following appear to be pertinent to rate-setting deliberations. Pricing judgments should be such as (a) to ensure the continuing and efficient provision of high quality and adequate levels of product or service; (b) to provide universal access to every basic product and service – energy, communication, transportation; (c) to guarantee noninvidious, non-discriminatory provision of product and service; (d) to ensure an environmentally sustainable performance, and (e) to reflect accountability by ensuring continuing responsible and responsive commission discretion over pricing policy.

In appraising commission pricing with such purposes in mind, what does one find? Pricing judgments that accept or reflect Ramsey pricing (the inverse elasticity rule) appear to be invidiously discriminatory. Placing disproportionate rate burdens for technological expansion on inelastic (including low-income) buyers threatens their continuing access to basic services. The 'stand alone' argument seems disingenuous; commissions must base pricing judgments and cost assignments on total operations, not on a contrived cost-burdening contention. The claims to alleged Paretian welfare consequences are unpersuasive. Their empirical realization and demonstration are not feasible; their import is to retain the status quo.[58]

Moreover, the stipulated institutional conditions required for the envisioned functioning of contestable markets – no sunk costs, no exit or entry barriers, etc. – are as austere and unrealistic as are those for purely or perfectly competitive markets. 'Contestable market' conditions are presumed to provide improved accountability by turning the pricing function over to this surrogate of the free market. Pricing discretion would be abandoned by commissions in favour of this substitute. But without the actual existence of these austere and unrealistic conditions that are assumed, discretion in fact devolves upon the megacorps that provide the products or services – thus directly serving their interests to retain and extend their power. This appears as a ceremonially-warranted judgment, although claims to the contrary are rife. Increased concentration of control and reduced accountability of existing power systems are the predictable outcomes in the regulatory sector. The vested interests of the conglomerate or megacorp become a surrogate for the public interest.

Among various instrumentally-warranted public purposes to be served by negotiational contracting in the military procurement field, the following are suggested. Pricing procedures and judgments should be such as (a) to facilitate the production and maintenance of materiel sufficient in design and number to support essential national military roles and responsibilities democratically determined; (b) to require that all non-sensitive records relating to pricing negotiations, especially after contracts are signed, becomes available as public knowledge, to hedge against fraud, diversions and excesses; (c) to ensure that Constitutionally specified initiating roles for the President and his executive agencies on the one hand, and for Congress and its oversight and accountability committees on the other, are observed; (d) to reflect continuing review and working of bilateral or trilateral negotiations to ensure that incentives for cost containment and integrity of deliberation are retained.

Has the administration of prices in the procurement of military materiel served these purposes in the last decade or so? Although the sea of controversy has been both wide and deep, the unparalleled magnitude of defence outlays in the 1980s and the concurrent disclosures of excessive costing and other forms of malfeasance have garnered enough Congressional attention to prompt significant corrective measures over the decade. Rules requiring increased public disclosure of contract negotiations have been enacted. Congress has, through new legislation, generated improved accountability. Allowable costing criteria have also been established. Fixed fee returns have been openly considered and set.

What is not yet clear, however, is the extent to which intrasector conflicts over pricing and costing in these bilateral and trilateral negotiations have contributed negatively to the provision of low quality materiel, to the devolution of public discretionary power upon private prime contractors, to the diversion of productive energies and resources to extralegal paramilitary purposes, to the waste of human and material resources, to the obstruction or impairment of inquiry, and to the generation of substantial environmental hazards. Definitive responses to these questions must await subsequent research. In addition, the effects of a significant reduction in the size of the defence establishment, corresponding to the aforementioned public purposes, are yet to be determined.

The concern here has been to extend the exploration of administered prices in the public sector as part of what hopefully will become a major research programme – the development of a more general neoinstitutional theory of administered pricing. Perhaps this analysis will also help to demonstrate that any such research agenda on pricing powers and practices must encompass both normative and positive dimensions of inquiry.

NOTES

1. Hamilton (1938); Means (1963); Galbraith [1952] (1980); Galbraith (1967); Galbraith (1973); Eichner [1976] (1980); Okun (1980); Tool (1991); Lee (1993).
2. Galbraith (1967), p. 296.
3. Ibid, p. 297.
4. Kefauver (1965), ch. 1.
5. Peterson (1991), ch. 3.
6. Munkirs (1985).
7. Dugger (1989).
8. Galbraith (1973), pp. 39–40.
9. See Munn vs. Illinois, 94 U.S. 113 (1876) in Commager (1948), pp. 91–4.
10. Successive public executives with power of appointment can, over time, reconstitute commission membership and therewith radically alter its perspective and behaviour.
11. Schwartz (1985), p. 312.
12. Ibid.

13. Sheehan (1991), p. 22.
14. Schwartz (1985), p. 314. For an historical summary of the emergence and assessment of public utility regulation, see Trebing (1984), pp. 223–50.
15. Miller (1978), p. 610.
16. Lower (1981), pp. 597–601.
17. Actually the deregulation pressure began in the 1970s, for example, with an effort to require commissions regulating the electric power industry to have recourse to marginal cost pricing techniques. Miller (1978), pp. 610–25.
18. Sheehan (1991), p. 21.
19. Trebing (1989). pp. 406–7.
20. Ibid.
21. The origin of the 'inverse elasticity rule' is attributed to Frank D. Ramsey, a young British mathematical economist of the early 20th century who was known to J.M. Keynes.
22. Sheehan (1991), p. 21.
23. Ibid, p. 23.
24. Miller (1990), p. 727.
25. Ibid.
26. Tye (1990), p. 1.
27. Ibid, pp. 2–3.
28. Ibid, p. 2.
29. Ibid, p. 124.
30. Ibid.
31. Ibid, pp. x–xiii; 119–28.
32. Marlin (1992), p. 25.
33. Stubbing (1986), p. 51.
34. Perhaps the largest and most recent inquiry, involving nine days of hearings, was US Congress, House Committee on Armed Services (1988), *Integrity of Department of Defense Acquisition System.*
35. Marlin (1992).
36. MacLaury, in McNaugher (1989), p. ix; US House (1986), *Defense Procurement.*
37. Barnet (1972).
38. McNaugher (1989), p. 150.
39. Barnet (1969), p. 59.
40. Yoshpe, Franke *et al.* (1968), p. 17; Baldwin (1967).
41. McNaugher (1989), p. 152.
42. Scherer (1964), p. 132.
43. Ibid, pp. 132–3.
44. Ibid, p. 133.
45. On profits: US House (1981), *Vinson–Trammell Act*; US House (1981), *Profit Limitations*; US House (1989), *Profit Policy Reporting.* On costs: US House (1985), *Allowable Cost Reform Act*; US House (1988), *Defense Acquisition Policy*; and US House (1988), *Integrity of Department of Defense.*
46. US House (1981), *Profit Limitations*, p. 1.
47. Ibid, p. 2.
48. US House (1984), *Defense Spare Parts.*
49. US House (1981), *Profit Limitations*, p. 2.
50. US House (1985), *Allowable Cost Reform Act*, p. 2.
51. US House (1981), *Profit Limitations*, p. 2.
52. Ibid.
53. A recent example is a study prepared by the MAC Group, a Harvard faculty based consulting team, on contract with three defence industry trade associations. A summary of their report and discussion thereon appears in US House (1988), *Defense Acquisition Policy.*
54. Bush (1988), pp. 125–66; Hickerson (1988), pp. 167–96; Tool (1993), pp. 119–59.
55. Bush (1983), p. 37.
56. Ibid.

57. Ibid, pp. 39–41.
58. Miller (1990), p. 729.

REFERENCES

Baldwin, William L. (1967), *The Structure of the Defense Market, 1955–1964*, Durham: Duke University Press.

Barnet, Richard J. (1969), *The Economy of Death*, New York: Atheneum.

Barnet, Richard J. (1972), *Roots of War*, New York: Atheneum.

Bush, Paul D. (1983), 'An exploration of the structural characteristics of a Veblen-Ayres-Foster defined institutional domain', *Journal of Economic Issues*, **17**, March.

Bush, Paul D. (1988), 'The Theory of Institutional Change', in Marc R. Tool (ed.), *Evolutionary Economics I: Foundations of Institutional Thought*, Armonk, N.Y.: M.E. Sharpe.

Commager, Henry Steele (1948), *Documents of American History*, 4th edn, New York: Appleton-Century-Crofts.

Dugger, William M. (1989), *Corporate Hegemony*, New York: Greenwood Press.

Eichner, Alfred S. [1976] (1980), *The Megacorp and Oligopoly*, White Plains, N.Y.: M.E. Sharpe.

Galbraith, John Kenneth (1967), *The New Industrial State*, Boston: Houghton Mifflin.

Galbraith, John Kenneth (1973), *Economics and the Public Purpose*, Boston: Houghton Mifflin.

Galbraith, John Kenneth [1952] (1980), *A Theory of Price Control*, Cambridge: Harvard University Press.

Hamilton, Walton *et al.* (1938), *Prices and Price Policies*, New York: McGraw-Hill.

Hickerson, Steven R. (1988), 'Instrumental Valuation: The Normative Compass of Institutional Economics', in Tool, Marc R. (ed.), *Evolutionary Economics I: Foundations of Institutional Thought*, Armonk, N.Y.: M.E. Sharpe.

Kefauver, Estes (1965), *In a Few Hands: Monopoly Power in America*, New York: Pantheon Books.

Lee, Frederic S. (1993), *From Post Keynesian to Historical Price Theory: Facts, Theory and Empirically Grounded Pricing Model*, Leicester: De Montfort University.

Lower, Milton D. (1981), 'Decontrol déjà vu', *Journal of Post Keynesian Economics*, **3**, Summer.

MacLaury, Bruce K., 'Foreward' to Thomas L. McNaugher (1989), *New Weapons Old Politics*, Washington, D.C.: Brookings Institution.

Marlin, John Tepper (1992), 'Tell the pentagon: the cold war is over' (an interview), *Challenge Magazine*, **35**, July/August.

McNaugher, Thomas L. (1989), *New Weapons Old Politics*, Washington D.C.: Brookings Institution.

Means, Gardiner C. (1963), 'Pricing Power and the Public Interest', US Congress, Senate, Committee on the Judiciary, Subcommittee on Antitrust and Monopoly, *Administered Prices: A Compendium on Public Policy*, 88th Cong., 1st sess., Washington, D.C.: US Government Printing Office.

Miller, Edythe S. (1978), 'Rate structure reform: a review of the current debate', *Journal of Economic Issues*, **12**, September.

Miller, Edythe S. (1990), 'Economic efficiency, the economics discipline, and the "affected-with-a-public-interest" concept', *Journal of Economic Issues*, **24**, September.

Munkirs, John R. (1985), *The Transformation of American Capitalism*, Armonk, N.Y.: M.E. Sharpe.

Okun, Arthur M. (1980), *Prices and Quantities*, Washington, D.C.: Brookings Institution.

Peterson, Wallace C. (1991), *Transfer Spending, Taxes, and the American Welfare State*, Boston: Kluwer Academic Publishers.

Scherer, Frederic M. (1964), *The Weapons Acquisition Process: Economic Incentives*, Boston: Harvard University Press.

Schwartz, David S. (1985), 'Idealism and realism: an institutionalist view of corporate power in the regulated utilities', *Journal of Economic Issues*, **19**, June.

Sheehan, Michael (1991), 'Why Ramsey pricing is wrong', *Journal of Economic Issues*, **25**, March.

Stubbing, Richard with Richard A. Mendel (1986), *The Defense Game*, New York: Harper and Row.

Tool, Marc R. (1991), 'Contributions to an Institutional Theory of Price Determination', in Geoffrey M. Hodgson and Ernesto Screpanti (eds), *Rethinking Economics: Markets, Technology and Economic Evolution*, Aldershot: Edward Elgar.

Tool, Marc R. (1993), 'The Theory of Instrumental Value: Extensions, Clarifications', in Marc R. Tool (ed.), *Institutional Economics: Theory, Method, Policy*, Dordrecht: Kluwer Academic Publishers.

Trebing, Harry M. (1984), 'Public utility regulation: a case study in the debate over the effectiveness of economic regulation', *Journal of Economic Issues*, **18**, March.

Trebing, Harry M. (1989), 'Restoring purposeful government: the Galbraithian contribution', *Journal of Economic Issues*, **23**, June.

Tye, William B. (1990), *The Theory of Contestable Markets*, New York: Greenwood Press.

US Congress, House, Committee on Armed Services (1984), *Defense Spare Parts Procurement Reform Act: Report* (to accompany H.R. 5064), 98th Cong., 2nd sess.

US Congress, House, Committee on Armed Services (1985), *Allowable Cost Reform Act: Report to the Committee of the Whole House* (to accompany H.R. 2397), 99th Cong., 1st sess.

US Congress, House, Committee on Armed Services (1988), *Integrity of Department of Defense Acquisition System and Its Impact on US National Security: Hearings before the Full Committee and the Acquisition Panel*, 100th Cong., 2nd sess.

US Congress, House, Committee on Armed Services, Acquisition Policy Panel (1988), *Defense Acquisition Policy (Industrial and Contract Policies): Hearing*, 100th Cong., 2nd sess.

US Congress, House, Committee on Armed Services, Acquisition Policy Panel (1989), *Profit Policy Reporting: Hearings*, 100th Cong., 2nd sess.

US Congress, House, Committee on Armed Services, Subcommittee on Procurement and Military Nuclear Systems (1981), *Profit Limitations on Defense Contracts: Report*, 97th Cong., 1st sess.

US Congress, House, Committee on Armed Services, Subcommittee on Procurement and Military Nuclear Systems (1981), *Vinson-Trammell Act of 1934 and the Necessity for Profit Limitations on Defense Contracts in the Current Contracting Environment: Hearings*, 97th Cong., 1st sess.

US Congress, House, Committee on the Judiciary (1986), *Defense Procurement Conflict of Interest Act: Report*, 99th Cong., 2nd sess.
Yoshpe, Harry B., Franke, Charles F. and others (1968), *Production for Defense*, Washington, D.C.: Industrial College of the Armed Forces.

6. Costing and valuation[*]

An acceleration of scholarship in neoinstitutional and evolutionary economics in the domain of pricing and costing theory is, in my view, an urgent and pragmatic matter. The pertinence and applicability of the neoinstitutionalist paradigm generally appear to me significantly to hinge on progress in this area. Earlier chapters addressed administered pricing and its valuational aspects. This chapter is intended to introduce a neoinstitutional formulation[1] of an empirically realistic and analytically defensible theory of cost and cost determination (costing). It encompasses a provisional application of instrumental value theory to the general area of discretionary costing. Its focus is exploratory. Its main purpose is to encourage the expansion of neoinstitutional analyses of cost determination as a research programme. Only in passing do I make comparisons with, or assessments of, the traditional approaches of neoclassicists in these fields of interest.

Although much significant attention has been given to social and environmental costs, beginning with John Maurice Clark, K. William Kapp, and Karl Polanyi[2] (with more provided below) too little study, in my view, has been devoted by neoinstitutionalist and evolutionary economists to more general theories of costs and costing. In addition, since neoinstitutionalists continuously demonstrate that all economies are discretionary systems, in which choices of institutional structure (including pricing policies and judgments) define and redefine the structural fabric of the economic order, this analysis must encompass costing judgments that parallel existing analyses of administered pricing judgments.[3] *Costing* refers to procedures agents use in setting pecuniary costs to determine cost-plus selling prices. *Pricing* refers to procedures agents use in setting selling prices. Indeed, costs and prices as such are distinguishable mainly through reference to the placement and/or roles of the discretionary participants in a firm's instituted processes of decision making. Pricing and costing determinations are forms and choices of institutional adjustments. And since all choices of structure, pricing or costing compel recourse to criteria of choice, analytical attention must continuously be directed to the social value premises reflected in cost setting as well as price-setting judgments. Costs, including the analyses that explain their determina-

*Paper presented at meetings of the Association for Evolutionary Economics, Boston, January 1994.

tion as costing and the criteria that define their character and assess their impact, constitute the universe of discourse addressed here.

Part I identifies and explores fundamental neoinstitutional tenets that undergird the analysis of costs and costing. Part II considers neoinstitutionalist concepts of costs, costing, opportunity costs and opportunity sets. Some recasting of constructs and meanings is undertaken. Part III presents an analytical characterization of pecuniary costs and costing as administered input prices. The concern here is to help reconstruct the analytical and discretionary domain of exchange as reflecting the possession and use of power and of the employment of normative tenets. Part IV undertakes an exploratory application of instrumental social value theory to the analysis of social costs. Particular illustrative consideration is given to social costs relating to the environment, to education, to unemployment and underemployment, and to the growth of knowledge and technology. The chapter concludes with Part V in which the major characteristics of a neoinstitutional theory of costs and costing are summarized.

I   BASIC TENETS

This formulation of neoinstitutionalist cost and costing theory rests especially upon the following four heavily abbreviated, but evidentially grounded, underpinnings: human nature, knowledge growth, institutional structure and social intercourse. These neoinstitutionalist constructs and postulates together provide a frame of reference for the following consideration of discretionary costing constructs, practices and agents.

Human Nature

It is the neoinstitutionalist view that people (producers, workers, buyers, sellers) are inherently capable of developing cognitive perceptions, framing reflective abstractions and discerning causal relations. From infancy they come to understand means-consequence connections, to interact in a social context, to develop habitual behaviour and to make judgments about conduct. Their attributes, preferences, personalities and behavioural regularities are acquired through participatory involvement in economic and cultural processes and are more or less constantly evolving. They are at once creators of, and created by, economic and cultural influences; they are educators even as they are themselves educated, formally and informally. As Walton Hamilton once put it: 'the individual and society [are] remaking each other in an endless process of [cumulative] change'.[4] As social and cultural beings, they are sensitive to and seek support from others. Being 'well thought of' is a motivating source of self-identification. Growth in knowledge and capabilities is a motivating source of self-realization. To confront substantive problems of choice is a motivating source of maturation and self-development. As Dewey observed, the emotion of pleasure or satisfaction is a sometime residual outcome of instrumental analysis and action, not its anterior *raison d'être*.[5] Cost setters – the object of subsequent discussions – are necessarily culturally emergent and discretionary agents exhibiting habitual behaviour and motivational complexities. Simplistic characterizations will not serve.

Knowledge Growth

It is the neoinstitutionalist view that, for both physiological and cultural reasons, people are the only theory-building organisms. Lingual, cognitive, analytical, and motivational capabilities permit the human agent to rehearse in the mind an ordered sequence of subsequent behaviour through perception of cumulative and complex causal relations. Causes generate effects; means produce ends-in-view, costing and pricing decisions induce consequences. Perception of such causation and its communication provide for the formulation and assessment of explanations. Doubts arise; questions are posed; explanations are offered; responses are sought. Knowledge evolves processually as the residual and cumulative outcome of continuously enhanced comprehension of economic phenomena, including cost and price administration. The fund of warranted knowledge expands cumulatively and exponentially. Hypotheses are conceived and appraised for explanatory merit. Warranted knowledge explains causal connections. People, drawing on past knowledge and experience, create new knowledge; knowledge is the premier resource. Knowledge defines ideational and material resources. Ironically, the growth of knowledge expands the areas of unknowns even as it enlarges the known. These created resources and capacities provide discretionary options for agents in making economic choices and assessments relating to costs and costing. Cost setters acquire and apply emergent knowledge of constructs and existential conditions in determining cost levels and structures.

Institutional Structure

It is the neoinstitutionalist view that production is generated and income distributed only through institutional structures. Correlation and coordination of all economic activities are accomplished through the establishment of rules, codes, laws, regulations, conventions, customs, beliefs and behaviours that stipulate how existing knowledge is to be implemented in the conduct of the provisioning process. Costing and pricing activity are institutionally constituted. The structural fabric of the economy is wholly embedded in the social order generally.

Accordingly, as Yngve Ramstad has explained: 'The term *market* refers only to a structured process of interaction between actual or potential buyers and sellers, not to a domain within which a single equilibrium price is presumed to emerge or exist'.[6] From the neoinstitutionalist perspective, 'a market *is*, and is nothing more than, a behavioral domain giving effect to a specific matrix of interrelated rules; competition, in turn, is the concrete pattern of behavior implicit in or allowed by those rules. In short, economic competition is understood to be an *instituted process*' (emphasis in original).[7] Neoinstitutionalists agree that the 'quantities produced, prices charged, incomes obtained ... are understood to be most fundamentally consequences of the specific rules consecutively adopted or authorized by those empowered to do so'.[8] In this light then, the 'costs of production are perceived as simply the pecuniary consequences of adherence to the practices mandated or authorized by the extant set of rules'; 'prices also are understood as socially constructed or instituted, not natural, phenomena'.[9]

In consequence, those persons in the public and private sectors who have discretion to formulate, reshape and implement rule changes that correlate behaviour in fact hold substantial power to direct production, distribution and the determinants of exchange. The universe of inquiry for cost setters must include and acknowledge the reality of a rule-governed economy and the loci and character of its discretionary control. Cost setters, then, are continuously engaged in the process of making institutional adjustments.

Social Intercourse

It is the neoinstitutionalist view that social life connotes extensive and continuing rule-governed interaction among individuals. In the economic provisioning process, these interactions are perhaps most significantly observed as *transactions*.[10] Transactions identify varieties of social interaction involving the delivering and receiving of something[11] – property, ideas, money, rights, goods, services and more. A transaction may involve an active-active or an active-passive connection; it may be a unidirectional or a reciprocal contact. If the receiver responds comparably to the deliverer, the interactive connection may constitute exchange. If the transaction is an exchange connection, it will encompass costing and pricing elements and aspects that are extensive, complex and significant. For example, path dependencies, anticipated consequences and normative purposes may each or all impinge on transactions as instituted exchange. *Delivering* connotes transfers. *Receiving* connotes acknowledgment; it may or may not connote acceptance. Implicit is the cognition of a means-consequence continuum of causality. Explicit is the recognition that transactions generate, in consequence, altered insights, rules, states or conditions for participating individuals. It must be emphasized that the delivering-receiving interaction is processual. There is no presumption of episodic culmination, no absolute path dependency, no inevitable sequencing, no pecuniary reductionism, no terminating arrivals. As Greg Hayden observed, 'there is no final demand, absolute requirement, or end to the process'.[12] Delivering-receiving interactions occur in real time, are guided by behavioural regularities, generate observable consequences, are conceptually replicative and amenable to appraisal. Cost setters are typically participants in, sometimes creators and often managers of transactional exchange.

II COSTS, COSTING, OPPORTUNITY COSTS, OPPORTUNITY SETS

My task here is to establish cost concepts and referential meanings which exhibit a consistent neoinstitutionalist perspective for use in subsequent discussion. Drawing contrasts with neoclassical meanings and usages will at times be a necessary aspect of the discussion.

Concepts of Cost

The neoinstitutionalist theory of costs rests on the instrumental theory of social value, with various warranted indices as measures. The neoclassical theory of costs rests on the utility theory of social value with price as the measure. If problem solving is to be enhanced, the former must displace the latter, in my view.

Social costs

For neoinstitutionalists, *social costs* are considered to be *real costs*. All social costs are real costs, not in the classic disutility sense of irksome and laborious effort or painful abstention from consumption, but in the neoinstitutional sense of demonstrable disruption or impairment of the knowledge-driven flow of real income and product. Real social costs are consequences of the underdevelopment of, and/or the failure to apply, instrumentally-warranted reasoning and judgments as provided and refined by the current state of reliable knowledge. They are reflected in the destructive consequences for the community of invidious or ceremonial judgments. Social costs as real costs are indicated by substantive inefficiencies, reductions and distortions in the economic provisioning process, as reflected in the physical tallies ('weight, tael measure and count') of lost output, conspicuous waste, environmental destruction, blighted lives, needless deaths, deprived learning, invidious discrimination, ethnic conflict and the like. If rooted in instrumental-value premises, pecuniary measures can sometimes be used to calculate real costs.

Indeed, real social costs are sometimes identifiable qualitatively even where quantitative indicators are absent or are difficult to establish.

For neoinstitutionalists, social costs as real costs are not the obverse of conventionally viewed, utility-based subjective private costs. Little use is made of the Pigouvian distinction between private costs and benefits and social costs and benefits. For neoinstitutionalists, these two foci of interest are not divorced. Given present high levels of interdependencies of individuals and their communities, whatever enhances or cripples an individual enhances or cripples the larger community as well. Substantive impairments, then, of the lives of 'private' individuals will generate social costs. Alternately, the quest for and realization of 'private' gain (income, wealth, status) may impose social costs on others. Indeed for Kapp, social cost was identified as 'all direct and indirect losses suffered by third persons or the general public as a result of private economic activities'.[13]

Finally, social costs as real costs, for neoinstitutionalists, are largely devoid of concerns about subjectivistic feeling states or other utility-based postures of individuals. Neoinstitutionalists do not incorporate or encompass notions of psychic pain as reflected, for example, (1) in the presumed 'positive time preference' that makes deferring consumption (waiting) the disutilitous source of neoclassical savings, or (2) in the 'irksomeness' of labour time embedded in commodities in the Marxist tradition. I return to a consideration of social costs and costing in Part IV.

Pecuniary costs

For neoinstitutionalists, pecuniary costs are reflected in the discretionary setting of most exchange ratios. Delivering and receiving will often occur as the exchange of a good or service for money at a price. Neoinstitutionalists acknowledge the fact and continuing significance of pecuniary exchange. Pecuniary costs refer to prices of component elements that enter into selling prices in pecuniary exchange. A price set is a cost to a buyer, whether at the level of primary, intermediate or final sale. As the foregoing chapters suggest, in sales at all levels administered prices are comprised in large measure of administered costs. Moreover, discretionary costing and pricing are not confined to megacorps. As I observed in earlier chapters, the continuing quest for control over exchange is endemic among firms and among economic market participants generally. The determination of costs by discretionary agents through facilitative institutional structures – costing conventions, rules, directives – is a significant exercise of achieved economic power. The decision processes exhibited as costing determinations, as we shall see, are structurally complex, motivationally diverse and normatively intended. In the setting of pecuniary cost levels (costing), in the rationale offered in their defence, and in assessing the consequences invoked by their imposition, value judgments are repeatedly made.

The purposes to be served by cost determinations will typically encompass both instrumental and invidious (or ceremonial) facets or aspects. Accordingly, the consequences of such costing decisions will be correlatively progressive or regressive or some combination thereof. A running assessment of such costs must remain on the inquiry agenda. Only specific inquiry in a particular case will disclose whether or not pecuniary costing decisions generate or identify real social costs as identified above. I return to matters of pecuniary costing in Part III.

Costing

Costing refers to the *determination* of costs, as noted. It is the neoinstitutionalist view that pecuniary costs are not typically determined by impersonal market forces in price competitive markets. Pecuniary costing involves the use of economic power heavily to affect, if not control, the direction and character of pecuniary exchange. It is a context in which discretionary cost-setting agents are called upon to make exceedingly difficult decisions. For instance, credible empirical cost data may be impossible to secure. The impact on market shares may be indeterminate. The effect on the continuity of cost-setting powers may be speculative. Cost determination is made difficult and complicated both for reasons political (invites public oversight) and sociological (impinges on working rules and contracts). The institutional configurations in and through which such power is acquired and used may well be quite diverse. In addition to the more familiar structures of legislative bodies, regulatory agencies, megacorps, mesacorps, trade and professional associations and union organizations, etc., one must include intricate interfirm networking, corporate cooperation and supplier-producer concords. However complex, the institutional structure creating and/or sustaining the relevant power system(s) must be analytically examined; its inter- and intra-networking connections understood; its criteria of cost setting investigated.

Opportunity Costs

I have suggested above that costs and their determination are in the main a discretionary matter. In an interactive and interdependent institutional context, agents choose to deliver an idea, product or service, a delivery that may be willingly or unwillingly received. This interaction is transactional; as noted, it may or may not constitute exchange. In any case, decisions to deliver or receive generate consequences for participating parties.

Opportunity cost is presumed conventionally to identify a continuing and governing attribute of choice making where transactional exchange occurs. As an analytic construct of neoclassicists, it is thought to be logically obvious and warranted a priori. Neoinstitutionalists can retain certain logical elements of opportunity costs analysis, but will abandon the neoclassical utilitarian content and warrant embedded therein.

Opportunity costs for neoclassicists are perceived as the 'value of all of the things which must be foregone, lost or given up in obtaining something'.[14] The key term in the foregoing is *value* and its admissible meanings. For neoclassicists, the concept *implicitly* embodies a comparison of the expected utilities of what is given up with what is obtained. The unstated referent for 'value' is the comparative utility, ordinally or cardinally construed, of what is lost and what is gained.

When incorporated in neoclassical analysis of pecuniary exchange, opportunity cost specifies that if one purchase is completed with the payment of money, another must be lost or foregone. Money spent on one item may not then be used for another. The perceived cost of the purchase is indicated by a comparison of utility, reflected in the pecuniary 'value' of that which was foregone with that which was acquired. *Utility*, then, is the *meaning* of value; *price* is the *measure* of value! In this context of basic pecuniary exchange, discretionary costing does occur. In making decisions to deliver or receive in pecuniary exchange, opportunity costs, so identified, are purported to represent the definitive method of distinguishing *implicit* gains or losses of utility.[15]

When, moreover, opportunity costs are incorporated in cost-benefit analysis, the neoclassical utilitarian content becomes *explicit*, but not more substantive. 'A benefit is ... any gain in *utility* and a cost is any loss of utility as measured by the *opportunity cost* of the project in question' (emphasis in original).[16] The orthodox quest is to find pecuniary measures for utility and disutility. Where such benefits and costs are not amenable to quantification in money terms (for example, clean air, safe water), they must be imputed. Their technique of imputation predictably exhibits a 'market mentality'. '[S]trictly pursued cost-benefit analysis would value all outputs and inputs at their shadow prices. Similarly, where inputs and outputs have no observable markets ... it is necessary to discover what the price would have been had a market existed.'[17] Surrogate markets and shadow prices are deemed sufficient to provide these pecuniary estimates as measures of comparative utility. Accordingly, if benefits exceed costs, so contrived, the exchange activity or project is 'worth' pursuing.

But for neoinstitutionalists, given the inability to identify or measure 'utils' or to determine the substance of preference ordering, the neoclassicist calculation of costs is at best conjectural. To incorporate conventional opportunity cost analysis in this pseudo price-determining manner undermines the conviction that utility value measured by price is a relevant criterion of judgment. The neoclassical construct of opportunity costs will not function in the encompassing normative role assigned. There are pecuniary costs and social costs, as noted, but the neoclassical concept of opportunity cost, as I perceive it, is an analytical cul-de-sac. It cannot escape an inherent dependence on the ethical relativism characteristic of utility-based judgments. In its acceptance of subjective norms, neoclassicists defer to the unknowable psyches of individuals and to the methodological individualism upon which such norms rest. Moreover, given the de facto inapplicability of utility value theory and the neoclassicists' admitted need to make choices, one must be alert to the presence of other undisclosed and unexamined criteria (for example, the retention or extension of power) that may actually be guiding the formation of judgments.

A neoinstitutionalists' formulation of opportunity costs, in contrast, rejects outright all utility value constructs and incorporates instrumental value theory. In addition, such a formulation will reject price as the measure of social value and incorporate a variety of other inquiry-specific indicators of costing.

Let me return to the original construct. Opportunity costs are perceived as the '*value* of all of the things which *must* be forgone, lost or given up in obtaining something'.[18] Two aspects are at issue: the referent for 'value' and the implicit either-or dimension of choice in the use of the term 'must'.

As for the former, I have recommended the rejection of utility as value (with price as its measure) and its replacement with instrumental value (with situation-specific measures). This shift means that instrumental value tenets define the options to which opportunity cost theory applies. Choices are no longer matters of more or less maximized utility reflected in more or less credible shadow prices in conjectural markets in pursuit of social gain. Choices are matters of distinguishing between the character of and differences between instrumental and ceremonial or invidious judgments and actions, and the comparative significance or (as feasible) magnitudes of these differences. In neoclassical theory, projected utility should exceed disutility; benefits should exceed costs so identified. In neoinstitutional theory, projected instrumental outcomes should displace ceremonial or invidious costs and consequences.

For neoinstitutionalists, for a social benefit to be realized, what is obtained must exceed in instrumentally-warranted significance and magnitude that which has been 'foregone, lost or given up'. Indicators of what is obtained and what is given up may or may not be measurable or quantifiable. For instance, one that might be quantitatively approximated is the opportunity cost of rehabilitating the national transport infrastructure through the redirection of the billions of public dollars rashly committed to the purchase of physicists' talent, scientific knowledge, military plant and resources dedicated to the procurement of 'Star-Wars' weaponry.

Alternatively, for a social benefit to be incurred, what is obtained through choice must exhibit fewer ceremonial and invidiously warranted opportuni-

ties or experiences than those 'foregone, lost or given up'. As an example, if
in choosing programmes and curricula for graduate study in economics, the
current insistence on the near exclusive consideration of standard orthodox
analysis (mathematically expressed and ceremonially defended) was eroded
and a pluralistic, open-inquiry 'competitive market in ideas' approach introduced, the prospect (instrumentally defended) of turning out graduates with
the capacity for imaginative and critical thinking would be enhanced. The
feasibility of quantifiably measuring such a shift to less ceremonial and
invidious institutional arrangements and judgments is not obvious, but not
necessarily impossible.

The foregoing suggests, of course, that the neoinstitutionalist interpretation of opportunity costs is cut from the same conceptual cloth as my earlier
identification of social costs as real costs, and the suggestion that pecuniary
cost setting and consequences be appraised together with instrumental value
theory.

I now return to the question of whether opportunity cost analysis, as
infused with instrumental value theory, logically imposes an either-or constraint on analysis. In my view, to choose one option may or may not require
the loss of another in the same context.

In a more general sense, opportunity costs reflect alternative choices.
Choices made will generally affect other persons and may reduce or enhance
their real options. Choices thus generate consequences. In the construct of
opportunity costs as alternative choices, then, we acknowledge causal and
consequential outcomes; we recognize and transform the inherent normative
dimension of choice making. At issue are the character and significance of
the choices made and the criteria utilized by the agent in selecting options.
What kinds of consequences ensued? What was their impact on others? Were
their lives enhanced or diminished? Were outcomes mainly invidious and
destructive or instrumental and constructive? Opportunity costs may thus be
conceived as involving the making of alternative choices.

Consider the logical case for either-or. In the context of alternative choices
for individuals, *time* used and required for one task clearly is not concurrently available to engage in another. An either-or condition obtains. To
engage in one activity is to forego another at the same time. 'Quality time'
(instrumentally warranted?) reserved by parents for children is obviously not
available for office work. Similarly, *energy* utilized for one purpose precludes
its use for another. Coal used to power an electricity generating plant is
'foregone' as a power source for home heating. The product is consumed in
its use. But the question of the presence or absence of social or real costs –
obstruction or impairment – remains to be examined. There are, obviously,
alternative uses of time and energy. Here, the logic of the either-or condition
is unassailable. Circumstances of decision making, at any particular time,

may compel an either-or decision. To choose in one way may deny another way. But the character of the choice made and its consequences must also be addressed. What are the alternative options for time and energy that were or might have been made available?

The exercise of discretion over property, conferred by legal ownership, may compel a non-owner or an adjacent or other owner to forego or give up options otherwise available. But discretion over property, obviously, is always prescriptively limited and often modified by public law. In these and similar examples, then, if one person uses his/her choice-making capacity, that person or someone else must forego, lose or give up an otherwise available option. But the contrary is also at least as plausible. The development of one's own property may *increase* options of adjacent owners to use, develop or sell their properties. Whether options are increased or decreased for the respective parties is significant, but at bottom the purposive use of owned property is normatively assessable. What impact is produced by the decision concerning the property? Whose interests are served? What is the nature of these interests?

Important either-or decisions may or may not be reversible, but the paths actually chosen are critically significant in defining future options and directions. To a significant degree, then, choices are path dependent. Accordingly, the assessment of consequences of choices is a continuing and essential responsibility of both agents and those to whom they are accountable. Do the choices made serve invidious or ceremonial ends in view? If so, their impact will increase social costs.

But let us proceed beyond the either-or constraint: The universe of delivering-receiving decisions also includes instances where the presumed condition of 'either-or' choices may not necessarily apply. As a familiar example, in real cost (as distinct from monetary or utility) terms, undertaking (say) public construction of roads and bridges may put already existing but idle or unemployed men, machines and resources back into the production process. There is then no 'production foregone', no significant invidiously-grounded opportunity cost imposed. Indeed the reemployment of labour preserves productive skills and generates an instrumentally-warranted 'opportunity gain', not an opportunity cost.[19]

Moreover, in decisions concerning the delivery and receipt of knowledge, for example, its creation and use by one does not preclude its use by another. Nothing is 'foregone, lost or given up'; the sum is not diminished by increased uses of parts. On the contrary, the sum is enhanced through incremental and cumulative processes of inquiry. In this sense, warranted inquiry is largely devoid of social costs.

Similarly, the 'tool-and-idea' combinations that choices generate as new technology are not diminished by their incorporation in subsequent technologies and techniques. The fact of technological obsolescence does not necessarily impose social costs as something foregone, lost or given up serving invidious purposes. Instrumental functions were once positively served by the technologies of steam locomotion, typewriters and telegraphic communication. Decisions directing their substantial abandonment do not necessarily represent an imposition of ceremonially-identified social costs. With the expansion of warranted knowledge, they have simply been supplanted in the interest of more instrumentally-efficient transportation and communication.

In addition, in their rejection of the neoclassical meaning and usage of opportunity cost, neoinstitutionalists also implicitly reject the endowment theory of resource creation and the accompanying dictum that all resources are finite and given. When we acknowledge that 'knowledge is truly the mother of all other resources'[20] and that knowledge defines the resource base, the referential meaning of 'resources' is profoundly changed.[21] Resources become whatever materials, substances and ideas that the knowledge continuum defines at any one moment as of instrumental economic use. At a given point in time, such defined resources, broadly construed, may or may not be relatively scarce. As with the growth of knowledge, the growth and transformation of the resource base are evolutionary and developmental. But the character of resource expansion is of continuing normative concern. If, for example, it violates warranted knowledge or enshrines unwarranted ignorance about destructive environmental consequences, it will be imposing what neoinstitutionalists call social costs.

Opportunity Sets

Allan Schmid defines an 'opportunity set ... as the available lines of action open to an individual'.[22] He correctly argues that the lines of action open to some are conditioned and constrained by the interdependence of their opportunity sets with those of others. Discretionary agents with opportunity sets interact with other discretionary agents and jointly produce consequences. They 'condition the outcome of human transactions'.[23] Schmid is especially concerned with constraints reflected in property rights.[24]

For present purposes, however, it is desirable to broaden and moderately reshape the construct of opportunity sets. Here, 'areas of discretion' will be used in a way that is compatible with Schmid's use of 'opportunity sets'; however, in order to incorporate processual and reflective content, we must substitute 'creative options' or 'effectual choices' for 'lines of action'. Areas of discretion, then, define and thus delimit the universe of choice and action that in a causal sense change circumstances and contribute to the reconstruction of the institutional order. But the shaping of areas of discretion is always processual. In this process, to choose among options always compels recourse to criteria of judgment. These criteria guide an expanding area of genuine choice over the determinants of institutional formation and adjustments, among which, as I explore below, are judgments observed as administered costing decisions. Areas of discretion expand and contract; their windows of implementation change over time. Discretionary judgments are revamped as experience and reflection dictate. In brief, discretion is bounded, but in an evolutionary and processual way; it is constantly being reconstituted. Thus 'free to choose' does not mean a consumer's Friedmanesque participation in an unfettered market; rather, it liberates an expanding area of discretion for affected individuals over the market structure itself!

Accordingly the areas of discretion for any individual or group are shaped and constrained (even as they may, concurrently and ironically, be enhanced) by the following factors, among others:

- levels of warranted knowledge and understanding;
- property ownership and its impact on others;
- extent and character of environmental and ecological impact;
- availability of financial resources or retained earnings;
- criminal codes that protect agency as well as channel options;
- 'customs of the manor', 'canons of decency', mores and folkways;
- access to credit creating sources and institutions;
- acquired skills and capabilities of discretionary agents;
- availability and appropriateness of physical resources;
- availability and appropriateness of tools and technology;
- purposes to be served by discretionary actions, and
- path dependencies in the area of discretion.

In sum, discretionary choices and actions are basically path determining but, inevitably and simultaneously, also somewhat path dependent. At any particular time, discretion is limited or bounded. Electing one option reshapes the character and availability of subsequent discretionary areas and options. To choose option A may mean foregoing option B. But that is not an anterior given; it is a consequential assessment in a processual context. For example, publicly to subsidize the development of an efficient electric automobile may mean that funds are not available to clean up toxic wastes. However, public and private debt-creating institutions can generate additional funding for such projects. The commodity of credit is *not* inherently scarce, notwithstanding 'crowding out' theories to the contrary.[25] A mature economic community can finance anything it technologically knows how to do.

Does the same reasoning apply to physical resources? If existing resources are indeed fully employed, say, in industrial production, then an increase in the use of a component resource in one productive context might require a cutting back of usage in another context and the consequent incurring of 'opportunity costs'. But the concept of 'full employment' of 'scarce resources' is equivocal. Two observations are offered. First, as statistically measured by GDP calculations, the US economy has known 'full employment' of 'scarce resources' on only one occasion in this century – for two to three years during World War II. The normal case is underutilized resource use. Second, resources are not given; they are created. Technology defines the resource base – the energy, material, machines and skills needed. Population levels, educational access and the character of labour demand define and shape labour resources. As a community, we are constantly engaged in the creation of resources. Their 'scarcity' even for particular uses is time- and site-bound only to a very limited extent. To analyse choice making as imposing opportunity costs in the traditional neoclassical sense, with reference to either funds or resources, thus reflects a static, nonevidential and largely irrelevant approach that neoinstitutionalists cannot accept.

Analytical deference to neoclassical opportunity costs misspecifies analytical questions and misguides policy formation. A rigid, narrow and nonprocessual conception of opportunity *sets* then undergirds a utility-based view of opportunity *costs*. A neoinstitutionalist concept of expansive and structural opportunity sets, on the other hand, permits an instrumental referent for opportunity costs.

III   PECUNIARY COSTS AND COSTING

Continuing Questions for Inquiry

Among the queries that must guide neoinstitutionalist investigation into the determination of pecuniary costs in exchange are the following:

- With what are costing decisions concerned? Expenses are incurred in assembling and utilizing the material and financial resources and in engaging the requisite productive and managerial personnel to create an output of goods and services. Those expenses represent costs to the organization so engaged. Such costs must be recovered in the administered prices at which output is sold. Costing is the administered determination of those input expenses.
- Where does discretion over costing lie? The capacity to choose cost levels and schedules is rooted variously in historic and cultural patterns of governance (hierarchical, democratic), in intra- or interorganizational agreements (cartels), in formal legal codes and stipu-

lations (statutory assignments), and in property ownership and rights associated therewith, among others. Discretion may be held by well-positioned individuals on managerial boards, by members of the 'technostructure', by officers of unions, organizations and associations, by leaders in politically empowered agencies, and the like. The costing function may be conducted on demonstrable evidence of prices paid for product and services. However, given the huge size and extraordinary complexities of contemporary multi-product megacorps, the exercise of discretion in cost determinations may in fact be quite arbitrary and even political.

- What characterizes the use of discretion over costing? Private purposes (intrafirm) served by the use of cost-setting power may include firm survival, sustaining employment by 'meeting a payroll', enhancement of market shares and control, promotion of increased productivity, destruction of rivals and broadening of political influence – thus exhibiting both instrumental and invidious facets and consequences. Public purposes (communal) served may include enhanced production, retention of political control, ecological and environmental protection, collusion with private power systems, enhancement of equity in distribution, enrichment of a selected elite, technological enhancement and innovation, and knowledge encapsulation for bureaucratic purposes – thus again exhibiting both instrumental and invidious facets and consequences.

- What are the consequences emerging therefrom? All cost-setting decisions impact upon participating individuals and the larger community. Both pecuniary and non-pecuniary instruments are needed to identify, trace and estimate the magnitude of outcomes of costing judgments. Their assessment in social value terms is also required if public instrumental purposes are to be served.

- Through what instruments, organizations or mechanisms can those wielding costing power be held accountable? How can their discretion be kept responsible? The neoclassical view that price competition generates accountability has been reduced to a textbook ideal. Its descriptive role appears to me to survive only in rhetorical flourishes of political controversy. In any discretionary economy, the only way private or public decision makers can be held to account is through the development of laws, rules and codes that (a) require the full release of all information bearing on the decisions and their consequences, and that (b) provide constraint and regulatory instruments so that the community can act on its own behalf to reverse or revise decisions when they fail to serve public instrumental purposes. As with any power system, public or private, the need to generate responsiveness and accountability is continuing and pervasive.

A Conventional Example of Costing

A stylized, factual characterization of costing judgments, reflecting the production expenses of a major oligopolistic firm, will provide a preliminary
focus for discussion about administered pecuniary costing. My immediate
concern is with the first two of the five questions posed above – the nature of
and discretion over costing. Such cost components of production and sales
may predictably include the following as a minimum:

1. wages of workers,
2. fringe benefits for workers (health insurance, holidays, pensions),
3. training costs,
4. salaries of managers,
5. perquisites of managers (health insurance, pensions),
6. interest on debt incurred (short and long term),
7. resources purchased (energy, materials, chemicals),
8. depreciation of existing plant and equipment,
9. acquisition of new plant and equipment,
10. advertising and marketing expenses,
11. research and development expenditures,
12. ecological and environmental compliance expenditures and
13. tax obligations.

Of the foregoing expenditure categories represented on the books of the
firm as costs of production, it is unlikely that any were set in consequence of
free, non-discretionary, unfettered market determination. Of course, only an
empirical review of a particular firm would provide adequate confirmation.
But since this is presumed to be a large oligopolistic industrial firm, in
continuing our stylized factual characterization, the following would be a
plausible set of expectations of administered costing.

(1–2): Wages and fringe benefits are the probable product of formal collective bargaining with union(s), of patterned wages reflecting collective bargaining agreements by industry cost leaders, of legislative minimum wage
stipulations, and/or of longstanding customs and practices of internal and
external comparable employments. (3): Training costs are provided inhouse
or contracted out at negotiated prices. (4–5): Salaries and perquisites of
management are negotiated on an individual basis and frequently are self-
administered. (6): Interest rates on debt are predictably a derivative of the
more general administration of interest rates by the FED and the dominant
banks. (7): Prices of resources purchased are typically administered by the
respective extractive or developmental firms. For example, public utility
commissions historically set limits on the cost-incurring and price-setting

discretion of regulated firms that provide energy, communication networks, and the like. (8): Depreciation on existing plant and equipment is set mainly in response to relevant tax rules and options. (9): New plant and equipment will usually be acquired from suppliers also routinely engaged in administered pricing of output. Part of the costs will sometimes be offset by governmental investment tax credits. (10): Marketing expenses are determined in contractual negotiations with advertising conglomerates. (11): Research and development personnel are recruited for technical and highly skilled positions and are paid salaries and 'fringes'. Research equipment (labs, resources, computers) are also secured from oligopolistic sources at negotiated/administered prices. (12): Ecological and environmental compliance costs are set in response to directives from, for example, the Environmental Protection Agency or its counterparts in other governmental jurisdictions. (13): Tax obligations are administered 'costs' set by political authorities at various levels of government.

Moreover, in addition to these items and areas of expense incurred, the cost-setting administrators in this stylized firm, in determining what will be the selling prices to their buyers, may have to make and incorporate (1) estimates of relative availability or 'scarcity' of the goods being priced; (2) estimates of demand elasticity; (3) experience-based judgments of what has been customarily viewed as a 'fair price'; and finally, (4) the inclusion of some cost-related (markup, cost-plus) margin of gain or profit.

In other words, the customary and institutionalized patterns of expectations, past purchasing and pricing practices, availability of alternative sources and the like, must continuously enter into the judgments of those exercising discretion over costing decisions. Relative availability reflects current market share estimates, delivery capabilities, fulfilment of product specifications, etc. Estimated demand elasticity (price and income) reflects predictable sensitivity to changes in aggregated costing as reflected in selling prices. Customary views of 'fairness' embody some sense that costing judgments mainly incorporate actual, not phantom, expenses incurred. Profit margins, as administered cost components, are thought essential to pay dividends to stockholders, to generate retainable earnings for investment and to sustain interest in the firm among participants in financial markets. Profits beyond this level rapidly come to be seen as 'excessive'.

An additional clarification for megacorp firms will be instructive. While the cost setter may have to address both the expense categories noted and aspects of relative availability, elasticity and fairness in cost setting, the actual pricing of products sold may be quite arbitrary. As Yngve Ramstad has recently observed, cost setters in multi-product, perhaps multi-industry and/ or multinational conglomerate firms

cannot identify objectively which of its (administratively-determined) costs should
be attributed, and certainly not in what proportion, to each of its many products.
Yet they each have to be priced. Conventions inherent in ... *highly arbitrary* cost
accounting practices are therefore used to assign costs to individual products. ...
[A] proper recognition of the role in pricing played by cost accounting conventions is not only significant to a comprehensive overview of 'administered costing' but the Trojan horse of conventional market theory. ... [A] recognition of the
inescapable need to have cost-allocation rules undermines the organization of
economic analysis via the abstraction 'markets' and necessitates instead that the
focus be on the multi-faceted enterprise as the central object of study [emphasis in
original].[26]

Such costing judgments occur in a context of institutionalized rules and
patterns of negotiation and exchange. What has become conventional and
customary cannot usually be modified without explanations of events and
circumstances that provide a rationale for and defence of changes introduced.
What is common to all entries is that the prices charged (costs to the firm)
appear, without exception, to be discretionary, if at times arbitrary. Cost
setting is a form of administered pricing. In many circumstances, the exercise
of that discretion will require changes in what has become customary pricing
behaviour. Choice-making agents in quite diverse institutional structures –
not impersonal atomistic markets – determine cost levels. Implied is a
negotiational economy in which costing and pricing *powers* are both held and
used. The locus and use of costing/pricing power then become the central
focus of inquiry.

Empirical Support of Administered Costing

In recent publications,[27] Frederic S. Lee reviews and summarizes an extensive literature that establishes empirical undergirding for neoinstitutionalist
theories of administered pricing and administered costing.[28] In so doing he
provides additional information and analysis in response to the first three
questions posed above: the nature of costing judgments, the loci of pricing
discretion and, briefly, purposes served.

For Lee, '*costing* refers to the procedures a business enterprise employs to
determine the costs that will be used in setting the selling price of a good
before actual production takes place and hence the actual costs of production
are known'. Prominent in cost setting are the historical cost patterns of the
firm. Similarly '*pricing* refers to the procedures the business enterprise uses
to set the price of a good before it is produced and placed on the market'
(emphasis added). Taking the estimated cost data, 'the business enterprise
then adds a costing margin to costs or marks up the costs to set the [selling]
price'.[29] Firm pricing policies generally reflect, then, a cost-plus pattern. Of
the three such patterns discussed – markup, normal cost, and target rate of

return[30] – the latter two were found heavily to dominate in actual business practices.[31] Their differences, though interesting, are not central to the present discussion.

What is critical, however, is the demonstration that 'the kind of costing and pricing procedures used within the business enterprise ... are administratively determined. ... [A]dministratively determined prices are administered to the market.'[32] A variety of empirical studies demonstrate that 'an essential facet of markup, normal cost, and target rate of return pricing procedures is that enterprises use them to set prices that they intended to maintain for periods of time and many sequential transactions'.[33] Price stability for periods of three months to a year or more, or through a particular selling season, is typical. Decisions on altering administered prices mainly occur at such periodic intervals. Changes in labour and material costs in particular will induce such alterations. Curiously, the evidence suggests the 'absence of any significant market price sales relationship in the short term'.[34] Prices set are intended to maintain 'a variety of sales volumes over time'. Price administrators 'believe that sales are almost entirely a function of buyer income, level of aggregate economic activity, government demand for armaments, population growth, product design, and perhaps advertising'.[35]

Retention of control over costing and pricing by administrators compels coordination among enterprises

> if destructive price competition is to be avoided and an acceptable, single market price is to be established. Therefore, business enterprises have turned to organizing secondary bureaucratic organizations in the guise of either market organizations, such as trade associations, cartels, open price associations, and price leadership organizations, or, if the purely market organizations fail in their tasks, quasi-, or purely governmental organizations, legal decrees, and laws.[36]

Coordination extends to the determination of which administered costing decisions and averages will be used in setting selling prices.

In Lee's view, the most important properties of the administered cost-administered price model he describes are the following: (a) 'it does not have a dual relationship between prices and quantities as typically assumed'; (2) 'it is not possible to reduce the model to a simple markup on labor costs'; (3) 'custom and competition are predominant among the determinants of the mark up for profit. ... [T]he role of custom and convention is significant enough to place the motivation of the price administrators outside the simple description of maximizing profits'; and finally, (4) 'its prices are tied to time, hence historical'. Accordingly, with long periods between price changes 'it would take years for market prices to converge to quasi long period prices'.[37]

For neoinstitutionalists, then, Lee marshals substantial empirical support for the fact of administered costing and pricing. He identifies where discretionary costing and pricing judgments are made, indicates something of the theoretical and policy-making significance of this altered pricing theory and, in passing, implies purposes served by such cost and price administrators.

Transactional Decision Structure

At this juncture, I add pattern to the analysis by incorporating a taxonomy of decision structures generated by A. Allan Schmid, reflecting the influence of John R. Commons.[38] His differential characterizations of *transactions* are all rooted in the fundamental assumption that the power to make choices and to implement those choices is both widely held *and used*. For Schmid there are three different kinds of transactions through which power is exercised: bargained transactions, administrative transactions, and status and grant transactions.[39] In using these characterizing categories, however, I go well beyond property rights and exchanges.

Bargaining transactions

In bargaining transactions, a delivery connotes receipt and reciprocity in exchange; it is an active-active transaction in which power is held and used by each party. 'In a bargained exchange system, rights are transferable upon mutual consent of the parties.' Participants 'are considered legal equals' in particular transactions. Each has 'certain rights that are antecedent to the transaction. ... Each party has an opportunity set ... and each is free within that limit to join or abstain from further transactions. ... Through a process of negotiation, the parties agree to transfer something they own in exchange for what the other owns ... a bargained transaction implicitly involves both coercion and consent.'[40] For example, conspicuous coercive instruments historically used in wage and salary setting are strikes and lockouts. In the last decade, partly as a legacy of the anti-labour Reagan and Bush administrations, 'striker replacement' has become an additional and effective coercive instrument of organized management.[41] The participating parties each has sufficient power to negotiate with the other concerning the specific transaction, but they may not otherwise be equals.

Administrative transactions

In administrative transactions, delivery does not necessarily connote reciprocity or exchange; formally, it is an active-passive transaction so far as power is concerned. (Parties experiencing consequences are far from indifferent, however.) The parties 'are not legal equals but are related as superior to inferior. ... Administrative transactions involve a position of authority whose occupant has some range of discretion as determined by the opportunity sets of the parties.'[42] The possessor of authority, the superior in the transaction, may be an individual owner, legislature, public or private administrator, law enforcement officer, or the like.[43] An 'individual administrative transaction involves a limited one-way movement of rights'. A third party may be the beneficiary. 'The political process often substitutes administration for former market relationships.' Administrative decisions are a 'method for making nonunanimous changes in opportunity sets, including those upon which bargained transactions take place'.[44]

Status and grant transactions

In status and grant transactions also, delivery does not connote reciprocity or exchange; this too is an active-passive transaction. In a *status* transaction, 'there is neither bid nor command. It involves a one-way movement of rights rooted in learned habits; ... transfers are governed primarily through the prescribed roles associated with social position. The amount and kind of good is prescribed and fixed by custom. The transfer is necessary to discharge a social obligation.'[45] Transfers within families and the practice of mutual aid among producers illustrate the status transaction.

A *grant* transaction 'is also a one-way transfer of rights but is distinguished from status in that the grant is less systematized and reflects more individual discretion and calculation'. Gifts to charities are examples. 'The essence of a grant is that the grantor receives no right in return', as with the transfer of wealth between present and future generations.[46] Ironically, the present abuse of environmental and ecological systems is a transfer from *future* generations to the present one at *our* discretion – a reverse grant.[47]

Those participating in or otherwise experiencing 'negative' consequences of bargaining, administrative or status-grant transactions may respond formally through political and legal avenues, and/or informally through social disapproval routes, in an attempt to alter outcomes. Choices are made; consequences ensue; assessments as value judgments follow; responses may be initiated.

Decision Structure in Dual Labour Markets

The use of this triad of transactions, all of which reflect the possession and use of power, will help to illuminate one major aspect of discretionary pecuniary costs and costing – wage and salary determination as administered costing. Each of the three discretionary routes to cost determination will be illustrated by reference to the empirically grounded dual labour market analysis developed by Michael Piore and others.[48] In a recent paper, Yngve Ramstad has argued persuasively that Piore's dual labour market analysis is fundamentally compatible with an institutionalist formulation of discretionary pricing and costing.[49] Indeed, 'at the core of the dual labor market theory is a presumption that, in general, prices are *not* determined by supply and demand, that is, that the "price mechanism" is *not* the operative force in allocating jobs among competing workers or in determining the wages to be paid to individuals occupying those jobs' (emphasis in original).[50] William M. Dugger arrives at a similar conclusion through an institutionalist analysis of feeder mechanisms that generate employees for internal and external labour markets.[51]

For Piore, labour markets are demonstrably segmented. Worker occupations are categorized hierarchically, by income levels and customary characteristics, into primary and secondary sectors. This is the basic duality. In addition there is an upper and lower tier in the primary sector, and a similar division, though less pronounced, in the secondary sector. The primary sector, *upper* tier, consists of professional and managerial categories; the primary sector, *lower* tier, is comprised of highly skilled, often unionized, jobs. The secondary sector contains mostly low skilled, largely non-unionized jobs. As Ramstad explains, 'in the primary sector, jobs provide relatively high wages, good working conditions, chances of advancement, equity and due process in the administration of work rules, and perhaps most important, stable employment'. In contrast, 'in the secondary sector ... jobs provide low wages, poor working conditions, little chance of advancement, a highly personalized relationship between workers and supervisors, harsh and capricious work discipline, unstable employment, and a high turnover among the labor force'.[52] The sectors are also distinguishable in the level and character of education needed, in the skill levels acquired, the job mobility routes available, and discretion over the determinants of one's income and related benefits, among other factors.

For present purposes, however, I must limit consideration to the question of where discretion over wages and working conditions actually resides in these occupational sectors. Where in these occupational categories will one find bargaining, administered, and status and grant transactions defining labour costs and income levels?

Bargaining Transactions

Collective bargaining in the legally structured sense will be found (a) principally in the lower tier of the primary sector, (b) to a limited extent, with professional unions, in the upper tier of the primary sector, and (c) where unions bargain on behalf of both skilled and unskilled workers in the same contract, to some extent in the secondary sector. Informal individual bargaining over salary levels and perquisites also occurs in the upper tier of the primary level as, for example, when participating medical doctors negotiate with healthcare companies (e.g. Kaiser Permanente) over their income levels.

In all these cases, bargaining transactions connote receipt and reciprocity in exchange. Power is held and used by each of the contending parties.

Turning briefly to legally structured bargaining, for some 60 years, beginning in 1933 with Section 7(a) of the National Recovery Act, workers in the US have held the legal right (1) 'to organize and bargain collectively through representatives of their own choosing' and (2) to join or not join a company union or a 'labor organization of [their] own choosing'.[53] Institutional arrangements (notably, the National Labor Relations Board) were created to facilitate the implementation of these and related rights. These laws *empowered* workers, through unions, to participate in decisions determining their levels of remuneration and the conditions under which they worked. Since that time, a structure to facilitate bargaining transactions has provided formal and continuing collective bargaining rights with respective employers in both the private (especially industrial) and public sectors.

As bargaining transactions, labour negotiations involve 'coercion and consent', as Schmid indicated. The ultimate lever of power that organized management holds and occasionally employs in its efforts to prevail is, as noted, the lockout (or 'striker replacement'). Organized labour's ultimate instrument of pressure is the strike. Arbitration and mediation structures and procedures are intended to forestall or moderate the use of either power instrument. But the financial resources of organized management to back up its imposition of a lockout or hold out against a strike are likely to exceed the ability of organized workers (from either stoppage) to forego money income over extended periods. It is, in any case, a power struggle concerning participatory rights to decide wage levels and conditions of employment.

What the dual labour market analysis adds, especially for the lower tier of the primary sector, is the recognition that the bargained agreements reached define and redefine a sociologically specified wage, in which various factors – customary job ladders, wage and salary schedules, fixed income differentials, customary working rules and other institutionalized specifications of relations among workers, and between workers and management – constitute the structural fabric of the employment connection.[54] Typically, the actual bargaining that occurs has to do with proposed *changes* in existing salary schedules, income differentials, working rules and the like.

Over the last decade and a half, the power position of organized labour has been continuously assaulted and in consequence has deteriorated, as evidenced in various spheres. (a) Politics: The national administrations of Presidents Reagan and Bush succeeded in eroding the relative power of organized labour through punitive legislation, conservative appointments to the NLRB, strike-breaking tactics, etc.[55] (b) Industrial flight: By 1992 union membership had dropped to 15.8 per cent of employed wage and salary workers,[56] in part because of unrelenting plant closures and the removal of productive industry overseas to tap cheap labour in Third-World countries.[57] (c) Technological displacement: Technological unemployment continues to be generated with the advent of computer-controlled production, information generating and processing, robots and other labour-saving innovations.[58]

Even so, collective bargaining processes in the US continue to account for a significant proportion of discretionary wage and salary setting, as pecuniary costing. Data from the US Bureau of Labor Statistics show (by economic productive sectors and by occupational categories) the extent of union representation, as of 1993, for wage and salary workers and therefore, by implication, the areas in which collective bargaining persists.[59] Collective bargaining by unions remains significant in such productive *sectors* as construction (21 per cent of workers represented by unions), manufacturing (21 per cent), transportation and public utilities (33 per cent) and, most particularly in recent decades, in government employment (43 per cent). It is of modest import in wholesale and retail trades and services (7 per cent) and financial positions (3 per cent). Collective bargaining remains significant in industrial *employments* for precision and production workers, and operators and fabricators (27 per cent represented by unions); somewhat less so for managers and professionals (18 per cent), service workers (16 per cent) and sales people (12 per cent). It is insignificant in agricultural occupations (6 per cent).[60]

Nearly 600 collective bargaining agreements were negotiated (expirations and reopenings) in 1994 in the US; nearly 1900 agreements, each covering 1000 or more workers, are currently in place.[61] Some of these set de facto industry standards, becoming cost leaders and generating 'market pressures' to which even unorganized firms must accommodate in some measure in setting administered wage rates for their own employees. In these cases of bargaining transactions, discretion is shared to some degree. That some unions are relatively weak in their bargaining roles is to be expected. Their leadership may be marginal; their share of the employed labour force may be relatively small. In consequence, their collective bargaining transactions may more accurately be characterized as Schmid's 'administrative transactions'.

Even after examining the character of the collective bargaining agreements reached, the normative question remains. The fact that agreements are struck does not in itself mean that such cost determining settlements necessarily serve the public's instrumental interests. The fact that agreements were reached and that productive processes continue uninterrupted is significant, of course. Continuity of income flows and unimpaired generation of product and service are instrumentally supportable, if they accommodate to ecological and environmental continuity. But the consequences generated for those not party to the contracts and to the community generally must also be appraised. The principle of agreed compromise – a tenet of bargaining theory – is not an instrumental value premise per se.[62] These consequences reflect the use of achieved power, as Kapp observed, to shift immediate pecuniary costs, and ultimately social costs, on to third parties and the community generally.[63]

Administered Transactions

The income levels of most wage and salary workers not covered by bargaining agreements are set by administrative authorities in both the public and private sectors. Administrative transactions, as seen by Schmid, involve the exercise of authority by one party over another; the parties are not legal equals.

Returning to Piore's labour market categories, clearly the salaries received by that portion of the upper tier of the primary sector (consisting of governmental managers and professionals) is an uncomplicated administered income set by political bodies holding discretion over appointments and income levels in the civil service. Here too, however, salary schedules, income differentials and working rules become customary and define expectations. Administrative salary setting then typically consists of modifications in an otherwise elaborate and complex institutional structure of remuneration.

Administered wage setting also seems wholly to dominate the secondary labour market, with the exception of those few unskilled who are included in skilled worker collective bargaining agreements. Firms in this sector do not operate in unfettered price-competitive markets but, even so, considerable 'market pressure' exists. The struggle is typically among franchised chains for market shares, using power instruments of price manipulation and aggressive advertising of differentiated products.

In this secondary market, the administered wage tends to be at or near the federal minimum wage level, set through formal Congressional action. The secondary labour force is largely unskilled; it tends to consist of young, disadvantaged, minority, migrant and/or women workers. Training is brief, turnover high, and the establishment of customary rules and levels difficult. Firms cannot legally pay less than the minimum, but their intense struggles for market shares make them reluctant to pay more. Accordingly, the statutory minimum wage set tends to become the actual wage paid. Piore demonstrated these characteristics of the secondary sector in empirical studies of labour markets in Boston and in Louisiana.[64] Interestingly, in the case of Boston, however, the wage set was a social minimum modestly higher than the statutory minimum. Worker pressure and local custom evidently succeeded in establishing the marginally higher differential over the statutory minimum.

More recently, modification of certain labour market segments has occurred, with primary sector structures eroding in some major firms. Instead, a core-periphery model has emerged in which 'a "core" of "primary" workers [are found] coexisting within the same workplace unit with a "periphery" of "contingent" workers doing the same tasks. Contingent workers occupy jobs in large part fitting the descriptions of "secondary" markets'.[65] Indeed, it must be expected that the structure of administered wage and salaries will continue to evolve.

Status and Grant Transactions

As for status transactions – administered transfers 'governed primarily through the prescribed roles associated with social position' – it is reasonable to presume that, for the upper tier of Piore's primary sector, salary setting (in which the recipient may also be the discretionary agent) reflects status judgments of what is appropriate and fitting for this CEO, that vice-president, or a particular plant manager.

But beyond this there is an element of status transaction in the salary structures that become customary in the lower tier of the primary sector as well. Here considerations of what is just and fair, given specified levels of training and experience that define status, enter into deliberations of administered income levels. In Piore's view, a salary schedule that becomes customary 'in the eyes of the work group acquires an ethical aura. Adherence to it tends to be viewed as a matter of right and wrong and violations are seen as unfair and immoral.'[66] Customary salary differentials usually define ceremonial status; they may also incorporate instrumental differences in responsibility held and productivity achieved. Mobility ladders reflect not only income and status aspects, but also the instrumental considerations of experience and performance. But however well wage and salary norms, schedules and differentials may be established in the customary sense, their initiation and, as importantly, their revision, are discretionary acts reflecting the possession and use of achieved power. In short, they are administered costing judgments.

Grants transactions may seem on first consideration to be incongruous. How could there be an administered wage or salary where the 'grantor receives no right in return'? But for some in the upper tier of the primary sector, the offering of stock options to executives and the provision of 'golden parachutes' (additional service credits) upon retirement appear to qualify. They in fact represent administered income shares for the eligible few.

If the construct of grants transactions were to be extended beyond wages and salaries to transfers in the public sector, a whole new sphere of application emerges with the recognition that some 40 per cent of public expenditure is now distributed as transfer payments to individuals in the form of administered income shares.[67] If one were to add to this net interest paid on government debt (risk-free income) to holders of government securities,[68] and tax expenditures (subsidies written into the tax code) as transfer payments to firms and some individuals,[69] total transfer income as grants would represent roughly 50 per cent of public expenditure. Accordingly, in the aggregate, public administered income grants of various sorts comprise a very large component of actual income received in addition to or in lieu of administered wage and salary income.

Recourse to Schmid's transaction categories, then, helps to identify the ways in which achieved discretionary power is used to administer income shares. How that power is acquired and retained is, of course, a related issue for inquiry. Piore's empirical analysis of the character of actual sectoral labour markets provides insights and examples of how income determination occurs and thus how administered costs develop.

In summary, then, wage and salary structures are examples of cost determining institutions. Wage and salary levels and schedules are the product of prior discretionary institutional creation and are embedded in the social order. Once established to serve coordinating and regulating functions, they become customary and habitual patterns and their retention becomes a prime concern of both organized management and organized labour. Divisions between labour and management tend to arise with proposals initiated and pursued by either to *change* the established wage-setting levels or patterns. Power is marshalled, positions staked out, deliberations pursued.

Explanations of wage determination must thus be approached through a recognition of the omnipresence of wage *structure*.[70] Two such structures illustrate the point. 'A job cluster is ... a stable group of job classifications or work assignments ... linked together by ... technology, ... administrative organization, or social custom.'[71] Similarly, 'a wage contour is ... a stable group of wage-determining units ... linked together by ... similarity of product markets', use of 'similar source for labor', or 'common labor-market organization'.[72] These structures define wage differentials, link productive segments, and establish patterns and schedules which order income relations among workers. Not unexpectedly, they incorporate both instrumental and ceremonial purposes. The wage determining process then is comprehensively *institutionalized* in myriad and complex arrangements and regularities. Much wage setting conforms to already established levels, structures, differentials and patterns.

Wages and salaries are thus administered costs; this means that they are set by the exercise of achieved power in bargaining, by administered and status and grant transactions, and are intended to endure. At any particular point in time, wage structures reflect past exercises of discretion. Any current agenda of proposed changes or new discretionary acts will presumably address only segments of the workforce or marginal issues in existing structures and patterns.

III SOCIAL COST

Social Cost and Social Value

The normative content of the concept 'social cost' now becomes the pivotal concern for this analysis. Although the foregoing discussion of opportunity costs and pecuniary costing has introduced aspects of the instrumental value theory of neoinstitutionalists, it will be helpful here to extend that normative analysis by considering the meaning and applications of the construct 'social costs'. Neoinstitutional analysis is in fact based on the Veblenian dichotomy[73] – technological or instrumental versus ceremonial or invidious valuation and behaviour. A value construct developed by the present author incorporating the Veblenian distinction is to do or to choose 'that which provides for the continuity of human life and the noninvidious recreation of community through the instrumental use of knowledge'.[74] This construct lies at the heart of the following discussion.

I have already introduced the view that, for neoinstitutionalists, social costs refer to the destructive consequences to individuals, their social order, their environmental and ecological systems and their ideational and material resources, of invidious and ceremonial judgments that impair or impede the social and provisioning processes. I also indicated that, under certain conditions, instrumental judgments could also generate social costs, but to a lesser extent. These views must now be extended.

In general, judgments in economic provisioning and distribution processes are instrumental in nature if they incorporate the creation and persistent and effectual use of warranted knowledge in formulating and utilizing institutional arrangements. As noted in Chapter 2 above, warranted knowledge is the evolutionary emergence and cumulative outcome of an inquiry process characterized by reasoning in causal terms, evidential grounding, creation and testing of hypotheses, and assessment of outcomes. Although the stock of warranted knowledge is necessarily under constant expansion, revision and correction, it is for neoinstitutionalists the universe of ultimate appeal in deciding how to produce and distribute real income.

Those judgments regarding structure that are based on unwarranted knowledge are primarily ceremonial or invidious when, in implementation, they preserve the status quo, protect entrenched power, sustain an ideological dominion, demeaningly discriminate among persons on the basis of colour, race, gender, national origin, age or wealth, and otherwise impair the application of knowledge to problematic situations.

Social costs arise in two related ways. First and most obviously, when outright invidious and ceremonial judgments are used to frame and implement economic policies that impede or impair the provisioning process. For example, denying educational access on discriminatory grounds (race, creed, colour) significantly deprives the community of more adequately educated employees and citizens. In the US, more than three decades of desegregation of schooling have followed this recognition. Second and less obviously, when warranted knowledge is not available or is insufficiently developed in a particular area, designedly instrumental judgments may generate unavoidable or unintended impairments or impediments in the provisioning process. For example, the early use of pesticides to enhance agricultural output appeared to be justified by quite adequate warranted knowledge. But as the hazardous consequences of their use, particularly on the health of handlers, consumers and wildlife, became reliably known, its continued use was rationalized on self-interest and invidious grounds of sustaining output. Recognition that instrumental judgments are inadvertently generating social costs, then, should stimulate further inquiry to find less hazardous means to achieve instrumentally efficient production.

In anticipation of the following brief overview of varieties of social costs in four areas – environment, education, unemployment and knowledge – two salient attributes of the generation of social costs must be noted. First, extraordinary and extensive complexities and interdependencies relating to social cost extend across the entire spectrum of economic functions and institutional structures. They reflect causal linkages that are multiple, cumulative and at times circular. Social costs of increasing environmental contamination, to return to my latter example, impinge adversely on individual and public health, that in turn impinge adversely on capacities for and extent of work performed, that in turn impinge adversely on productivities in the economy, that in turn impinge adversely on the ability of the community to restore and sustain its socio-biotic continuity. Avoiding the onset of such an extensive set of adverse consequences should, of course, be given priority, but it is exceedingly difficult analytically to isolate causal sequences into specific linkages or episodic segments. However, causal patterns can be traced, complexities clarified and problematic elements identified. In attempting to transform institutions to reduce social costs, such complexity must be tackled by instrumental methods and conceptual tools, multidisciplinary approaches and imaginative inquiry.

Second, although K. William Kapp, among others, correctly viewed the emergence of social costs as a consequence of cost shifting by private enterprise to third parties or to society as a whole,[75] such costs in fact adversely impinge directly or indirectly on the whole community, including originating individuals and firms. Levels of interdependence are such that what Kapp calls 'negative' consequences are spread widely and are jointly, if unevenly, shared. Shifting occurs but does not sufficiently identify the spread effects of environmental disruption and the impairment of the provisioning process.[76]

Communities are increasingly integrated. The widening circle of consequences resulting from the generation of any social cost, then, not only affects the initiator and the immediate community, but the larger community as well. Given such interdependence, to impair any significant part of the community is to impair the whole. Acid rain from the US poisons water bodies in Canada; radioactivity from Chernobyl contaminates crops in Scandinavia; the crime and poverty of urban city centres now extend into the suburbs; potentially hazardous atmospheric warming is global. With continuing increases in world-wide population densities, social interdependencies will necessarily also continue to increase.

Social Costs in the Environment

With respect to the environment, the governing normative premise to which most neoinstitutionalists would assent is that the interdependencies of social and biotic communities are so extensive and critical that neither can survive without the other. Co-evolutionary development and continuity in a sustainable environment are the purposive inferences to draw from instrumental reasoning about the ecological aspects of economic and social processes.[77] Whatever disrupts, impairs or threatens that continuity is a social cost. Whatever does not support or validate that continuity is contra-instrumental and ceremonial. For a business firm, for example, short term profit maximizing may appear as a sufficient criterion for judgment and behaviour regarding resource use and productive techniques. From an instrumentalist perspective, however, its single-minded pursuit may entail environmentally destructive and ecologically damaging practices adversely affecting its own continuity and that of the larger community.

Social costs appear, following Kapp,[78] as *disruptions* and *impairments*. Socio-biotic disruption takes many forms: habitat destruction, ozone depletion, intrusions on fertility/reproduction cycles, the destruction of genetic varieties and forms, among others. Impairment encompasses air and water pollution, soil erosion, deforestation and overgrazing, among others. Structural debates that prompt ceremonially-justified claims and instrumentally-warranted arguments concerning these evident impairments continue over property rights, riparian water rights, regulations constraining polluters, regulations on land use, environmental impact assessments, rules concerning the creation and disposal of wastes, etc. Institutional adjustments reflecting instrumental judgments are required if environmental and ecological protection, restoration and continuity are to be assured. The environmental and ecological disruptions and impairments reflected, for example, in the chemical pollution of the Rhine at Basel, Exxon's oil spill in Alaska, depletion of the mid-continent Ogallala aquifer, absence of safe disposal of radioactive wastes, among others, remind us of major and threatening social costs incurred in the last decade or so, many of which still await correction or resolution.

Policies to reduce or eliminate the social costs of environmental disruption and impairment have evolved rapidly in recent years, building on the early work of Kapp, Leopold, Commoner[79] and others. Neoinstitutionalists including Swaney[80] and Hayden[81] have joined in the effort, contributing refinements in instrumental value theory. These include the development of an environmental ethic that fosters organic cultivation and sustainable yields in agriculture; preservation of seed varieties, genetic banks and habitat of non-human flora and fauna; persistent reduction in dependencies on nuclear and fossil fuels as sources of energy; recycling of wastes; persistent reductions in global levels of air and water pollution. Policies that provide for co-evolutionary restoration, development and continuity are instrumentally warranted.

Social Costs in Education

With respect to education, the governing normative premise to which most neoinstitutionalists would assent is that all individuals should have the opportunity and support to develop their inherent and acquired capabilities (reflective and behavioural) to the fullest extent possible. This means that the institutional structures and behaviours that *deprive* children and adults of educational access, and invidiously *discriminate* in ways that negate the educational experience, generate social costs. Central is the recognition that education is fundamentally a continuing process of helping persons to develop 'the capacity to think critically and coherently over the entire range of their experience'.[82] For John Dewey, the goal of education was to promote continual growth in understanding and participatory capacity. Teaching children to think was only an expansion of ordinary cognitive activity. '[T]he native and unspoiled attitude of childhood, marked by ardent curiosity, fertile imagination, and love of experimental inquiry', he suggested, 'is near, very near, to the attitude of the scientific mind.'[83] Whatever prevents, thwarts or distorts this universal quest for growth of reflective and causal understanding generates significant social costs.

Social costs, then, appear as deprivation and discrimination. Deprivation of continuing and stimulating instruction generates a lifetime of under-fulfilment and dependency. The cumulative maturation of lingual, cognitive and manipulative skills must be assured at every stage of development. Failure to acquire these attributes can only partly be compensated for in subsequent years. Early deprivation fosters subsequent impoverishment. Discrimination (gender, race, ancestry) impairs the learning process by destroying self-confidence and self-image, by shrinking options and promoting hostility. The social cost of failed education can only be hinted at by calculations of foregone income, narrowed job options, and stunted lives.

Deprivation of educational access and effective instruction takes many forms: the absence of insightful, supportive and stimulative parenting that equips children for formal education; the dearth of support (as income, taxes and resources) that diminishes programmes, curriculums and the hiring and retention of capable instructors; the bureaucracies of educational management that drain off resources, and the absence of governmental regulations that would help equalize support levels among differing educational jurisdictions. Discrimination arises, for example, in the invidious sorting (tracking) of students, by gender, race or income of parents, for differing curriculums; in the de facto invidious quota systems that sometimes still operate for admission to institutions of higher learning; and in the tendency of teachers to prejudge students' abilities by invidious identifications.

A reduction in the social costs of educational deprivation and discrimination can be undertaken with specific policy initiatives: to dramatically enhance and extend programmes like 'Head Start' that give otherwise insufficiently prepared young children a chance to achieve early success in learning; to divert an increased fraction of total support funds to the education of the very young (k–4 years); to restore creative arts to curriculums; to introduce legislation that continues and extends prohibitions against differential support levels on invidious grounds; to restore predictable and acceptable tax bases (progressively constituted) to more adequately fund formal education; to raise income levels, quality of preparation and accountability standards of teachers; to restore and revitalize structures that involve parents more extensively in the education of their children; and to accelerate cross-cultural and integrative education of children from different backgrounds.[84] Policies that generate capacities for and interest in lifetime educational growth and maturation are instrumentally warranted.

Social Costs of Unemployment and Underemployment

With respect to unemployment and underemployment, the governing normative premise to which most neoinstitutionalists would assent is that, in any exchange economy, all adult individuals who are able to work should have access to continuing employment at jobs/positions they regard as significant. This means that, in a democratic society, individuals have a *right* to gainful and meaningful employment comparable to their civil rights. In most modern societies, income from employment provides the primary pecuniary means to participate in the economy generally. (A sizeable fraction of the community – seniors, disabled – must depend, of course, on prior earnings and income transfers.) The size of income usually defines the extent of social and economic choice. Nearly as importantly, employment connections generate self-identification and provide social recognition. People become habituated to perceiving themselves as computer-specialists, plumbers, professors, pilots, CEOs or nurses. Denial of access to meaningful employment, then, generates a double hazard: without work the individual has no earned income to provide sustenance and no social standing from recognition of contributions to the larger community. Both lead to an erosion of confidence and capacity.

Social costs, then, appear as *waste* of skills and productivity and *demoralization* and *impoverishment* of workers. Substantial unemployment and underemployment mean a vast waste of un- or under-utilized acquired skills and capacities for the community and hence a dramatic loss of real product and services. If such unemployment continues for an extended period of time, a profound and frightening loss of skills and capabilities occurs from non-use and from failure to keep abreast of innovative techniques. Invidious discrimination against women and minorities accounts for much underemployment. Consequential demoralization and loss of incentives of the unemployed and underemployed are widely acknowledged. The social costs both to individuals affected and to the community are accordingly dramatic and extensive.[85]

Over most of this century, scholars have been estimating income and real product losses from unemployment. The decade of the Great Depression, including a period during which one-quarter of the labour force was involuntarily unemployed, evidently deprived the US community of the equivalent of one to two years of production at end-of-decade output levels.[86] Data continue to be generated showing the differences between potential full-employment levels of output and actual levels achieved.[87] Archaic, market-oriented theories (pre-Keynesian) did not actually explain the determinants of unemployment (allegedly, workers were choosing leisure over work!) and 'corrections' (let the market rule) did not reduce it. These theories and 'policies', as with counterparts generated recently by monetarists and new classicists, inadvertently provoked a large and invidious expansion of social costs. Theories perpetuating the status quo and conservative policies (limited monetary policy, no credible fiscal policy) failed to contribute to the restoration of fuller employment.[88]

Policy recommendations coming from neoinstitutionalists (and Keynesians and Post Keynesians) would predictably include, as a minimum, an activist fiscal policy, a managed monetary policy and extensive job-training programmes to prepare skilled workers for jobs currently available.[89] In an age of rapid technological change, automatic and comprehensive retraining options, together with transition income support, should be routinely provided to workers displaced, for example, by automated and robotic systems. Consideration should be given to legislation that makes the *right* to a job universal (guaranteed employment); those unable to find employment in the private sector would be hired in the public sector; government becomes the employer of last resort. Although discussed in the 1960s[90] and considered in legislative terms in the mid-1970s,[91] the restoration to the policy agenda of the right to work has not yet occurred. Policies that assure full employment, public or private, that provide adequate income, dignity and purpose are instrumentally warranted.

Social Costs in Growth of Knowledge and Technology

With respect to the growth of knowledge and technology, the governing normative premise to which most neoinstitutionalists would assent is, following Charles Sanders Peirce, 'do not block the way of inquiry'.[92] Any community seeking continuity and well-being must ensure that the intellectual freedom of its members is not impaired. Scholars, thinkers, technologists, students, teachers, researchers and policy makers must have and retain unfettered opportunities to pursue scientific and social (causal) inquiry and its applications to experience, to report outcomes of formal and informal investigation, and to incorporate new warranted knowledge into the knowledge and experience continuum of the whole community.

Social costs appear as *impairments* of the inquiry process and as *encapsulations* of its outcomes. Impairments take many forms: intimidation and coercive insistence on particular methodologies whose basic elements cannot be challenged, ideological dominion over research, perpetuation of orthodox modes of inquiry, withholding economic support (grants, promotions, contacts) from those who question establishment positions and policies, and discouraging the publication of provocative and challenging materials.[93] Such intimidations effectively truncate the process of generating warranted knowledge. They eliminate uncomfortable questions and hypotheses from inquiry; they constrain inquiry into path dependency; they convert assumptions into dogma and policy alternatives into blueprints for structural change.[94] The acquisition and retention of discretionary control over the direction and character of inquiry, for the express purpose of sustaining received doctrine, is profoundly invidious behaviour. The social costs are cultivated ignorance, perpetuation of flawed theoretical analyses and structural changes that aggravate rather than resolve institutional malfunctions.

Social costs also arise with the encapsulation of knowledge.[95] When discretionary authorities, public or private, act to sequester or withhold warranted knowledge from instrumental use in order to serve ceremonial or invidious purposes, social costs are incurred. Constraints on the timing and extent of release of new knowledge deny to the larger community the intellectual resources with which to address the poor performance of institutions as well as technological inefficiencies. Encapsulation is accomplished by a variety of institutionalized restrictions involving, for instance, corporate control over 'in house' inventions and innovations, property rights in ideas and technologies, manipulation of patent systems (patent blocks, patents pending), research and development cooperation, coordination and control agreements, the granting or withholding of funding to initiate and sustain research agendas, and the like.

Finally, the encapsulation of warranted knowledge and associated social costs may result from formal or informal attacks on warranted knowledge itself. Religious, economic or political zealots offer simplistic, non-evidential and often mono-causal 'explanations', grounded in hagiographic, cultish and/ or salvation literature. Talk-show hosts, editorial writers, religious leaders, TV evangelists, doctrinaire politicians and financial 'advisers' are among those who belittle and negate warranted knowledge. While there is no suggestion here that discourse from the above sources should be stifled, an increased alertness to, and continuing rebuttal of, such attacks is essential. Their success in enlisting popular support corrupts the deliberative processes of a functioning democratic order. The social cost of ignorance is increased.

Fashioning policy initiatives to reduce levels of intimidation and encapsulation will not be easy for neoinstitutionalists and others similarly concerned. Continuing efforts to reform educational institutions in order to create and maintain pluralistic approaches to inquiry and instruction in respective disciplines are badly needed. Other measures include support for formal and informal efforts to sustain intellectual freedom; assistance for those generating demonstrable successes in problem solving (through institutional adjustment) in ways which undermine or disarm the simplistic and self-serving; assistance with the formulation of legislative measures to support inquiry and ensure the availability of its outcomes for the community's instrumentally defined benefit. As noted above, warranted knowledge is the community's premier resource. Policies that provide for the creation, protection, expansion and availability of the expanding fund of reliable knowledge are instrumentally warranted.

IV TENETS FOR A NEOINSTITUTIONALIST THEORY OF COSTS AND COSTING

The following is a summary of the provisional neoinstitutionalist theory of costs, costing and valuation discussed above:

- Neoinstitutionalists provide an instrumental mode of inquiry with which to formulate criteria for the assessment of pecuniary costing judgments and for the identification and appraisal of social costs.

- A neoinstitutionalist analysis of pecuniary and social costs is grounded neither in the utility theory of value nor in the labour theory of value. It encompasses neither disutility incurred nor labour time embodied as 'real' costs.

- Opportunity costs for neoinstitutionalists are identified through instrumental value theory. What are foregone or given up in choice making are instrumentally-warranted or ceremonially-warranted options and their differing outcomes.

- Because of the sterility and static character of its preconceptions of utility value measured by price, neoclassical opportunity costs cannot serve as the foundation for a credible analysis of costs and costing.

- There are pecuniary costs, the determination of which may serve progressive or regressive purposes, and there are social costs, the imposition of which obstructs or impairs social and economic processes.

- Pecuniary costs are demonstrably a form of administered prices, set by discretionary agents.

- The power to determine pecuniary costs is widely held in both the private and public sectors and, in the interest of the community's welfare, must be held accountable.

- The exercise of power over pecuniary costs may be unidirectional (as in administered and status and grant transactions) or reciprocal (as in bargaining and/or negotiated transactions).

- Administered pecuniary-cost decisions are generally set through extensive and complex institutional structures that typically have become habitual and resistant to change.

- Pecuniary costs are set mainly to cover administered prices of inputs and only partly in response to conditions of relative scarcity and estimates of elasticity of demand.

- Neoinstitutionalists, utilizing instrumental value theory, may normatively assess and appraise judgments made in setting pecuniary costs. Costing judgments may be instrumentally or ceremonially warranted or reflect aspects of each.

- Social costs are real costs. Real social costs emerge in part because of the tardy development of instrumentally-warranted reasoning and judgments and/or insufficient knowledge about causal linkages of decisions made and consequences experienced.

- Social costs result in part from the failure fully to apply instrumental reasoning and judgments to minimize waste, disruptions, environmental hazards and productive impairments in and to the provisioning process.

- Social costs originate in part in the invidious use of differences of race, gender, nationality, ethnicity, wealth, etc. to deprive, impair, demoralize and/or impoverish individuals in their access to and participation in the economic process.
- Neoinstitutionalist fact-based, theory-driven, value-laden inquiry into policy formulation and implementation can contribute significantly to the reduction of social costs.

NOTES

1. As noted earlier, neoinstitutionalists tend to follow and extend the tradition of Thorstein B. Veblen, John Dewey, Clarence E. Ayres and J. Fagg Foster, with special emphasis on instrumental analysis and social value theory.
2. Clark [1923] (1971); Kapp (1969), pp. 334–47; Kapp (1970), pp. 15–32; Kapp (1971); Polanyi (1944); Polanyi (1947), pp. 109–17; Swaney, (1989), pp. 7–33.
3. Means (1963), pp. 213–39; Means (1972), pp. 292–306; Means (1983), pp. 467–85; Lee (1993a); Lee (1993b); Tool (1991), pp. 19–39.
4. Hamilton (1929), p. 185; quoted by Ramstad (1993), p. 186.
5. Dewey (1939), pp. 33–40.
6. Ramstad (1993), p. 196.
7. Ibid, p. 188.
8. Ibid, pp. 188–9.
9. Ibid, p. 189.
10. Schmid (1978), pp. 10–19; Commons (1950), pp. 43–57.
11. Hayden (1982), pp. 637–62.
12. Ibid, p. 645.
13. Kapp (1971), p. 13.
14. Pearce (1986), p. 84.
15. Ramstad (1994), personal correspondence.
16. Pearce (1986), p. 84.
17. Ibid.
18. Ibid.
19. Interestingly, although neoclassicists arrive via a different route and with utilitarian luggage, they probably would agree that the pragmatic implications of the foregoing examples (of spillover effects from ownership and the reemployment of idle persons and resources) do not necessarily generate 'opportunity costs' as they would define them.
20. Zimmerman (1951), p. 10.
21. DeGregori (1985), pp. 56–84.
22. Schmid (1978), p. 6.
23. Ibid, p. 7.
24. Ibid, ch. 1.
25. Wray (1991), pp. 951–75.
26. Ramstad (1994), personal correspondence.
27. Lee (1993a), (1993b).
28. For background sources, see also Lee (1990) and Lee and Samuels (1991).
29. Lee (1993a), p. 29.
30. Ibid, p. 30.
31. Lee (1993b) has provided a comprehensive empirical survey, particularly of Post Keynesian studies over the last two decades, of *actual* pricing and costing practices in categories of markup, normal cost, target rate of return, labour-based pricing, and labour- and material-based pricing.

32. Lee (1993a), p. 30.
33. Ibid, p. 35.
34. Ibid.
35. Ibid, pp. 35–6.
36. Ibid, p. 37.
37. Ibid, pp. 39–41.
38. Ibid, pp. 10–19.
39. Ibid.
40. Ibid, p. 11.
41. Ramstad (1994), personal correspondence.
42. Schmid (1978), pp. 12–13.
43. Ibid, p. 13.
44. Ibid, pp. 14–15.
45. Ibid, pp. 15–16.
46. Ibid, pp. 16–17.
47. Swaney, James A. (1994), personal correspondence.
48. Piore (1979), pp. 5–16, 134–43, 197–206; Doeringer and Piore (1971), pp. 13–92.
49. Ramstad (1993), pp. 173–233.
50. Ibid, p. 207.
51. Dugger (1981), pp. 397–407.
52. Ramstad (1993), p. 200.
53. Bernstein (1950), p. 37.
54. Piore (1979), pp. 134–49.
55. Goldfield (1989); Bowles, Gordon and Weisskopf (1989), pp. 107–34.
56. Bureau of Labor Statistics (1993a), *News*, p. 1.
57. Lustig (1985), pp. 123–52; Bluestone and Harrison (1982).
58. Cyert and Mowery (1988).
59. Bureau of Census (1993), *Statistical Abstract* p. 436.
60. Ibid.
61. Bureau of Labor Statistics (1993b), *News*, p. 2.
62. Tool (1986), pp. 126–34.
63. Kapp (1971), pp. 13–25.
64. Piore (1979), pp. 197–206.
65. Ramstad (1994), personal correspondence.
66. Piore (1979), p. 136. See also Hutton (1993), p. 21.
67. *Economic Report of the President* (1993), p. 440. Regrettably, no consideration can be given here to the extensive and provocative literature on the 'grants economy' originated by Kenneth Boulding and his students.
68. Ibid.
69. Peterson (1991), pp. 57–93.
70. Dunlop (1979), p. 64.
71. Ibid, pp. 64–5.
72. Ibid, p. 66.
73. Waller (1982), pp. 757–71.
74. Tool (1986), pp. 292–314.
75. Kapp (1971), pp. xiii, xxvii; Kapp (1969), pp. 334–47.
76. For Kapp, 'disruption' and 'impairment' constitute the 'negative' impact of private decisions on environmental continuity and are the generators of social cost. Kapp (1970), pp. 15–32.
77. Swaney (1988), pp. 329–34.
78. Kapp (1970).
79. Kapp (1971); Leopold (1966); Commoner (1971).
80. Swaney (1988).
81. Hayden (1984).
82. My recollection of a statement often made by J. Fagg Foster in his class lectures.
83. Dewey, quoted by Westbrook (1991), p. 169.

84. Marshall and Tucker (1992), chs. 8–10.
85. Gallie (1994); Ginsburg (1983), pp. 85–107.
86. Lubin (1939); cited by Mitchell (1947), p. 363.
87. Ginsburg (1983), pp. 85–8; Peterson (1988), pp. 7 and 18.
88. Cornwall (1990), pp. 73–90; Cornwall (1983).
89. Marshall and Tucker (1992), chs. 14 and 15.
90. Theobald (1967).
91. Congress (1974), *Humphrey-Hawkins Full Employment and Balanced Growth Act*; Ginsburg (1983), pp. 63–84.
92. Peirce; quoted in Buchler (1955), p. 54.
93. Kuttner (1985), pp. 74–84.
94. Hildred (1991), pp. 781–97.
95. The definitive work on encapsulation has been done by Paul D. Bush (1986), pp. 25–45; Bush (1988), pp. 125–66.

REFERENCES

Bernstein, Irving (1950), *The New Deal Collective Bargaining Policy*, Berkeley: University of California Press.

Bluestone, Barry and Harrison, Bennett (1982), *The Deindustrialization of America*, New York: Basic Books.

Bowles, Samuel, Gordon, David M. and Weisskopf, Thomas E. (1989), 'Business ascendency and economic impasse: a structural retrospective on conservative economics, 1979–1987', *Journal of Economic Perspectives*, **3**, Winter.

Buchler, Justus (ed.) (1955), *Philosophical Writings of Peirce*, New York: Dover Publications.

Bush, Paul D. (1986), 'On the concept of ceremonial encapsulation', *Review of Institutional Thought*, **3**, December.

Bush, Paul D. (1988), 'Theory of Institutional Change', in Marc R. Tool (ed.), *Evolutionary Economics I: Foundations of Institutional Thought*, Armonk, N.Y.: M.E. Sharpe.

Clark, John Maurice [1923] (1971), *Studies in the Economics of Overhead Costs*, Chicago: University of Chicago Press.

Commoner, Barry (1971), *The Closing Circle*, New York: Alfred A. Knopf.

Commons, John R. (1950), *The Economics of Collective Action*, New York: Macmillan.

Cornwall, John (1983), *The Conditions for Economic Recovery*, Armonk, N.Y.: M.E. Sharpe.

Cornwall, John (1990), *The Theory of Economic Breakdown*, Cambridge: Basil Blackwell.

Cyert, Richard M. and Mowery, David C. (1988) (eds), *The Impact of Technological Change on Employment and Economic Growth*, Cambridge, Mass.: Ballinger Publishing Co.

DeGregori, Thomas R. (1985), *A Theory of Technology*, Ames: Iowa State University Press.

Dewey, John (1939), *Theory of Valuation*, Chicago: University of Chicago Press.

Doeringer, Peter B. and Piore, Michael J. (1971), *Internal Labor Markets and Manpower Analysis*, Lexington, Mass.: D.C. Heath.

Dugger, William M. (1981), 'The administered labor market: an institutional analysis', *Journal of Economic Issues*, **15**, June.

Dunlop, John T. (1979), 'Wage Contours', in M.J. Piore (ed.), *Unemployment and Inflation*, White Plains, N.Y.: M.E. Sharpe.

Economic Report of the President (1993), Washington, D.C.: U.S. Government Printing Office.

Gallie, Duncan (1994) (ed.), *Social Change and the Experience of Unemployment*, New York: Oxford University Press.

Ginsburg, Helen (1983), *Full Employment and Public Policy*, Lexington, Mass.: D.C. Heath.

Goldfield, Michael (1989), *The Decline of Organized Labor in the United States*, Chicago: University of Chicago Press.

Hamilton, Walton (1929), 'Charles Horton Cooley', *Social Forces*, **8**, December.

Hayden, F. Gregory (1982), 'Social fabric matrix: from perspective to analytical tool', *Journal of Economic Issues*, **16**, September.

Hayden, F. Gregory (1984), 'A Geobased National Agricultural Policy for Rural Community Enhancement, Environmental Vitality, and Income Stabilization', in Marc R. Tool (ed.), *An Institutionalist Guide to Economics and Public Policy*, Armonk, N.Y.: M.E. Sharpe.

Hildred, William M. (1991), 'Antidemocratic elements of the Reagan revolution', *Journal of Economic Issues*, **25**, September.

Hutton, Will (1993), 'Choice does not pave the road to happiness', *Manchester Guardian Weekly*, 14 November.

Kapp, K. William (1969), 'On the nature and significance of social costs', *Kyklos*, **22**, Fasc. 2.

Kapp, K. William (1970), 'Economic disruption: general issues and methodological problems', *Social Science Information* (International Social Science Council), Nr. 9–4.

Kapp, K. William (1971), *The Social Costs of Private Enterprise*, New York: Schocken Books.

Kuttner, Robert (1985), 'The poverty of economics', *The Atlantic Monthly*, February.

Lee, Frederic S. (1990), 'G.C. Mean's Doctrine of Administered Prices', in P. Arestis and Y. Kitromilides (eds), *Theory and Policy in Political Economy*, Aldershot: Edward Elgar.

Lee, Frederic S. (1993a), 'Facts, Theory and the Pricing Foundation of Post Keynesian Price Theory' in John Groenewegen (ed.), *Dynamics of the Firm: Strategies of Pricing and Organization*, Aldershot: Edward Elgar.

Lee, Frederic S. (1993b), *From Post Keynesian to Historical Price Theory: Facts, Theory and Empirically Grounded Pricing Model*, Leicester: De Montfort University.

Lee, Frederic S. and Samuels, Warren J. (1991), *The Heterodox Economics of Gardner C. Means*, Armonk, N.Y.: M.E. Sharpe.

Leipert, Christian (1989), 'National income and economic growth: the conceptual side of defensive expenditures', *Journal of Economic Issues*, **23**, September.

Leopold, Aldo (1966), *A Sand County Almanac*, Oxford: Oxford University Press.

Lubin, Isador (1939), TNEC Hearings, Part 1, *Economic Prologue*, Washington, D.C.: US Government Printing Office.

Lustig, R. Jeffrey (1985), 'The politics of shutdown: community, property, corporatism', *Journal of Economic Issues*, **19**, March.

Marshall, Ray and Tucker, Marc (1992), *Thinking for a Living: Education and the Wealth of Nations*, New York: Basic Books.

Means, Gardiner C. (1963), 'Pricing Power and the Public Interest', US Senate,

Committee on the Judiciary, Subcommittee on Antitrust and Monopoly, *Administered Prices: A Compendium on Public Policy*, 88th Cong., 1st sess., Washington, D.C.: US Government Printing Office.

Means, Gardiner C. (1972), 'The administered-price thesis reconfirmed', *American Economic Review*, **62**, June.

Means, Gardiner C. (1983), 'Corporate power in the market place', *Journal of Law and Economics*, **24**, June.

Mitchell, Broadus (1947), *Depression Decade*, New York: Holt Rinehart Winston.

Munkirs, John R. (1985), *The Transformation of American Capitalism: From Competitive Market Structures to Centralized Private Sector Planning*, Armonk, N.Y.: M.E. Sharpe.

Pearce, David W. (ed.) (1986), *The MIT Dictionary of Modern Economics*, 3rd ed., Cambridge: MIT Press.

Peirce, Charles Sanders, 'The Scientific Attitude and Fallibilism' in Justus Buchler (ed.) (1955), *Philosophical Writings of Peirce*, New York: Dover Publications.

Peterson, Wallace C. (1988), *Income. Employment and Economic Growth*, 6th edn, New York: W.W. Norton.

Peterson, Wallace C. (1991), *Transfer Spending, Taxes, and the American Welfare State*, Boston: Kluwer Academic Publishers.

Piore, Michael J. (1979), 'Fragments of a "Sociological" Theory of Wages'; 'Pricing Rules'; and 'Wage Determination in Low-Wage Labor Markets and the Role of Minimum Wage Legislation' in M.J. Piore (ed.), *Unemployment and Inflation*, White Plains, N.Y.: M.E. Sharpe.

Polanyi, Karl (1944), *The Great Transformation*, New York: Einehart and Co.

Polanyi, Karl (1947), 'Our obsolete market mentality', *Commentary*, **3**, February.

Polanyi, Karl (1957), 'The Economy as Instituted Process', in Conrad M. Arensberg and Harry W. Pearson (eds), *Trade and Market in the Early Empires*, Glencoe, Ill.: Free Press.

Ramstad, Yngve (1993), 'Institutional Economics and the Dual Labor Market Theory', in Marc R. Tool (ed.), *Institutional Economics: Theory, Method, Policy*, Boston: Kluwer Academic Publishers.

Schmid, A. Allan (1978), *Property, Power, and Public Choice*, New York: Praeger Publishers.

Swaney, James A. (1988), 'Elements of a Neoinstitutional Environmental Economics' in Marc R. Tool (ed.), *Evolutionary Economics, II: Institutional Theory and Policy*, Armonk, N.Y.: M.E. Sharpe.

Swaney, James A. (1989), 'The social cost concepts of K. William Kapp and Karl Polanyi', *Journal of Economic Issues*, **23**, March.

Theobald, Robert (ed.) (1967), *The Guaranteed Income*, New York: Anchor Books.

Tool, Marc R. (1986), 'Equational Justice and Social Value', in M.R. Tool, *Essays in Social Value Theory*, Armonk, N.Y.: M.E. Sharpe.

Tool, Marc R. (1991), 'Contributions to an Institutional Theory of Price Determination' in Geoffrey M. Hodgson and Ernesto Screpanti (eds), *Rethinking Economics: Markets, Technology and Economic Evolution*, Aldershot: Edward Elgar.

US Bureau of Census (1993), *Statistical Abstract of the United States* (113th ed.), Washington, D.C.: U.S. Government Printing Office.

US Congress (1974), House Bill 15476, Senate Bill 3947, *Humphrey-Hawkins Full Employment and Balanced Growth Act*, 93rd Cong. 2nd sess.

US Department of Labor, Bureau of Labor Statistics (1993a), *News*, Washington, D.C.: US Department of Labor 93–43, 8 February.

US Department of Labor, Bureau of Labor Statistics (1993b), *News*, Washington, D.C.: US Department of Labor 93–518, 1 December.

Waller, William T. Jr. (1982), 'The evolution of the Veblenian dichotomy: Veblen, Hamilton, Ayres, and Foster', *Journal of Economic Issues*, **16**, September.

Westbrook, Robert B. (1991), *John Dewey and American Democracy*, Ithaca: Cornell University Press.

Wray, L. Randall (1991), 'Savings, profits and speculation in capitalist economies', *Journal of Economic Issues*, **25**, December.

Zimmerman, Erich (1951), *World Resources and Industries*, rev. ed., New York: Harper and Brothers.

7. Social value theory and regulation*

Whatever else the administrations of Presidents Carter, Reagan and Bush may or may not have accomplished, they succeeded in keeping the theory and practice of public regulation of economic activity on the research and policy agenda of both neoclassical and neoinstitutional economists. While I cannot here explore this interesting economic history, it does provide a rationale and setting for the following analysis.

My purpose in this chapter is to analyse some basic social value aspects of economic regulation, including those relating to exchange ratios. In so doing, I intend to join, and in part to reflect, the contributions of institutionalists – including John R. Commons, J.M. Clark, James Bonbright, Harry M. Trebing and others – who developed 'the public interest theory of regulation'. In their view, regulation is 'viewed as a method for resolving conflicts and coordinating social objectives in an industrialized economy and, more importantly, as a means for curbing monopoly power and preventing the abuses associated with the unrestricted exercise of that power'.[1]

The conclusion towards which the argument moves is that instrumental value theory, as developed by neoinstitutionalists in the Dewey tradition, provides guidance for the formulation of judgments regarding the regulation of economic activity, including pricing and costing power, in the public interest. One of the main contentions offered is the recognition that instrumental value theory (although not formally recognized as such) has typically provided the actual criteria employed when regulation has been deemed progressive – that is, when it contributed at least temporarily to the resolution of actual problems encountered. Other sorts of criteria have generated regressive regulation and have failed significantly to contribute to a public-interest view of problem solving.

In this essay, I am incorporating Paul D. Bush's distinction between progressive and regressive social change. '"Progressive" institutional change occurs when, *for a given fund of knowledge*, ceremonial patterns of behavior are displaced by instrumental patterns of behavior'. In contrast, '"regressive" institutional change' is generated by 'the *displacement* of instrumentally

*Paper presented at meetings of the Association for Evolutionary Economics, Atlanta, December 1989, and published in the *Journal of Economic Issues*, June 1990. Reprinted with permission.

warranted patterns of behavior by ceremonially warranted patterns of behavior'
(emphasis in original).[2]

Here I take the view that economic regulations prescribe and proscribe
economic behaviour; they comprise a large part of the institutional structure
through which behaviour is correlated in providing the material means of
life. Economic regulations consist of rules and their enforcement. Most economic regulations impose public constraints on private judgment, for instance by defining areas of discretion over ownership of property, use of
resources, creation and utilization of technology, negotiation of labour relations, provision of products and services, administration of prices, disposal of
wastes, etc. Regulations may reduce areas of discretion for some and expand
those for others. For example, rules that limit managerial prerogatives and
compel 'good faith' bargaining by organized employers simultaneously enhance the discretionary options of organized labour. All economic regulations, then, advantage some and disadvantage others. At issue is whose
interests or advantages *ought* to be served.

All regulations arise as products of discretionary agents who are usually,
but not always, in governmental bodies. They reflect choices made in the
effort to achieve one or more objectives or outcomes. The creation and
implementation of regulations, then, always require the application of criteria
of choice. Normative questions abound. When and under what circumstances
should public (or private) bodies attempt to expand or contract areas of
discretion on economic matters for particular groups through regulatory action? When and under what circumstances should the character of discretion
be specified or delimited? What public purposes should guide the creation
and implementation of regulations? Identification and assessment of expected
consequences are required. But how ought we to choose a criterion to appraise consequences? Does the above distinction between progressive and
regressive institutional change provide a principle of appraisal that cannot
easily be dismissed on common experience grounds as inappropriate or non-
contributing – as is the case where self-serving, ethnocentric, utopian or
status-quo standards are employed? Perhaps.

Some years ago, Warren Samuels argued, in effect, that no such principle
was available.[3] After first demonstrating (correctly) that, in conventional
regulatory analysis, normative assumptions do 'prefigure the decision results', he asked analysts to 'make values as explicit as possible, perhaps most
effectively by making alternative value premises'. He then insisted that 'to
avoid building in either the status quo or the analyst's private prejudices or
ideology', a position of 'functional nihilism' was necessary.[4] He did not
suggest how to choose among value premises. Yet clearly one could not
reject the inappropriateness of judgments reflecting the status quo and private
prejudices or ideology without employing some justifying standard or crite-

rion of appraisal. Functional nihilism will not serve. Can we move beyond this dilemma?

I UNDERBUSH CLEARING

Functional nihilism is not the only impediment to normative inquiry. The traditional postures of ethical relativism and ethical absolutism also obstruct the inquiry process. The former affirms that values are relative to the person or culture and hence unknowable. The latter affirms that some values are anterior to, and unapproachably aloof from, normative inquiry. In both cases, ethical criteria are ejected from the inquiry process.

Regressive Principles of Appraisal

We can get little help from orthodox neoclassicists on the matter of social value theory. Even when they abandon their positivistic postures, the utility-based, ethically relative criteria they recommend turn out to be analytically unacceptable and pragmatically inapplicable. Elsewhere, many institutionalists have undermined the credibility of the Paretian optimum,[5] cost-benefit criteria,[6] economic efficiency,[7] constrained maximization,[8] and the normative use of the competitive model,[9] among other principles. All of the above imply, in different ways, the a priori acceptance of wants, tastes and preferences as given and unknowable. Wants are incommensurable! In consequence, these standards are, on the whole, status-quo preserving and thus regressive.

Similarly, as Samuels has also argued,[10] efforts to employ Kantian-like, ethically absolute criteria will not provide relevant standards for creating and assessing regulations. The a priori and uncritical acceptance of property rights (rooted in natural law), anterior economic interests (identified by status, ancestry or power), and other prejudicial or ideological categorical imperatives that specify, *prior* to inquiry, whose economic interests really matter, suppress the value question. It does not enter inquiry. The *ought* question is never really posed; the 'answer' precedes analysis. These, too, are regressive criteria.

Assessing Rights and Interests

Any regulation will probably have an impact on existing property rights. It will change options and constraints for some – that is its purpose. Rule changes reorder discretionary prerogatives in the service of some conception of what ought to be; they may be progressive or regressive. Newly intro-

duced regulations are designed to respond to perceived problematic consequences arising from the (mis)use of discretion by owners and/or other institutional power sources. Persons have either judged those consequences to be
destructive in some significant way or have sought to enhance constructive
options not presently available.

We routinely construe 'private ownership' to mean a legally specified area
of discretion over an item – to hold, use, gain from or sell that for which title
is held. Legal ownership, however, *never* connotes *absolute* discretion, since
regulations inevitably constrain and/or modify it. Public authorities have
long been responsible for defining and redefining precisely these ownership
prerogatives. In the principle of eminent domain, as is well known, public
authority may even compel transfer of property (and therewith discretion)
from private to public ownership, with compensation. But the affirmation of
a public purpose in such a transfer or in any new regulation must itself be
rooted in and validated by progressive criteria of judgment. Again the public
interest validation cannot be presumed; it is absolutely required.

Moreover, any regulation will probably have an impact on existing and/or
future economic interests. It must, as Samuels has often insisted,[11] specify
whose interests really matter and are to be served. I perceive private economic interests to consist primarily of existing legally established (under-
ground economy excepted) claims to, and discretion over, the following
matters: access to, and size of, real and money income, participatory control
over economic functions and structure, perquisites of status and position, and
power to impinge on the economic circumstance of others. To affirm the
obvious, the greater the money income, ordinarily the wider the discretion.

Private interests become the subject of public regulation when, as Dewey
observed, 'indirect, extensive, enduring and serious consequences of conjoint
and interacting behavior call a public into existence having a common interest in controlling these consequences'.[12] That is, private interests must always be subject to regulation when the public interest is significantly impaired or threatened by the perpetuation or dominance of the former. Of
course the public interest must also be rooted in and validated by progressive
criteria of judgment.

I turn now to the proposition that instrumental value theory provides such
progressive criteria, permits an identification of the public interest, and offers
a defensible rationale for regulation.

II INSTRUMENTAL VALUE THEORY

Is there a social value theory available to guide regulatory judgments that
neither reinforces the status quo nor reflects private prejudices or ideology?

Is there a progressive principle of social value? The argument of this paper is that instrumental value theory, drawn principally from the Deweyian contribution to the neoinstitutionalist tradition, does provide an affirmative answer for a democratic society. Using it, we can move beyond 'functional nihilism', ethical relativism and ethical absolutism.

That principle of social value, as I have formulated it, is this: choose or do that which provides for 'the continuity of human life and the noninvidious recreation of community through the instrumental use of knowledge'.[13] Such provision represents progressive regulatory change; its impairment or rejection represents regressive regulatory change. I have discussed this principle of social value at length elsewhere.[14]

Its relevance for a democratic society, however, merits reiteration. Here, again following Dewey, I perceive democracy to mean that those who receive the incidence of policy must have and retain ultimate discretion over that policy. Restraints and constraints are self-imposed through responsive and responsible political participation and may be revised as the evolving consensus dictates.[15] An instrumentalist can regard the democratic process as an efficient means through which to identify and promote regulatory changes which, by continuing and successive approximation, will generally tend to reflect an implicit use of the instrumental value principle. They will represent progressive changes. Stated another way, those who experience consequences of problems have a continuing and pragmatic interest in experimenting with reforms (i.e. regulations) so long as they and the problems persist. This processual deliberative effort can succeed only if the political process is and remains responsive and regulated, providing for wide and non-invidious participation.

Although the three main conceptual elements of the instrumental value principle – continuity, non-invidiousness, and instrumental use – are normally regarded as interdependent and mutually reinforcing, it will be useful, as an analytical exercise, to separate them. Thus we can show, historically, how broad patterns of regulatory efforts in the economy have, often successfully, emphasized one or other of these elements. To these three, I will add examples of judgments that have provided continuing democratic control over regulatory reform efforts. The fundamental point to be made is this: much of the regulatory experience in the American economy over the last century has been a common sense, if unacknowledged, implementation of the instrumental value principle. Given present constraints, the examples provided can only be illustrative.

A caveat. I am well aware that a number of the regulations introduced did not wholly accomplish the envisioned intent. Some were subsequently modified, some were subverted, some abandoned. Indeed, a few may well have been regressively designed to create invidious differential advantages for the few. But overall, most of the economic and social regulations introduced in recent decades, prior to the Carter-Reagan-Bush deregulation era, were generally fashioned to serve instrumental functions.

III   INSTRUMENTAL VALUE AND REGULATORY EXPERIENCE

Instrumental judgments reflect the application of warranted knowledge to the discretionary fashioning of effective institutional structures that correlate and organize the social order. Ceremonial judgments, on the contrary, reflect a deference to established institutions as customary or traditional, to discrimination in the participatory access and options of people, and to coercive control by the few over the many. The instrumental value principle, as noted, affirms the continuity of human life, the noninvidious recreation of community and the instrumental use of knowledge through the democratic process. Institutional adjustments reflecting this normative focus will often appear as new or modified regulations of social and economic behaviour.

Regulations concerning the Continuity of Human Life

The continuity of human life obviously depends importantly on access to quality medical care and an environment as free as possible from threats to physical well-being. Thus, progressive regulations reflect a continuing concern to make emerging medical knowledge and treatment widely available, and to eliminate or reduce hazards to health. These regulations include Medicare coverage, occupational safety protections, food and drug legislation, cost containment and pricing rules, public health measures, rules governing smoke emissions, water and air pollution, and the like. The regulation of medical quality may have a mixed impact, however. A progressive licensing measure seeking to provide protection against incompetent medical practice may inadvertently provide licensees with regressive differential economic power and market control.

Secondly, in any exchange economy the continuity of human life hinges on the adequacy of money income flows.[16] Given prevailing levels of economic interdependence, public provision of income maintenance transfers has become commonplace in all major economies. Regulatory structures addressing this concern include, for example, social security, unemployment compensation, aid to dependent children, aid to the blind and disabled, and negative income tax. However, given the political influence of the 'privileged', we have also introduced regressive regulatory measures to benefit the rich through transfer schemes, for example ones that allow tax avoidance through tax shelters and subsidies through tax expenditures.

Regulations concerning the Noninvidious Recreation of Community

If, as I suggest, economic power is primarily exercised to serve vested, private and self-serving 'interests', thus generating invidious discrimination, then progressive regulations are required, in the public interest, to control such power. If not, this legally or extra-legally acquired power may have deleterious effects: it may well reduce levels of money or real income for the relatively powerless, generate excessive levels of costs and prices, deny access to employment and education, and increase inequality of income distribution. Centres of power will clearly resist efforts which would hold them accountable for their actions. The centuries-old concern to regulate monopoly power in all its forms is a prime example.[17] Regulatory measures addressing this area of concern include rules governing the operations of commercial banks, savings and loans, and insurance companies; control over interest rates and administered prices, antitrust legislation and the like.

But here again, a mixed outcome may occur. Control over 'natural monopolies' through public utility regulation – presumed to cover prices and quality and availability of service – is sometimes subverted. Corporate professional/political forces may dominate such regulatory commissions in the quest for pricing power, higher profits and protection of market shares (as noted in Chapter 5). The perverse use of neoclassically grounded criteria regarding rate structures, including the commissions' normative use of the competitive model, transforms progressive into regressive regulatory rules.

If we turn now to regulations which aim to remove or reduce invidious discrimination rooted in such human differences as race, gender, age, ancestry, ethnicity and the like, a different broad range of constraints has evolved to help create and maintain community. Included would be affirmative action programmes, fair housing legislation, constraints against discrimination in employment, and the removal of discriminatory access to public education, among others. Regressive corruption of these efforts is found in pro forma, rather than de facto, compliance, and in the reintroduction of invidious discrimination among and between ethnic groups themselves.

Regulations concerning the Instrumental Use of Knowledge

All regulatory measures that contribute to the creation of warranted knowledge and its efficient use in problem solving are here viewed as progressive and reflective of instrumental use. Regulations and policies as various as the following illustrate the point: public education including mandatory attendance rules, public funding of research in universities, public funding of experimental industrial production efforts, and the education and skill enhancement provided by the historic G.I. Bills of Rights.

However, mixed outcomes may again occur, for example concerning patent rights. A progressive regulatory measure designed to encourage invention and innovation, by conferring discretion for a specified period on 'the sole true inventor', is sometimes converted into an elaborate regressive constraint. Corporate hegemony over knowledge generated and held under patent regulations may be encapsulated and withheld from wider use as a market-share control device.[18]

Provisions for Assuring Democratic Control

If the political process is to provide for democratic control of the creation and use of regulations, it, too, must be structured by rules and constraints that provide (1) access to relevant knowledge and (2) power and opportunity to act on that knowledge in political terms.[19]

Regulations addressed to these concerns include voter rights to registration, etc., stipulated limits on campaign spending and reporting requirements, rules that provide for secret ballots, recurrent elections, rotating terms of office, access to legislator performance information, and the creation and operation of 'watch dog' bodies including, for example, the Government Accounting Office. That these progressive regulations are sometimes corrupted by negative campaigning, voter fraud practices, political action committee financing, etc., needs no elaboration here.

In sum, my claim is that much of the social and economic regulatory reform efforts of this century, until a decade or so ago, implicitly reflected a common sense employment of progressive instrumental criteria in identifying the public interest, in defining problems and in proposing new rules and regulations. That regressive regulatory efforts, and especially subversion of progressive regulation, has also occurred, is acknowledged. I consider the recent deregulation campaign to be an abandonment of this progressive tradition and a 'return' to mainly regressive, neoclassically warranted, but generally irrelevant, criteria. But the democratic community, in assessing the consequences of regressive changes, is already rediscovering which direction really is 'forward'.

NOTES

1. Trebing (1984), p. 353.
2. Bush (1988), pp. 150–51.

3. Samuels (1978), pp. 100–113.
4. Ibid, p. 113.
5. Tool (1986), pp. 94–101; Schmid (1987), pp. 210–18.
6. Swaney (1987); Söderbaum (1987), pp. 146–53.
7. Trebing (1984), pp. 356–63.
8. Samuels (1978), p. 108.
9. Tool (1986), pp. 104–25.
10. Samuels (1978), pp. 111–13.
11. Samuels (1978).
12. Dewey [1927] (1946), p. 126.
13. Tool [1979] (1985), p. 293.
14. Ibid, chs. 14 and 15; see also, Tool (1986).
15. Tool [1979] (1985), ch. 10.
16. For a perceptive development of the concept of economic security, see Waller (1992), pp. 153–71.
17. Montgomery (1940), p. 13, cites an early effort to regulate monopoly (in the manufacture of playing cards) in the case of *Allen vs. Darcy*, Court of the King's Bench, 1602.
18. Hamilton (1957), ch. 3.
19. Myers (1956), pp. 236–44.

REFERENCES

Bush, Paul D. (1988), 'The Theory of Institutional Change' in Marc R. Tool (ed.), *Evolutionary Economics I: Foundations of Institutional Thought*, Armonk, N.Y.: M.E. Sharpe.

Dewey, John [1927] (1946), *The Public and Its Problems*, Chicago: Gateway Books.

Hamilton, Walton (1957), *The Politics of Industry*, New York: Alfred Knopf.

Montgomery, Robert H. (1940), *The Brimstone Game*, New York: Vanguard Press.

Myers, Francis M. (1956), *The Warfare of Democratic Ideals*, Yellow Springs, Ohio: Antioch Press.

Samuels, Warren J. (1978), 'Normative premises in regulatory theory', *Journal of Post Keynesian Economics*, **1**, Fall.

Schmid, A. Allan (1987), *Property, Power, and Public Choice*, 2nd ed., New York: Praeger.

Söderbaum, Peter (1987), 'Environmental management: a non-traditional approach', *Journal of Economic Issues*, **21**, March.

Swaney, James A. (1987), 'Valuing the environment: a critique of benefit-cost analysis'; a paper presented at meetings of the Association for Social Economics, Chicago (unpublished).

Tool, Marc R. [1979] (1985), *The Discretionary Economy: A Normative Theory of Political Economy*, Boulder: Westview Press.

Tool, Marc R. (1986), *Essays in Social Value Theory*, Armonk, N.Y.: M.E. Sharpe.

Trebing, Harry M. (1984), 'Public control of enterprise: neoclassical assault and neoinstitutional reform; remarks upon receipt of the Veblen-Commons award', *Journal of Economic Issues*, **18**, June.

Waller, William T. Jr. (1992), 'Economic Security and the State', in William M. Dugger and William T. Waller Jr. (eds), *The Stratified State: Radical Institutionalist Theories of Participation and Duality*, Armonk, N.Y.: M.E. Sharpe.

PART III

Economic Systems

8.   The evolution of economic systems*

All major economies are everywhere engaged in a systemic evolution in pursuit of economic transformation. The character, credibility and relevance of the theory employed to initiate, guide and appraise this evolution are fundamentally determinative of outcomes actually experienced. Accordingly, the significance of such inquiry and problem solving endeavours can hardly be exaggerated.

In this chapter, I briefly sketch fundamental theoretical characteristics of neoinstitutional economics and, in this context, develop the neoinstitutionalist argument that the problem-solving process itself accounts, in large measure, for the evolution of economic systems.[1] This commentary on the basic neoinstitutionalist perspective of social and economic change will undergird the concluding chapters in this volume that compare and assess analyses of and modifications in economic systems. Brief reiterations of some earlier identified premises and constructs will serve to clarify and reinforce pertinent aspects of the neoinstitutionalist paradigmatic approach.

Most are aware that institutional economics began in the United States with Thorstein Veblen's writings in the late 1890s.[2] In this century, a distinctive and comprehensive institutionalist literature has evolved that incorporates this Veblenian legacy, among others. In the last 30 years, in particular, this literature has become more extensive, sharply focused and tightly integrated.[3] I draw here on some of these recent contributions: first, in reviewing the historical perspective and, second, in explaining the evolution of economies.

I   THE NEOINSTITUTIONALIST PERSPECTIVE

The purpose of neoinstitutionalist analysis is to provide an evidentially grounded, causal account of processual reality. The *social process* in all its complexity is the object of inquiry. This social process is evolutionary and developmental,

*Originally published in Kurt Dopfer and Karl-F. Raible (eds) (1990), *The Evolution of Economic Systems: Essays in Honor of Ota Sik*, New York: St Martin's Press. Permission granted by St. Martin's Press (New York) for republication within the US and by The Macmillan Press, Ltd. (Basingstoke UK) for republication elsewhere.

but not necessarily cyclical, episodic or epochal. Two continuing and interrelated functions or categories of activity dominate this process: the economic process of social provisioning – the generation and distribution of goods and services – and the political process of determining and administering social policy. Although separately identifiable as continuing and dominating aspects of the social process, they are everywhere structurally interdependent and intertwined. The neoinstitutionalist focus is primarily on the evolutionary transformation of this institutional fabric called political economy.

In all cultures, institutions organize behaviour in pursuit of differing facets of these interdependent economic and political functions. *Institutions* are here defined as socially prescribed patterns of correlated human behaviour and attitudes. However obscure the origin, all institutions are formed by human choice; none is specified by 'nature'; none is divinely invoked. They are, in principle, amenable to revision. Institutions reflect the acquired value structure of the society.[4] They represent historically successive determinations of what ought to be the controlling patterns of behaviour.

Socially correlated patterns of behaviour are internalized by individuals and become habitual. Institutions, then, are made up of habits but are not determined by habits. Being constituted of habits, institutions are often resistant to change. Rules, codes, customs and attitudes, once established and embedded as habits, define expected behaviour and are presumed to be continuing. However, when expectations are unfulfilled, questions of how come? or why so? arise. As people reflect on the consequences produced by existing institutional structure, they are prompted to appraise habitual behaviour. They come to see a difference between what is and what ought to be. Those with discretion in the community may decide that ineffectual or destructive consequences from the performance of existing institutional forms should be corrected through institutional adjustment.

To give meaning or content to 'ineffectual' or 'destructive' consequences – even to distinguish between 'what is' and 'what ought to be' – requires the use of normative criteria of judgment. As economic systems evolve through problem solving, the character of the institutional adjustments that comprise that evolution is specified by the criteria of appraisal chosen and employed.

But in explaining the evolution of economic systems, institutions cannot themselves credibly serve as criteria for choosing institutions. To propose the existing structure of 'what is' as the determiner or criterion of 'what ought to be' is to reaffirm the status quo and, in effect, to deny the existence of real economic problems. Obviously, pertinent structural change cannot be effectively conceived and implemented until *after* actual institutional malfunctions have been identified and understood.

Similarly, a priori patterns for economic systems – for example, the ideological models of capitalism, socialism or communism – cannot serve as criteria; they appear rather as utopian designs. Their *basic* system character is given; their distinguishing institutional components are not amenable to revision. They are, at best, of only remote or accidental relevance to the continuing real-world task of making choices among institutional options. The recent insistence that 'reform' be conceived as a return to Friedmanesque free market allocation (as in the Reagan and Thatcher administrations in the 1980s) is an example of this illusory quest. The normative use of the competitive market model, as I explore more fully in the following chapter, is inadmissible and irrelevant precisely because it will not permit the identification or resolution of actual problems of institutional malfunctioning.[5]

The *modification* of institutional structures – institutional adjustment – is the process through which any community solves its economic and political problems. Problem solving is accomplished by revamping the problematic elements of prevailing institutions to bring them into congruity with what the expanding fund of reliable knowledge indicates is feasible and constructive. The evolution of any economic system is punctuated with institutional modifications initiated to correct what is perceived as inefficient performance, insensitive direction or pervasive sabotage of the economic process. What is the source of such institutional modification?

According to the neoinstitutionalist view of human agency, discretionary persons assume the role of initiators of evolutionary change. 'Human nature' is an emergent product of continuing and complex interactions between genetically equipped human organisms and their physical and cultural environment. This genetic inheritance permits the development of a lingual facility, cognitive capability and social interdependence. But specific behaviours, beliefs, motivations and attitudes are acquired through cultural conditioning. 'All socially relevant behavior is learned and is, for the most part, habitual.'[6] Cultures impose attitudinal and behavioural configurations on genetically endowed and educable beings. That educability permits subsequent critique and revision of cultural impositions. People are capable of developing the capacity to perceive means-consequence connections implied in such assessments. This developmental potentiality is the neoinstitutionalist referent for *rationality*. (There is no reliance here on maximizing assumptions.) Men and women, to the extent permitted or encouraged by cultural constraints, choose among available options; in their choosing, they change both themselves and the cultural context of their own modes of living and livelihood. This indicates, then, that a credible explanation of the evolution of economic systems cannot deny human agency. No 'law of motion' of society, no geographic or psychological determinism, no 'great man' theory of history will suffice. The evolution of economic systems is primarily a function of the exercise of human will. The questions of whose will governs and what purposes are served comprise the domain of inquiry in the political process.

The neoinstitutionalist mode of inquiry is addressed to an understanding of causality; prediction is of secondary interest. Inquiry originates with the appearance of doubt about the adequacy of received explanations or of expected behaviour; through evidentially grounded and logically coherent analysis, it seeks to restore congruity of understanding and experience. As I noted in Chapter 2, inquiry incorporates the generation and examination of relevant evidence, the creative formulation of possible explanatory hypotheses, the use of such hypotheses to guide inquiry and sharpen its focus, the election of the hypothetical account that most accurately, simply and completely explains the causal phenomena under review, and the tentative assertion of truth (for Dewey, 'warranted assertability') as the outcome of inquiry. Recourse to inductive, deductive *and* abductive modes of reasoning is commonplace. Such inquiry is not characteristically dialectical, episodic or equilibrium-seeking. It is a continuing processual juxtaposing of evidential assessment and theoretical accounting.

Inquiry is value-driven in its concern with problem solving. The latter is accomplished by revamping the obstructive elements of the prevailing institutional structure of provisioning in accord with what the expanding fund of reliable knowledge permits as options. The significance of this or any social inquiry perspective is derived, by common consent, from its demonstrable relevance for problem solving in this sense.

The scope of neoinstitutional analysis then, is not pre-defined by, or confined to, narrow academic disciplines as such; the concern is always necessarily with political economy. The breadth of inquiry is set by, and adjusted to, the emerging and encompassing recognition of the loci and significance of actual determinants of real problems as confronted. The outcomes of such inquiry are provisional and tentative; what is being sought are instrumentally-warranted elements of reliable knowledge. Inquiry, so conceived, will explain the evolution of economic systems.

Inquiry is value-laden. Since choices must be made at every stage of inquiry, and since such choices logically require the use of criteria, value judgments are endemic in all social inquiry. The inquiry mode of neoinstitutionalists, then, is both positive in its pursuit of the causal determinants of what is going on, and normative in its explicit consideration of what ought to be done to define and resolve problems. The conventional dichotomy divorcing the positive from the normative is wholly rejected. Institutionalist inquiry into the problem-solving process that explains the evolution of economic systems must, then, be evaluative as well as analytic.[7]

II   THE EVOLUTION OF ECONOMIC SYSTEMS

In the context of the neoinstitutionalist perspective as described above, it is now possible directly to address what is meant by 'the evolution of economic systems'. How can their evolution be explained? Can the character of evolution be guided? Provisional answers are provided by the neoinstitutionalist theory of social change.[8]

An economic *system* is the structural composition of the myriad interrelated institutions through which people organize and correlate behaviour to carry on a host of social functions that sustain and enhance the life processes of the community. Among these functions are the production of food and fibre, the determination of exchange ratios, the distribution of income, the generation and dissemination of knowledge, the education of the young, the provision of health and medical care, the communication of word and image, the protection of environmental quality and ecological balances, and the like.[9] The generation and delivery of such products and services require specified institutional arrangements. The extant economic system reflects the continuance of cultural heritage, past judgments of public and private discretionary agents, and complexities and constraints imposed by external powers and circumstance.

In any modern economic system, the institutional structure is constantly being transformed. Its emergent character does not reflect either an autogenetic quest for equilibrium, or accommodation to a law of succession of 'modes of production and exchange', or the implementation of a preemptive utopian design. Neither is it merely an ad hoc pragmatic arrangement. Neoinstitutionalists see the economic system as a product of deliberative, discretionary actions that are in principle knowable and reflect value judgments. They customarily initiate inquiry in social value theory through consideration of the Veblenian dichotomy.

This dichotomy appears in one form or another in all of Veblen's writings.[10] A representative formulation appears in his *Leisure Class*: 'Institutions ... may be roughly distinguished into two classes or categories, according as they serve one or the other of two divergent purposes of economic life[:] ... acquisition or production ... pecuniary or industrial [activity] ... [an] invidious or non-invidious economic interest.'[11] What is especially significant in this context is the distinction between ceremonial and technological behaviour and institutions.[12]

In a paper that significantly refines and extends this dichotomy, Paul D. Bush has written the following: 'The institutional structure of any society incorporates two systems of value: the ceremonial and the instrumental, each of which has its own logic and method of validation. While these two value systems are inherently incompatible, they are intertwined within the institutional structure through a complex set of relationships.'[13] The distinction between these two value systems is a central construct in the neoinstitutionalist explanation of the evolution of economic systems. Bush continues: 'Ceremonial values correlate behavior within the institution by providing the standards of judgment for invidious distinctions, which prescribe status, differential privileges, and master-servant relationships, and warrant the exercise of power by one social class over another'. In contrast, 'instrumental values correlate behavior by providing the standards of judgment by which tools and skills are employed in the application of evidentially warranted knowledge to the problem-solving processes of the community'.[14]

Note that *both* sorts of value judgments are reflected in the institutional structure, although their relative importance will vary with time and circumstance. Behaviour may thus be wholly ceremonial, wholly instrumental or, more likely, may contain elements of each mode. Either behavioural mode may incorporate elements of the other, but the value traits are discrete and dichotomous. Examples of wholly ceremonial behaviour would include fascist use of coercive power or parental child abuse. Examples of wholly instrumental behaviour would include appeals to reason in political deliberation or teaching lingual skills to children. Examples of behaviour reflecting both modes would include defence of democratic institutions (preservation of tradition *and* providing genuine choice) or the insistence that children obey school rules (exercise of unilateral authority *and* provision of a safe environment). Ceremonial behaviour will be correlated by a ceremonial value, as in the invidious use of coercive power. Instrumental behaviour will be correlated by an instrumental value, as in the furtherance of political freedom and of effectual reflective communication. Where a ceremonial value correlates both ceremonial and instrumental behaviour, Bush argues that 'ceremonial encapsulation' of instrumental behaviour occurs.[15] An example would be fascist control of the instrumental flow of real income: provisioning must not threaten the continuity of autocratic control. Available knowledge and technology must be rendered 'ceremonially adequate'. With encapsulation, ceremonial considerations will dominate instrumental ones.

Some measure of 'ceremonial dominance' will be found in all cultures. Ceremonial dominance defines the degree of permissiveness a culture provides for instrumental behaviour and judgment. An 'index of ceremonial dominance', then, would indicate the extent to which a culture will permit its available instrumentally-warranted knowledge to be utilized. It follows that the higher the index of ceremonial dominance, the more retarded the evolution of an economic system.

For an economic system to evolve progressively, the levels of ceremonial dominance must be reduced by the substitution of instrumental patterns of behaviour for ceremonial patterns. An economic problem exists, for example, when the flow of real income and/or its equitable distribution are impeded; in other words, where unemployment, poverty, discrimination and/or stagnation demonstrably prevail. The neoinstitutionalist approach is to discover, through empirical research and theoretical analysis, the levels and character of ceremonial dominance that generate these conditions and to seek ways to enhance the prevalence of instrumental correlation of behaviour by formulating implementing institutional modifications.

The dynamic element in the evolution of economic systems is the growth of reliable (instrumentally-warranted) knowledge and its application as technology to the productive process. Although it overstates the case to say that gunpowder destroyed feudalism and that the steam engine spawned capitalism, such innovations continue to modify the community's knowledge fund and technological applications, to stimulate fresh consideration of the adequacy of existing institutions, and to encourage reflection on new options of coordination. While the attribution of causal potency for evolutionary change to class conflict, great men, entrepreneurial spirit or 'innate' greed may provide political strategies of limited usefulness, none offers an instrumentally credible account.

This technological continuum has cultural origins and roots. As Bush explains: 'Technology for Veblen was a process that arose out of the human proclivity for workmanship and the exercise of intellectual curiosity. It was embodied in the tool-skill nexus of problem-solving activities. The essence of technological change, therefore, was the change in the "prevalent habits of thought" associated with a given state of the arts and sciences.'[16] All the evidence appears to confirm that 'technological innovation is developmental in the sense of being cumulative, combinatorial, and accelerating in character'.[17] Given its cumulative attribute, the fund of knowledge that underlies technology is expansive and irreversible. The interdependence and mutual promotion of tools, skills and ideas expand the knowledge fund. Such growth is the source of the emergence and identification of problems as people, with knowledge, perceive a difference between what is and what might be. At the same time, the 'knowledge fund' is the primary resource on which thoughtful people draw in efforts to resolve problems.

The community's fund of knowledge, then, 'is either "encapsulated" within ceremonial patterns or "embodied" within instrumental patterns of behavior'.[18] But it is the community's index of ceremonial dominance that determines the extent to which the knowledge fund – the source and sanction for instrumental behaviour – is made available for problem solving purposes. With ceremonial dominance, only that part of the knowledge fund that can be reconciled with the existing ceremonial value structure will be implemented. Instrumental knowledge is encapsulated and made to serve invidiously-based power systems and their status demands.[19] To the extent that such conditions prevail, the evolution of economic systems is sabotaged and misdirected to serve ceremonial or invidious purposes. The imposition of a test of ceremonial adequacy overrides instrumental valuing.

When the index of ceremonial dominance is high enough to permit ceremonial encapsulation of important elements of the knowledge fund, instrumentally-warranted patterns of behaviour may be replaced by ceremonial or invidious patterns. Where this happens, there is *regressive* social and economic change. When, however, with a given stock of knowledge, instrumental patterns of behaviour displace ceremonial or invidious patterns, *progressive* institutional change occurs. Problem solving is accomplished only with progressive change. The *character* of the evolution of an economic system is thus reflected in the distinction between progressive and regressive change and hinges on the degree of ceremonial dominance that prevails.

The *rate* of progressive change is largely determined by three considerations (more fully explored in Chapter 9 below).[20] The first concerns the availability of knowledge. Unless a culture permits and encourages the growth of reliable knowledge, including a willingness to borrow and/or exchange information and techniques with other cultures so as to gain an insightful understanding of the actual determinants of problems, progressive change will be severely constricted. The stock and sophistication of the knowledge fund, however acquired, will define the scope and character of investigations of problematic conditions. A paucity of knowledge will limit progressive evolution.

A second factor concerns the ability of a community to absorb and adapt to new knowledge and technology. Changes in habits of thought and behaviour which might be required in the shift from ceremonial to instrumental values are always difficult. Unless extensive efforts are made to inform the relevant communities of what changes are contemplated, why they are thought necessary, what their implications are (that is, how adequately people will be able to function under the new prescriptions), and unless the prior approval or acquiescence of those affected is secured, change will be resisted, sometimes vehemently. A top-down imposition of rule changes will usually retard or prevent progressive evolution.

The third limitation concerns the timing and extent of change. So far as possible, initiating change must be 'minimally dislocative'. While any change is disruptive in some measure, successful instrumental change must be limited to that which is demonstrably essential for problem resolution. Facets of the economy not suffering significant invidious impairment should not be disturbed. Massive, convulsive, economy-wide changes usually fail to reduce ceremonial dominance because they are excessively dislocative.

In sum, the neoinstitutionalist theory of social change, supported by fundamental tenets of neoinstitutionalist thought, introduces non-traditional and pertinent tools of inquiry, identifies the dynamic element in the transformation of economies, provides a causal explanation of how and why the evolution of economic systems occurs, and offers credible principles for the normative assessment of economic change. Given such understanding, the policy agenda for the discretionary management of the progressive evolution of an economic system can be fashioned with both confidence and humanity.

NOTES

1. I note at the outset that the Veblen-Dewey-Ayres-based neoinstitutional economics addressed here is fundamentally incompatible with contemporary, neoclassically based 'new institutionalism', public choice analysis, and the neo-Austrian perspective.
2. After Veblen, major contributors include John Dewey, John R. Commons, Wesley Clair Mitchell, Walton H. Hamilton, John Maurice Clark, Clarence E. Ayres, Allan G. Gruchy, J. Fagg Foster, John Kenneth Galbraith; also, since the 1960s, many scholars in the Association for Evolutionary Economics and the Association for Institutional Thought. Contributions to this mode of inquiry of Europeans – Gunnar Myrdal, Karl Polanyi, K. William Kapp – and others have also been most important.
3. A sampling of this more recent literature would include: Munkirs (1985), Tool (1986), Tool (1988a), Tool (1988b), Hodgson (1988), Samuels (1988), Dugger (1989), Dugger and Waller (1992), Hodgson (1993), Tool (1993), Hodgson, Samuels and Tool (1994). See also recent issues of the *Journal of Economic Issues*.
4. Bush (1988), p. 128.
5. Tool (1986), pp. 104–25.
6. Bush (1988), p. 127.
7. Tool [1979] (1985), pp. 274–336.
8. In this section, I draw extensively on the work of Paul D. Bush. See Bush (1988); Bush (1986), pp. 25–45.
9. Tool [1979] (1985), pp. 105–37.
10. Listed in Tool (1986), pp. 34–7.
11. Veblen [1899](1934), p. 208.
12. Veblen [1915] (1939).
13. Bush (1988), p. 129.
14. Ibid, p. 130.
15. Ibid, p. 134.
16. Ibid, p. 137.
17. Ibid.
18. Ibid, p. 141.
19. For a consideration of 'past-binding', 'future-binding' and '"Lysenko" type' forms of 'ceremonial encapsulation', see Bush (1988), pp. 142–9.
20. Bush (1988), pp. 155–7; Tool [1979] (1985), pp. 172–6.

REFERENCES

Bush, Paul D. (1986), 'On the concept of ceremonial encapsulation', *Review of Institutional Thought*, **3**, December.
Bush, Paul D. (1988), 'The Theory of Institutional Change', in Marc R. Tool (ed.), *Evolutionary Economics I: Foundations of Institutional Thought*, Armonk, N.Y.: M.E. Sharpe.

Dugger, William M. (1989), *Corporate Hegemony*, New York: Greenwood Press.
Dugger, William M. and Waller, William T. Jr. (1992) (eds), *The Stratified State*, Armonk, N.Y.: M.E. Sharpe.
Hodgson, Geoffrey M. (1988), *Economics and Institutions*, Cambridge: Polity Press.
Hodgson, Geoffrey M. (1993), *Economics and Evolution*, Cambridge: Polity Press.
Hodgson, Geoffrey M., Samuels, Warren J., and Tool, Marc R. (eds) (1994), *The Elgar Companion to Institutional and Evolutionary Economics*, Aldershot: Edward Elgar.
Munkirs, John (1985), *The Transformation of American Capitalism*, Armonk, N.Y.: M.E. Sharpe.
Samuels, Warren J. (ed.) (1988), *Institutional Economics*, Aldershot: Edward Elgar.
Tool, Marc R. [1979] (1985), *The Discretionary Economy*, Boulder: Westview Press.
Tool, Marc R. (1986), *Essays in Social Value Theory*, Armonk, N.Y.: M.E. Sharpe.
Tool, Marc R. (1988a) (ed.), *Evolutionary Economics I: Foundations of Institutional Thought*, Armonk, N.Y.: M.E. Sharpe.
Tool, Marc R. (1988b) (ed.), *Evolutionary Economics II: Institutional Theory and Policy*, Armonk, N.Y.: M.E. Sharpe.
Tool, Marc R. (1993) (ed.), *Institutional Economics: Theory, Method, Policy*, Dordrecht: Kluwer Academic Publishers.
Veblen, Thorstein B. [1899] (1934), *The Theory of the Leisure Class*, New York: Modern Library.
Veblen, Thorstein B. [1915] (1939), *Imperial Germany and the Industrial Revolution*, New York: Viking Press.

9. Institutional adjustment and instrumental value*

Only the wholesale, complete replacement of ... [the Soviet command economy's] defining characteristics opens room for an alternative, market-based system. ... An entire world must be discarded, including all of its economic and most of its social and political institutions. ... Radical reformers are correct to seek the total replacement of the traditional system. Richard Ericson[1]

Russia has had a plethora of big bang crash programmes of impossibilist technical reform, none of which has survived – and whose failure is beginning to discredit the whole idea of a market economy. Will Hutton[2]

The significance and implications of current efforts to 'stabilize', 'privatize' and 'restructure' the political economies of Eastern Europe and the Commonwealth of Independent States can, of course, hardly be exaggerated. In most such countries, after three to five years of dramatic institutional adjustments, 'production is in sharp decline, the distribution of income is worsening, unemployment is increasing'.[3] Indeed the percentage *decrease* in output for the period from 1989 to 1992 for nine countries in Eastern Europe ranged from 17 to 51 per cent; the average drop was 29 per cent![4] Political instability continues. Did an effort to implement Ericson's observation (above) generate the consequences Hutton perceives?

The conventional wisdom is that these economies must be 'reformed' by transforming them from inefficient command and planning systems into efficient capitalist and free market-governed systems. It is alleged that such 'reform' is essential if they are ever to join the ranks of, and compete with, modern Western and Asian industrial economies. This paper raises questions about the meaning of 'reform' as reflected in the triadic recipe (stabilize, privatize, restructure) of Western advisers.

While it is evident that leaders in Eastern Europe wish to establish economies similar to those in Western Europe – in a so-called 'return to Europe' – their Western advisers have successfully argued that the first phase must be the creation of 'a common core of market institutions found in all of Western

*Paper presented at meetings of the European Association for Evolutionary Political Economy, Barcelona, October 1993. Published in *Review of International Political Economy*, November 1994. Reprinted with permission .

Europe: private ownership protected by commercial law, a corporate structure of industry, an independent financial system, and so forth'.[5] It will be my argument that, with only quite modest modifications, this first phase involves the introduction of a neoclassical model of a free competitive economy, grounded largely in what R.H. Coase calls 'blackboard economics'. It is 'a system which lives in the minds of economists but not on earth'.[6] The fact that this model does not accurately characterize Western and Pacific Rim economies seems not to have been a deterrent to Western advisers.

The orthodox neoclassical views characterized here will be drawn primarily from the writings of Professor Jeffrey D. Sachs of Harvard University, who served in the early 1990s as a primary adviser to the governments of Poland, Russia and other Eastern European countries. Although Sachs contends that 'the current revolutions under way in Eastern Europe are not utopian, nor do they seek to impose a new social experiment as was the case in Lenin's revolution' and that 'today's revolutions are of a relentlessly pragmatic character',[7] he also insists that the 'core institutions' of capitalism must be installed as the first priority. Capitalism is the model sought.[8] His 'endpoint' is ideologically identified.[9]

Largely missing from both popular and professional deliberations and recommendations on the restructuring of economic systems in Eastern Europe and the Commonwealth of Independent States is the formulation and analytical use of *credible theories of institutional adjustment*. Surely it is one of the supreme ironies of the age that the neoclassical theoretical model of an economic system now being used to guide the transformation of command economies through 'shock therapy' is itself largely *devoid* of a credible theory of institutional adjustment and of applicable criteria for institutional choice.

Institutional adjustments require recourse to theoretical explanations of how institutional choices are and should be made. Obviously, to judge between institutional options requires that attention be given to the character of the structural choices made. Choosing an institutional structure can never be undertaken without criteria. Discourse on institutional adjustment, including its derivative policy recommendations, is, and must be, both positive and normative, factual and valuational. This chapter is addressed to institutional choice and adjustment and the criteria of social value incorporated therein.

More particularly, in Part I, I will present major tenets and principles of a contemporary neoinstitutional theory of institutional adjustment. That framework will then be used, in Part II, to present and appraise a heavily abbreviated version of the mainstream neoclassical position, especially as it is reflected in Western advice for Eastern European economies. Part III offers brief concluding observations. Space constraints preclude consideration of specific circumstances in, or problems of, individual national economies.

I TENETS FOR A NEOINSTITUTIONAL THEORY OF INSTITUTIONAL ADJUSTMENT

The tenets of neoinstitutionalist theory introduced below are primary and foundational. They are drawn from multiple disciplines including philosophy, political theory and sociology, as well as from what is ordinarily construed to be institutional economics. It will be helpful to recognize at the outset, as Kurt Dopfer has observed, that 'what is exogenous to neoclassical theory constitutes the very theoretical core of institutional economics. Just as one would not expect an atheist to demonstrate the metaphysical validity of religion, so one does not expect a neoclassical economist to make institutions a topic of theoretical inquiry.'[10] A comparative absence of institutional *theory* in orthodoxy notwithstanding,[11] neoclassicists' advocacy of 'stabilization', 'privatization' and 'restructuring' of Eastern European economies *quite obviously* constitutes a comprehensive programme of institutional adjustment.

I turn now to six neoinstitutional tenets which contribute to an applicable theory of institutional adjustment. Considered in turn are principles relating to human agency, creation of institutional structure, problem solving, loci of discretion, criteria of judgment, and conditions facilitating institutional adjustment.

Human Agency

The human agent[12] is a physical and cultural product of her/his environment, but also is discretionary in guiding and shaping that context. As choosers and actors, agents make institutional adjustments reflecting and modifying the cultural fabric – mores, folkways, structures, values – of which they are a product.[13]

Agents are educable. Evolutionary transformations have enhanced human capacities for reflective and cognitive apprehension of causal reality. Rationality is the capability to perceive means/consequence connections, including circular and cumulative causation. 'Cognitive development' and 'cognitive facilitation' enhance reflective and judgmental capacities.[14] Developmental self-consciousness permits the agent to define a social space or context, acquire an individual identity in that social context, and exercise causal rationality as a discretionary agent. Motivations are genetically rooted as drives but are culturally configured and appraised, not antecedently given. Tastes and preferences are acquired as learned attributes; their origin and character are of analytical significance. Maturation of perception is enhanced by the pursuit of causal understanding of uncertainties and judgmental responses thereto in all aspects of experience.

Agents create knowledge. Acquisition and use of lingual, cognitive, analytical and communicative skills generate a cumulative stock of common, and increasingly more extensive and complex, knowledge. Warranted knowledge – logically coherent and grounded in evidence – cumulatively expands through imaginative tool-and-idea combinations and becomes an ever more elaborate communal resource with which to enhance learning and guide behaviour. Technological knowledge is interdependent with, indeed a facet of, warranted knowledge generally and reflects the application of such knowledge and created tools (material and conceptual) in problem-solving experience.

Agents are problem-solvers. They are continuously engaged in appraising factual reality and in adapting to and modifying circumstances in their quest for continuity of culture and experience. Their behaviour is habit-ridden but not habit-determined. Discretion exists regarding which habits to continue. They make choices of institutional adjustments reflecting these cognitive, habitual and developmental capacities and proclivities.

Agents in Eastern Europe are not atypical in reflecting the habits of mind and regularities of behaviour specific to their respective environs and history. A fundamental precondition for institutional adjustment is clear recognition of these distinctive and conditioned behavioural patterns, attitudes, motivations and loyalties. A fundamental condition for institutional adjustment is the extensive and imaginative use of the acquired skills and knowledge of existing cadres of agents. Human agency is always a culturally and perceptually delimited exercise of judgment, even as it is a reflection of deliberate and analytical assessment.

Neoclassical reductionistic enthronement of rationality as a maximization of net returns does not begin to acknowledge or accommodate the profound complexities, subtleties and resiliencies of culturally rooted patterns of behaviour and judgment. Neither does it reflect or tap the extraordinarily creative and knowledge-based capabilities of agents. For neoinstitutionalists, rationality connotes causal comprehension and cognitive perceptiveness, not maximization.

In sum, human agents are culturally emergent, self-aware, educable, rational, discretionary and judgmental beings. An economy is their creation. 'The concept of "institutional man" is distinct from that of "neoclassical man" in that it recognizes a historical [reality and] plasticity of the preference and behavioural disposition of economic agents.'[15] Homo oeconomicus is a convenient, but misleading, fiction.

Creation of Institutional Structure

Economic orders or systems are comprised of institutions; as structural arrangements, they prescribe and proscribe behaviour in the pursuit of social and economic functions. An institution is 'any correlated behavior of agents that emerges either by self-organization or by policy prescription'.[16] Institutions determine patterns of coordination and cooperation. They generate order and a measure of predictability in economic activity; they provide for coherence and integration of behaviour. They appear as codes, rules, laws, conventions, attitudes and activity patterns. They give form and shape to conjoint conduct; they constrain and direct the conditioning of individuals. They constitute the structural fabric of the economic order.[17]

Any social and economic order must be created; it is not 'naturally' emergent or specified a priori. It is a product of human agency; there is no other credible source. However obscure the origins, however leaden the 'cake of custom', all institutions are products of human reflection, formulation and election. '[T]he fact remains that the new pattern of behaviour must be specified in conceptual form before it can emerge into the new pattern of behaviour.'[18] Although ideas for new or altered correlations, coordinations or patterns must originate with an individual mind, the actual introduction of new structures is generally accomplished through conjoint, always social, often formal or legal, means.

Three positions characterizing institutional change are now briefly explored in a methodological context. *Path-determinant* change implies that direction is significantly discretionary and moderately culturally embedded; the forward path is by design open, though referenced in the cultural past. *Path-dependent* change implies that direction is minimally discretionary and heavily culturally embedded; the forward path must reflect primary deference to tradition and history. *Path-independent* change implies that direction is significantly discretionary but not culturally embedded; the forward path is largely autonomous in its pattern of ideas and is constructed with minimal reference to culture or tradition.

Path-determinant initiations of prescriptive rules characterize the basic neoinstitutionalist position. The core of its instrumental inquiry process is a procedural recasting and retesting of the relevance and capacity of ideas to explain circular and cumulative causal reality. This inquiry is induced by doubts concerning both the adequacy and the continuity of current structure as it correlates behaviour. Inquiry generates new ideas and proposals for structural change from an emerging causal understanding of events and their consequences. One is 'locked in' to inquiry by the logic of instrumental analysis, but is not 'enslaved' by that commitment.[19] Utilization of instrumentalists' methodological procedures, the 'locking-in', is temporal and transitional; it is not perpetually ideationally path-dependent. The ideas themselves may appear to be path-independent, but they are derived from an instrumental inquiry process that is evidentially grounded, inherently self-sustaining, and, in reference both to analytical and experiential applications, self-correcting.

There is, however, a contextual aspect of path-dependency in this path-determinant view of change. It is the recognition that, as inquiry is initiated, any individual participant is inescapably dependent on the intellectual and material resources at hand. Such situational constraints/resources define the reality in which inquiry is begun and continued. Such contextual path-dependency need not preclude or narrowly channel inquiry; it merely locates the preliminary universe of discourse. Prior habits of mind and behaviour will of course be operative. In this sense, inquiry and recommendation are provisionally dependent on prior investigative paths. But the overarching path-determinant purpose of instrumental inquiry – to fashion analyses for neoinstitutionalist problem solving – prevents contextual path-dependency from becoming a dominant view. Since instrumental inquiry is processual rather than episodic, open rather than closed, contextual, ideational and material resource constraints are continuously under critical scrutiny in determination and redetermination of their pertinence and contribution. Their inquiry standing and role are always provisional and contingent, not fixedly given and exclusionary.

When doubt about institutional performance prompts questions, inquiry is initiated in context. A knowledge-based perception may emerge of a discrepancy between what is going on and what could be going on. The immediacy of its appearance may suggest spontaneous insight, but all proposals for institutional adjustment necessarily reflect emergent intellectual habits of factual ordering (inductive), hypotheses creation (abductive), consequence assessment (deductive) and the like. In this sense, institutional creation is always deliberate. Processually it is mutational; substantively it is addressed to problem solving. Path-determinant institutional change is thus inherently normative. Which direction *is* forward? The only forward path is that which provides for the cognitive maturation and continuity both of the discretionary agents and the community more generally. An instrumental creation of structure provides for this continuity through the growth and application of warranted knowledge. In contrast, the creation of structure to implement a utopian design, to perpetuate coercive power, to establish discriminatory arrangements or to erode free inquiry – these threaten or even preclude that maturation and continuity. The creation of structure is thus always *purposive*. At issue are *which* purposes and *whose* interests are to be served by institutional adjustment. Neoinstitutionalists support instrumental and noninvidious purposes democratically identified.

Path-dependent initiations of prescriptive rules (as the term is used herein) are largely limited in substance and scope to what is thought to reflect or be compatible with prior correlations. Basic parameters remain unassaulted; fundamental alterations of direction are not contemplated; the past continues to shape and limit, if not to preclude, options. It is a mores dependency.

Indeed, new knowledge and insights that threaten established belief may well be ceremonially encapsulated. Changes to preserve or buttress the status quo delimit, if not define, the adjustment agenda.

However, in some circumstances, efforts to manage and delimit path-dependent change may generate unpredictable consequences. The significance of small departures from established rule may be underestimated.[20] If these rule changes trigger recognition of long suppressed unresolved problems, chaotic results may be precipitated; unanticipated problems of major structural recasting may demand attention. Indeed, a condition of *path-indeterminacy* may ensue when path-dependent regularities are discredited and replacement (theory-driven, value-guided) adjustments are stillborn. In such a cognitive vacuum, chaos induced, fragmentary and expedient adaptations and accommodations, legal and extra-legal, may be attempted to restore order and forestall further erosions in the flow of real income, personal and communal. Any instrumental problem *solving*, however, would be accidental.

Path-independent initiations of institutional structure originate as logically derived, systemic reform packages without constraints of time, space or habit. They are perceived to be both conceptually autonomous and analytically rigorous, in the sense of independence from prior historical circumstance, ideational habit or behavioural regularity.[21] Here institutional adjustments become a matter of following a pan-cultural recipe, of applying a universal model, to any and every need for structural change. The introduction of the neoclassical design for Eastern Europe is an example. This model reflects the presumption of the feasibility of a revolutionary transformation of structure, of a sharp rupture, via 'market shock', from prior ordered relations; it is path-independent.

Problem Solving

The *raison d'être* of economic analysis is, and always has been, to contribute to the resolution of problems encountered in generating and distributing the flow of real income. The conception, then, of what a 'problem' is goes to the very heart of the discipline. And since no one can conceive of a problem, logically or pragmatically, except by recourse to criteria that distinguish between 'what is' and 'what ought to be', all such considerations must be normative as well as positive. Thus, the theoretical content of the discipline is inherently and inescapably social value laden.

Institutionalists, with and since Dewey, have both formally and informally rejected the normative-positive dualism as logically, analytically and experientially unacceptable. Neoinstitutionalists, with a policy-oriented paradigm, have long insisted that the concept of an economic problem must incorporate the appearance and recognition of disruption, discontinuity and lack of rapport in and among the institutional structures providing the flow of real income. Economic problems, one way or another, involve institutional malperformance or nonperformance. '[A]ll answers to all real economic problems necessarily take the form of institutional adjustment.'[22] Adjustments – as revisions, corrections or replacements in the institutional structure – are required to create or restore the correlation of behaviour that will provide for continuity, adequacy and efficiency in the flow of real income. Structural change is required to restore congruity of purpose and experience.

Eastern Europeans, of course, well understand that comprehensive structural change from a collapsed old order is mandatory. At issue is whether or not a comprehensive and convulsive change to neoclassical institutions will generate the required levels of growth and income.

Loci of Discretion over Institutional Adjustment

All economies are discretionary or managed. The structure and functioning of economic systems reflect the exercise of discretion by those who hold economic power – public and private.[23] The command economy–free economy dichotomy is a charade; the zero-power market is a fiction. All major markets are managed, but not all in the same way nor for the same purposes. As Grahame Thompson put it recently: 'The European economy is being, and will continue to be, "managed". In an era ... where there is a reaction against notions of active economic management ... all economies demand to be managed ... whatever the political or rhetorical intention, the temptation to managerially intervene is overwhelming.'[24]

In modern industrial economies, major institutional complexes (public and private) hold substantial discretion over structure and processes: price setting/coordination vehicles are everywhere operative;[25] corporate cooperation is commonplace.[26] Corporations are engaged in extensive interdependent ordering of markets through investment strategies, research and development programmes, joint ventures, strategic alliances and networks.[27] Competitive rivalry for market shares is continuous. More specifically, power is held (publicly and privately) and used to design and shape pricing practices as institutional structure. Examples include the administered pricing of resources and industrial products;[28] setting wage and salary levels;[29] determining transfer income shares;[30] pricing government services and products;[31] formulating agricultural price support subsidies;[32] and controlling utility prices through commission regulation.[33] Power is used to create and control technological innovation and its utilization; to influence the character and impact of economic regulations; to grant or withhold access to financial resources. At issue is the locus of power, the character of its use, and the consequences that result.

Central here is the recognition that holders of discretion determine who will have the opportunity to frame, and the political capacity to implement, institutional adjustments as shifts in economic policy. Except in totalitarian regimes, such power is normally shared between public and private loci of control. However, those who acquire the power (public or private) to grant or withhold the provision and distribution of real income tend to dominate the social order generally – as the medieval church demonstrated centuries ago,[34] as Marx argued at length,[35] and as contemporary corporations make palpably evident.[36]

Where power resides in the economies of Eastern Europe, the *uses* to which it is put, and the *justifications* advanced in its support, are not peripheral to the transformation of their economies. They are central and determinant.[37] What has been undertaken is a shift in the locus of power from public bureaucracies to private corporate centres of control. The question of accountability arises in both spheres.[38]

Criteria of Judgment for Institutional Adjustment

The creation or modification of institutional structure will contribute to the resolution of problems when, in consequence, levels of instrumental judgment and performance displace and increasingly exceed levels of ceremonial or invidious judgment and performance.[39] As we noted in Chapter 8 above, where such is the case, institutional adjustments are progressive; where the reverse obtains, institutional adjustments are regressive.[40]

Progressive criteria
Progressive criteria are warranted by their contribution to the continuity and efficiency of the social process and include the following:

• *The Democratic Test*: Can the determination of structural change be established and sustained as a democratically responsive process? At issue is whether those who experience the consequences of policy are themselves able to find and employ the means to change such policy. Can they acquire and retain a significant substantive and noninvidious impact on the determination and implementation of newly introduced institutional adjustments?

John Dewey articulated the democratic ethic for many neoinstitutionalists: 'The keynote of democracy ... [is] the necessity for the participation of every mature human being in formation of the values that regulate the living of men together'.[41] 'Democratic political forms', then, 'rest back upon the idea that no man or limited set of men is wise enough or good enough to rule others without their consent. ... [A]ll those who are affected by social institutions must have a share in producing and managing them.'[42] '[T]he moral criterion is that individuals are free to develop, to contribute and to share, only as social conditions break down walls of privilege and of monopolistic possession' through the elimination of 'those external arrangements of status, birth, wealth, sex, etc., which restrict the opportunity of each individual for full development of himself.'[43]

At issue again is accountability. Can those who hold and use power be constrained and kept insecure about the continuity of their discretionary roles? Can discretion be more widely and noninvidiously shared? The discretion required for democratic participation encompasses (a) the continuing right of access to relevant warranted knowledge, and (b) the continuing right of opportunity to make genuine choices based on that knowledge – choices that, when taken, actually alter institutional outcomes.[44] Democratic freedom should represent an expanding area of genuine choice over the institutional structures that organize and correlate experience.

●   *The Instrumental Efficiency Test*: Can decision makers identify, introduce and support instrumentally efficient productive and distributive mechanisms? An underlying neoinstitutionalist social value principle provides for 'the continuity of human life and the noninvidious recreation of community through the instrumental use of knowledge'.[45] This principle defines a processual mode of inquiry for determining which institutional adjustments ought to be recommended. This approach incorporates warranted knowledge; it characterizes the modern inquiry process for problem solving;[46] it generates provisional and pragmatic policies. It does not recommend an ideological menu of institutions, nor an 'endpoint' to be realized.[47] It does not serve an invidiously defined power system, class or cadre.

At issue with instrumental efficiency is the character, pertinence and extent of use of warranted knowledge in organizing the economic process. 'Instrumental efficiency calls for the most skillful use of appropriate conceptual tools in defining problems and of formulating options as institutional changes.'[48] But how are pertinence and appropriateness to be identified? Elsewhere I wrote:

> The term *instrumental* connotes means-consequence connections. The continuing inquiry question is how can ideas, principles, constructs, and hypotheses *function* as means to achieve consequences as ends-in-view. *Instrumental valuing* encompasses the knowledge-guided use of 'tool-and-skill configurations' as means to transform an indeterminate situation – don't know, don't understand, can't explain, can't act – into a more ordered and determinate end-in-view where consequences are observed, causal understanding is enhanced, connections are disclosed, unknowns become knowns, questions are answered and some congruency between expectations and outcomes is achieved. ... *Instrumental valuing* is not 'merely' incidental to the judgment process; it is the *heart* of it. As the means are chosen in inquiry, so are the outcomes determined. Outcomes or consequences

become means to further outcomes. ... The 'ought to be' is implicit in sustaining and enhancing the continuum of inquiry itself.[49]

Instrumental efficiency is realized in the application of instrumental value theory to the determination of institutional adjustments in the political economy. Indeed, for many neoinstitutionalists, it is the primary criterion with which adjustments in economic structure are evaluated and identifies what they perceive to be economic reform.

• *The Growth of Knowledge Test*: Can maximal effort be directed to increasing warranted knowledge and causal understanding of economic performance? Instrumentally efficient judgments depend on the development of and access to warranted knowledge. At issue are the support and maintenance of educational access, open inquiry, intellectual freedom and full provision of public information.

The generation of warranted knowledge is enhanced by domestic material support and encouragement for progressive education generally, for scholarly inquiry in higher education and research institutions, for research and development in industries, and for cross-cultural borrowing. Exchange of technological and institutional innovations has been commonplace among developed economies since World War II. Expansion and communication of knowledge are enhanced by full and public disclosure, publication and sharing of ideas and information. Encapsulation of warranted knowledge, its sequestration by private corporations or public agencies, cripples the growth of knowledge.[50]

• *The Minimal Needs Test*: Can priority be given to the maintenance of at least minimally adequate real income flows, non-invidiously accessible? At issue is protection of major segments and sectors of the economy from drastic reductions in their provisioning levels and from their opportunistic exploitation by the well positioned and powerful. The 'basic needs strategy' in development economics of the 1970s and 1980s is, or can be made, compatible with the instrumental valuation proposed here. This approach 'focuses on assisting poorer people in lower-income countries to meet their basic needs on sustainable bases by creating employment, output, and income'.[51] It is distinctive in that efforts are made to promote institutional adjustments that specifically address the plight of the poor. No 'trickle down' development model is proposed. Particularly supported are efforts to assist the poor in generating sustainable real income and in gaining access to education, health facilities and skill acquisition – all means to enhance their own well being.

In pursuit of similar concerns, Len Doyal and Ian Gough have developed an extensive and sophisticated (but non-relativistic) theory of human needs that is implicitly corollary with instrumental value theory. Their analysis of human needs is intended to provide specific criteria for the evaluation of economic performance of diverse economic systems.[52] They identify *physical health* and *autonomy* as the two fundamental basic needs. Physical health is a prerequisite for virtually all forms of social and economic participation.[53] 'Autonomy of agency' is a function of achieved understanding, psychological capacity and opportunities to act; it implies discretionary roles.[54] Basic needs are met by 'universal need satisfiers' that contribute to basic health and autonomy. Examples of these 'need satisfiers' include adequate nutrition and housing, non-hazardous environments, physical and economic security, and basic and cross-cultural education, among others.[55] Those subject to increased threats to their health and autonomy through discrimination based on race, gender, class or age will require 'additional and specific satisfiers and procedures to address and correct them'.[56] An agenda for institutional adjustment is suggested.

• *Environmental Continuity Test*: Are institutional adjustments of a kind that provides for the continuity of social and biotic interdependencies? In an earlier work, I argued that 'a social community must exist and seek continuity within the ecological limits of the biotic community'.[57] At issue is the appraisal of structural change with reference to its impact on the maintenance of this fragile socio-biotic relationship in a context of continuing disregard for such ecological hazards as radiation, pollution, deforestation, habitat destruction, ozone depletion, and the like.

The interdependence of life forms is a critical consideration, including the emerging recognition that as many different forms of life as possible must be preserved. Maintenance of biodiversity has become a priority concern for medical and economic reasons.[58] Moreover, 'sustainability', as in agriculture, may no longer be a sufficient criterion of environmental compatibility. Unless a burgeoning population growth can be slowed, just to sustain real income flows will generate major environmental stress.[59] Reductions in rates of environmental destruction (including biodiversity) and restoration of environmentally damaged areas are essential for continuing biotic interdependence and compatibility. Central also is the recognition that current levels of warranted knowledge concerning the environmental impact of present and proposed adjustments are quite inadequate, especially with reference to the longer-term consequences of present actions.

Regressive criteria

Regressive criteria are warranted on some assumption of authority and/or status and include the following.

• *The Possession of Power Test*: Can the fact that a few *hold* power to impose institutional adjustments itself serve as a credible justification or validation for its *exercise*? Can the use of power be defended simply by its acquisition? Authoritarians so argue. 'Might makes right' is the fascist form. At issue is political legitimacy. By what warrant is power held by the few and exercised over the many? 'Rationalizations' for the possession and use of autocratic power are legion. Two are noted here.

Democracy is impossible. In the guise of Michels's 'iron law of oligarchy',[60] autocrats insist that authoritarian control is the inevitable result whatever contrary forms of governance are attempted. The quest for power is innate; in a Hobbesian war of each against all, only the possession of power ensures self-preservation. 'I put for a general inclination of all mankind, a perpetual and restless desire of power after power, that ceaseth only in death.'[61]

That possession of coercive power is a 'heady brew' that conditions the psyche, defines status and enhances self-esteem will not be denied. But this is no genes-rooted proclivity. Achievement and status warranted on instrumental grounds are quite obviously accessible and evident in democratic contexts. Moreover, democratic institutions have demonstrably existed for decades, even centuries, without an 'iron law' takeover.

Democracy is inefficient. Autocrats insist that democracy means rule by the ignorant masses who are unable to generate solutions to problems. A military elite can impose 'efficient' solutions; it can command and require obedience. Parliamentary deliberations are tedious, time-consuming and fraught with schisms. An autocrats' referent for 'efficiency' is expediency, unquestioning response, absence of deliberation. Neither ignorance nor dissension is permitted to impair performance. Discretion is unidirectional – from the top, down; obedience is from the bottom, up. The character and quality of directives are not at issue. Rather, decisions are not informed by assessment of consequences on the life process.

Neoinstitutionalists hold a vastly different view of 'efficiency'. Because deliberations in a democratic society are more likely to be informed, cultivated and appraised by those who experience the consequences of policy, there is continuing pressure to formulate and implement pragmatic, grounded and realistic institutional adjustments. Democratic institutions are more efficient in providing for the generation and application of warranted knowledge. They also provide control by holding power responsible and revocable. Discretionary roles and powers can be modified or withdrawn. Legitimacy is a function of accountability.

● *The Status Quo Preservation Test*: Can an economy be sustained where a governing criterion is to retain present structures (and the decision-making cadres dependent thereon) because they conform with the past? At issue is the extent to which a political economy seriously and impartially considers revised structures that acknowledge and utilize the past but may for instrumentally warranted reasons depart from it.

The pertinence of the conservatives' defence of the status quo can only be granted in those circumstances where credible institutional alternatives have not been generated. The present structure is of course a reflection of past problem-solving judgments, however archaic they may currently appear. The known is more appealing than the unknown until and unless the latter's instrumentally warranted benefits are made evident. But the 'is' – present structure – cannot serve as a credible *criterion* of what 'ought' to be new institutional arrangements.

• *The Invidious Defence Test*: Should important judgments of structural change be designed, coloured or distorted by discrimination grounded in ethnicity, tribalism, nationality, race, gender, ancestry, religious affiliation and the like? At issue is the recognition that the invidious use of any such distinctions – by precluding a shared sense of community, engendering denigrative conflict and destroying instrumental motivation – impairs the community's ability and capacity to provision and sustain itself.

The invidious use of distinctions among persons defines participatory involvement in a discriminatory fashion. Property ownership, educational choices, health care access, professional opportunities, credit availability, and the like are denied in a way that excludes and demeans segments of the community. An ingrained master-servant attitude places those invidiously identified in the servile class. In current budget debates, for example, it is interesting to observe that only the 'entitlements' of the poor are at issue; those relatively more generous entitlements, such as tax expenditures routinely received by middle and upper income classes, are 'deserved' benefits. Notions of 'better off' and 'worse off' order relationships and corrupt institutional functioning. Denials based on discrimination cripple the whole community: (a) by impairing the growth of individuals' capabilities and intellect, (b) by excluding instrumental contributions such individuals could make to the community, and (c) by fostering internecine conflict or tension.

• *The Pecuniary Gains Test*: Can pecuniary measures of output, performance, incomes, profits and the like serve as surrogates in determining economic success and well-being? At issue is a gargantuan Midas illusion: possession of money (and the property and status it buys) is the premier measure of standing and merit; personal acquisition of money income is the ultimate goal; ability to pay the going market price is the measure of social worth and value.

To be sure, pecuniary formulations are sometimes necessary to track the 'weight, tael measure and count' (a) of the delivery and receipt of product and service within and among participating productive units, and (b) of the origin, magnitude and dispersion of the aggregate flow of real income. This view does not disparage the analysis of 'a monetary economy' (as developed by Keynes and Dillard) to explain the determinants of income and employment in order to fashion stabilization policies.[62] But critical performance appraisals must reach behind pecuniary tallies to examine the substantive flow of real income itself and assess its adequacy, continuity and distributional equity.

Moreover, in any exchange economy, the possession of money and the continuity of money income (including access to credit) are enormous sources of personal power. To have discretion is to be able to create and choose among options. In most areas of the provisioning process, discretion is largely determined by the size and continuity of the flow of money income. Its acquisition, as a means of gaining access to real income, is and will remain a major concern of individuals. But the *instrumental* merit of acquisition and use of money income may not be assumed; it must be demonstrated. As the foregoing comments on progressive criteria imply, price cannot serve as a surrogate for social value.

Judgments of social value cannot be avoided in making institutional adjustments. The full disclosure of their presence and character is a first step in determining their appropriateness for problem solving. Applying the distinction between progressive and regressive criteria is a necessary second step in framing institutional change. The character and consequences of economic 'reforms' in Eastern Europe can be reassessed by using these differing progressive and regressive criteria.

Conditions Facilitating Institutional Adjustments

In formulating institutional adjustments, as I noted briefly in the previous chapter, there are certain continuing conditions that tend both to impinge upon their design and character, and to delimit the extent to which they can be realized. Although versions of these conditioners of social change had appeared elsewhere, J. Fagg Foster reformulated and consolidated them as evolutionary principles of institutional adjustment which he regarded as pertinent contributions to the institutionalists' perspective.[63] Because of their relevance for appraising the 'market shock' approach to 'reform' in Eastern Europe, I here quote his views at some length:

The principle of technological determination

The principle of technological determination is simply that social problems can be solved only by adjusting the institutional structures involved in the problem so as to bring them into instrumentally efficient correlation with the technological aspects of the problems. What is meant by 'instrumentally efficient correlation' is that the instrumental functions of the institutions in question be carried on at a level of efficiency tolerable to the members of the institution in view of the possibilities indicated by those same technological factors. The members of the community cannot 'unknow' anything which they do know as a technological or physical fact; and no amount of coercion short of complete destruction, can alter that situation. The members of an institution cannot avoid seeking adjustments because they cannot avoid the human incidences of a problematic situation which requires adjustments.[64]

The principle of recognized interdependence

The principle of recognized interdependence is simply that the immediate pattern of any institutional adjustment is specified by the pattern of interdependencies recognized by the members of the institution. Institutional structures are made up of habitual behavior in most part, but an adjustment in any such structure requires that a deliberate choice be made among the possible alternatives recognized by those who must alter their behavior. A new pattern of behavior requires that the behavior be 'directed' in its initiation. It becomes habitual through repetition, but its initial performance requires conscious direction. Since all adjustments, and therefore the whole of institutional structure, are specified at initiation, it necessarily follows that the conceptual apprehension precedes the course of action differentiating the new pattern from the old. ... However unwillingly the persons involved accept the new pattern and however little discretion they may have in specifying the adjustment, they must recognize their actual relationships as specified in the new pattern. Otherwise the pattern simply does not eventuate into action.[65]

The principle of minimal dislocation

All institutional modifications must be capable of being incorporated into the remainder of the institutional structure. It is convenient to call this the principle of minimal dislocation. It discloses the limits of adjustment in terms of rate and in terms of degree and area. ... [M]odifications cannot stand alone; they must be incorporated into the institutional structure of which they are parts. This circumstance sets certain limitations on the rapidity and extent of institutional adjustments. In the first place, the adjustments must be in tolerable rapport with the noninstitutional factors. Attempted adjustments must make instrumentally better use of the technological factors, else they simply increase the human incidences that initially motivated the adjustments. ... In the second place, attempted or contemplated adjustments must be brought as problematic factors into the comprehension of the persons involved; and those projections must do no violence to the factors not considered problematic.[66]

The first principle discloses what data and information are required to identify a problem, to distinguish between 'what is' and 'what ought to be', and to frame alternative adjustments. The second principle discloses the character of institutional adjustments that are to be undertaken and the levels of understanding needed for acceptance and resolution. The third principle helps identify limits of rate and scope of change that will be confronted.[67]

In my view, the foregoing six tenets and their implications constitute a sufficiently comprehensive perspective with which to review and appraise the neoclassical 'market shock' approach to structural change in Eastern Europe.

II THE NEOCLASSICAL MODEL AND INSTITUTIONAL CHANGE

Human Agency

The 'psychological creed' of discretionary actors in neoclassical orthodoxy characteristically encompasses the following: egoism (hedonism), intellectualism (rationalism), quietism (passivity) and atomism (individualism).[68] Egoism connotes utilitarian underpinnings; intellectualism undergirds the maximization principle as the referent for rationality; quietism affirms inaction as the normal state which is episodically disturbed by egoistic wants; atomism confirms an individualistic focus – asocial, ahistorical. Characterized by these attributes, human agency is a *given*; it is not emergent, developmental or even experiential. Choice – consumer or producer – is a continuing quest for personal gain in utility or profit, with a minimum cost in disutility or pecuniary position.

Accordingly, the neoclassical perspective admits of no discretionary or agency role in creating new structural fabric for correlating and coordinating economic activity. Constrained by its reductionist, rationalistic view of discretion, human agency is reduced to the manipulation and opportunistic exploitation of whatever pecuniary options exist or can be created.[69] Orthodoxy does not explore the creative decision-making process in conceiving of new ways and new rules for generating material well-being. No *analytical* account is taken of habitual modes of thought and behaviour; no reference is made to path-determinacy or path-dependency and its implications; little tracing out of the consequences of decisions and their significance (trivial or chaotic) is admitted to the inquiry agenda. To insist that profit and utility maximization are motivational constants, to claim their universality, and to pose them as primary determinants of systemic change, is, for example, grossly to ignore the significance of power and its retention, of status and ethnicity (among others) upon the systemic restructuring effort. It is also largely to ignore the uncertainties of indeterminacy, insufficient knowledge and the impact of unforeseen events.

In appraising structural transformations in Eastern Europe, Sachs professes to witness the reemergence of this stylized neoclassical man: 'In all of the countries, new entrepreneurs are coming to the fore, with a flair that dispels old notions that socialism had created a "homo sovieticus" in which the market-spirit had been vanquished'.[70] The 'market-spirit' evidently embodies the 'psychological creed'.

Yet Sachs identifies psychological *greed* as a problem. Managers, 'with a speed that is reassuring for neoclassical economists(!) ... jumped at the chance to get out from under bureaucratic controls'.[71] But such managers also engage in 'dysfunctional' activities; these include 'intentionally bank-rupting firms to buy them back cheaply; establishing private firms to do business, in sweetheart deals, with the state enterprises that they manage; accepting unfavorable joint venture and takeover offers that provide personal benefits for the manager'.[72] The 'creed' evidently supports the 'greed'. Mem-bers of the newly created corporate boards, in whom Sachs would vest basic economic discretion through 'privatization', must be presumed sometimes to behave *dysfunctionally*. Accountability remains a central concern.

Creation of Institutional Structure

The neoclassical model, as noted, is a path-independent approach to struc-tural change. Institutional adjustment by means of 'implementing the model' is incapable of effectively resolving problems, either in analytic or behav-ioural terms. The past cannot be abandoned; habitual beliefs and behaviours cannot *comprehensively* be overturned without inducing chaotic, wholly des-perate conditions of disrapport, discontinuity and disruption in the flow of real income. Maximum dislocation is foreshadowed.

Moreover, a self-referencing propensity appears to operate which insulates the initiator of the reform from criticism. As Kurt Dopfer hypothesizes, 'when-ever an explanation about an event in the external world is called forth, a set of answers [the stabilizing, privatizing and restructuring of Eastern Europe] is provided that not only provides an answer to the problem but also – in answer-ing the problem – confirms the status of the ideology [neoclassicism] on which the answer is based'.[73] Such a 'self-referential and self-maintaining ... closure judgment'[74] becomes an analytical cul-de-sac that forestalls critical assessment of the convulsive institutional adjustments imposed.

There is no encompassing theory of institutional adjustment put forward in neoclassical microeconomics. The institutional fabric of the capitalist economy, whose operation is explained by the determination of price in the exchange process, is a *given*; it is incorporated by *assumption* (along with technology, resources and preferences[75]); that structural fabric is not *itself* an object of inquiry or assessment. The historical and processual transformation of struc-ture, from which institutions are presumed to have evolved, is never addressed.

This assumed institutional fabric consists of the following: (a) the univer-sal behaviour assumptions (motivations and attitudes), as noted, of economic rationality referenced in utility maximization; (b) the private ownership of all material resources and labour;[76] (3) consumer demand, reflecting given tastes and preferences, as the driving force, both in the particular and in the aggregate, that determines the level and character of production of goods and services; (4) demand-responsive, cost-sensitive, privately-owned firms under entrepreneurial discretion that organize the productive process; (5) the presence and primary dependence upon competitive markets (no participant can affect price by her/his own efforts) as exchange arenas to induce order and assure coherence;[77] (6) markets that move inherently and continuously towards a quiescent state in equilibrium, (7) a passive money stock as a post-barter exchange facilitator (that implicitly denies the monetary theory of production), and (8) governments that function in the economy solely as protectors of property, enforcers of contracts, promoters of competitive markets and keepers of the peace.[78]

What is critical to recognize is that this structural fabric is presumed to be historically *autogenetic*. The removal of competing or rival institutions – especially the erosion of governmental 'intrusions' or 'interventions', or of central autocratic planning – permits the automatic emergence of the capitalist structure. But in the case of restructuring Eastern Europe, with little reference to an evolutionary institutional emergence, newly established governments are expected, virtually at a stroke, to privatize state enterprise and create new capitalistic corporate structures. Once established, they can be presumed to thrive under their own inherent drives and mechanisms. Thus throughout Sachs's discussion of stabilization, privatization and restructuring, there is a desperate urging for the most rapid possible conversion of productive facilities from public bureaucratic governments to privately-owned corporations and enterprises.[79] Privatization, he recognizes, is 'the most difficult and novel of the three, both conceptually and politically'.[80]

But as J.A. Kreger and Egon Matzner put it:

> The 'big bang' not only ignores the lessons of history, it fails to provide the social and economic conditions necessary to create a market economy. The basic error lies in the mistaken belief in the *spontaneous* appearance of a capitalist market economy once property is privatized, prices are set free, the currency is stabilized and unregulated competitive markets are introduced [emphasis added].[81]

For Sachs, however, original institutional choice is unnecessary; indeed choosing structure at variance with the model is perverse and can only lead to inefficiency in economic performance. But what Sachs does not address is the fact that the emergent corporate form of enterprise itself remains a largely undigested and ill-accommodated organizational form in orthodoxy in large part because it facilitates and exhibits (as viewed by neoclassicists) a pathological quest for, and amassing of, economic power over prices and markets.

Does the neoclassical model actually serve Sachs as a template for the 'reform' of Eastern European and former Soviet economies? The answer must be affirmative, although there are modest exceptions or departures pragmatically dictated by events and circumstances. However, *the theory dictating or warranting the 'exceptions' is not provided.* Compare the foregoing neoclassical model with the reform package proposed below for Eastern Europe by Sachs and others.[82] His summary of the adjustments needed to introduce the model was the following [in bracketed italics, I identify reflections of the neoclassical *model*].

> Economic liberalization: freeing of most prices; open trading policy (low tariffs, elimination of quotas, ending licensing of trading firms); and a legal basis for private property (commercial code, company law, judicial enforcement of contracts). [*Free markets, uncontrolled prices, private ownership, government as enforcer of contracts and protector of property.*]

> Macroeconomic stabilization: sharp cuts in subsidies, devaluation of the exchange rate and subsequent currency convertibility; positive real interest rates; and restriction on domestic credit expansion. [*Shrinking role and responsibility of government, restoration of exchange function of money, constraints on credit expansion, neutrality of money.*]

> Privatization: conversion of state enterprises into corporate form, followed by transfer of ownership of state enterprises to the private sector. Transfers may be through sales, free distribution or other means.[83] [*Shift of production responsibility to private enterprises as corporations, movement of public to private ownership in dramatic ways, implicit deference to private owners' discretion over economy as inherently constructive.*]

'Liberalization' has been introduced generally, if convulsively. 'Stabilization' has been attempted but has been largely overwhelmed by inflation. 'Privatization' has lagged; its rapid pursuit is Sachs's primary concern.[84] However, even if this reform package were fully realized, Eastern European systems would not substantially replicate the intricate and idiosyncratically managed systems in Western Europe.

In Sachs's more recent discussion of 'reforms' in Poland, the triad of 'stabilization, liberalization and privatization' – his 'three pillars of economic transition to a market economy' – is no longer deemed sufficient. Evidently in response to chaotic conditions introduced by the 'market shock' approach, Sachs has added 'creation of a social safety net' and 'economic support from the West' for a total of 'five pillars'. The transition cannot be completed without substantial achievement of the last three of these – privatization, safety net and more help from the West.[85] How the two new 'pillars' can be generated from, or even accommodated to, his 'endpoint' of capitalism is not clear. But it does suggest that, in confronting the reality of dislocation, unemployment and deprivation in the Polish transition, Sachs's view underwent something of a 'compulsive shift'[86] to a more pragmatic approach.

To return now to my main argument, I repeat my contention that *orthodox neoclassicism has no theory of institutional adjustment*.[87] Flexible market pricing presumably permits an existing structure to accommodate changing tastes, the growth of knowledge, emerging technology and other 'disequilibrating forces'. All such changes are reflected in market exchange through their bearing on supply and demand. When anomalies are observed (that is, when the reality does not conform to the market model, and it rarely does), the defence is usually that government interference, lack of information or high transfer costs were responsible. In the case of Eastern Europe, divergence from the model is explained as resulting from an insufficient time lapse, bureaucratic and political instabilities, and absence of sufficient support from the West which prevented rapid and comprehensive privatization.[88] The capitalist institutional fabric *itself* cannot be the locus of problems of malperformance. Institutional choice is constrained by a priori acceptance of, and deference to, capitalist modes of motivation and organization – a path-independent posture.

Expressed more generally, the only structural change one could derive from the neoclassical paradigm is the recommended shift from what is *not* capitalist structure as identified above, to what *is* capitalist structure. This view of change is episodic, non-processual, unidirectional, discontinuous and devoid of theoretical or empirical foundation. Its employment in Eastern Europe is also convulsive; it is a behavioural cul-de-sac. No non- or post-capitalist structure can be analytically envisaged or sanctioned. It is ahistorical in that it does not adequately reflect major and evolutionary systemic change in any of the modern economies.

As Polanyi shows with his 'double movement' thesis, 19th-century efforts to introduce self-regulating market capitalism were *concurrently* matched with attempts to regulate and constrain that transformation.[89] More particularly, the post-World War II restoration of Western European economies with the support of the Marshall Plan, together with the modernization and expansion of Japan and other Pacific Rim economies, were 'based on an undogmatic recognition that markets must be *managed* in order to provide support for entrepreneurial activities'.[90] Indeed, their development was, arguably, largely public-sector led. A neoclassically warranted, singular shift view of institutional change cannot guide institutional adjustment in the real world, claims to the contrary notwithstanding.

Problem Solving

For neoclassicists generally and for Western advisers in Eastern Europe particularly, the perception of a 'problem' is the failure fully to incorporate an ideologically designed model into a struggling political economy. Complaints that the privatization of industry and the transfer of industrial control to corporate owners have not been fully carried through are reflective of this tortured concept of an economic problem.[91] Indeed, the referential meaning of 'economic reform in Eastern Europe' now comes clearly into view. For neoclassicists, *reform means* moving directly and comprehensively to a dominantly capitalist model. The *problem* is a failure to do so. As Sachs observes,

> Managerial authority is sufficiently watered down by workers' councils, and the long-range ownership and economic prospects of the enterprises are so clouded that the behavior of workers and managers tends to be exceedingly short-sighted and geared to wage increases, asset-stripping, and job protection, rather than to long-run restructuring. ... The continuing industrial crisis is widely blamed on the economic reform program, rather than on the failure to proceed with real privatization.[92]

The real problem for workers and managers is to sustain their income flows in a chaotic world. Having been largely denied discretion over their own economic welfare under the Soviet regime, any increase in control over their own well-being post-Gorbachev will not easily be surrendered in the service of Sachs's agenda. Workers can hardly be expected to renounce concern about their income in the short run in the interests of questionable goals in the long run. In the long run, they and we are all dead, as Keynes observed. Without a credible theory of institutional adjustment that provides principles for the evolutionary transformation of prescriptive and proscriptive arrangements, neoclassical theorists can only bewail the 'short-sighted' proclivities of those who bear the real consequences of failed policy.

Loci of Discretion

As Kurt Rothschild observes, '[T]here is a strange lacuna of power themes in mainstream (neoclassical) theory'.[93] Except for the efforts to extend neoclassical analysis into inconclusive oligopoly theory, into industrial organization as an applied field,[94] and into game theory to describe and model the strategies of organizations and the regulatory process,[95] orthodoxy does little analytically to confront the fact and use of economic power. The reality of market 'imperfections' and corporate manipulation of demand make academic claims to consumer sovereignty through price-competitive markets increasingly tenuous. Massive advertising budgets that seek to create 'tastes and preferences' make entrepreneurs' claims of powerlessness and of deference to consumer tastes and preferences unpersuasive. Analysis of economic power, except as pathology, is not a major item on their agenda of inquiry.

Neoclassicists have long exhibited a need-hate attitude towards governmental structure and functions.[96] Their perception of the economic role of government as a centre of power is therefore ambivalent. The *need* is for ordered relationships and protection; the *hate* reflects a fear of public intrusion upon, and constraint over, private economic behaviour and purposes. While neoclassicists would acknowledge that institutions such as governmental bodies must exist as repositories of power through which the community can choose and revise institutional structure, the possession and use of governmental power are constantly perceived as a threat: through taxation governments drain enterprise resources; through expenditures they advantage some firms against others; through regulations they intrude on private discretion ('managerial prerogatives') and incentives.

At least since Hayek's *Road to Serfdom*,[97] orthodox economists have identified governmental regulation and planning with authoritarian control, and free markets with democratic control. This mistaken dualism resurfaces in Western advice for restructuring Eastern economies. Remnants of this ideological conflict are reflected in debates over privatization, stabilization and restructuring. While democracy is often identified with the capitalist market economy, most understand that competitive markets are not the economic counterpart of ballot boxes. Actually, income levels largely determine access to markets; citizen status determines access to participatory rights. The democratic condition has always meant popular control over rule making; policy constraints are directly or indirectly self-imposed. However, the extent of popular control actually realized depends heavily on increasing accountability over economic power centres and on enhancing equity in income distribution.

In the experience of Western and Pacific Rim industrial economies in the last half century, development has most often been led by their public sectors.[98] Governments lend; governments subsidize, governments generate new knowledge and technology, governments initiate; governments support; governments protect; governments educate and train; governments build infrastructure; governments manage; governments cooperate in joint ventures; governments absorb pecuniary risk; governments insure; governments manage competition as rivalry, governments solicit investments from abroad, and more. All modern industrial economies are continuously and heavily dependent upon public sector participation in, and direction of, macromanagement policy, trade policy, industrial policy and monetary policy. At issue are the character and extent of that participation. Changing the economic rules that matter, changing the institutional fabric of the economy, can be accomplished only through the political process using governmental institutions, as Sachs has advised in both Poland and Russia. Establishing and maintaining democratic control in Eastern Europe are clearly the critical conditions for a transition to more viable economies. The primary concern is, and will continue to be, to hold all those who wield private and public power to account.

Sachs's commentaries on governments and their functions in Eastern Europe reflect the same need-hate relationship of his cohorts. While his long-term analytical goal is evidently the closest feasible approximation of the neoclassical model (including, economically, a minimal state), his short-term recommendations in fact place heavy responsibility on newly-constituted national democratic governments. Note his announced de facto agenda of assigned governmental functions. They must: (a) assume primary responsibility for designing and implementing the most rapid possible restructuring (commercializing and privatizing) of major industrial enterprise;[99] (b) provide a comprehensive 'safety net' (unemployment insurance, retraining, welfare, pensions, etc.) for the 'losers' from 'reform';[100] (c) reform legal codes and systems to regulate acquisition and transfer of privately owned assets;[101] (d) establish boards of directors of corporate enterprise and find ways to hold these newly constituted corporate boards accountable and free of fraud (asset stripping, collusion, profit absorption, etc.);[102] and (e) promote international agreements, looking to free-trade policies and membership in the European Community.[103]

Sachs contends that Eastern European 'economies can indeed be converted to the Western European model in a reasonable period of time'.[104] But his longer-term view regarding government's role is neither hinted at nor implied in the initial neoclassicist definition of 'reform' as 'macroeconomic stabilization', 'liberalization' and 'privatization'.[105] What he omits is a longer-term governmental agenda that addresses institutional adjustments that do not necessarily mimic, but may still resemble, structural changes that have occurred in major West European countries over the last half century. Within a 'reasonable time', in my view, Eastern European governments will need to: (a) retain and extend democratic governance, including supervision over private-sector decision making; (b) serve as the leading sector in investment and growth promotion, as Post Keynesians recommend;[106] (c) accept primary responsibility for the restoration and expansion of infrastructure; (d) heavily invest time, energy and resources in promotion of education at all levels; (e) develop and borrow technology; (f) initiate and direct environmental and ecological restoration and enhancement; (g) assure minimum levels of real income, access to health services and the like, and (h) provide for noninvidious participation in all aspects of the economic process for increasing proportions of the community.

Finally, Sachs's position on the locus of discretion reflects his unease over worker participation in policymaking. He appears to have little patience with workers' councils, especially those (as in Poland) that collude with state managers 'to raise wages and salaries sufficiently to absorb the cash flow of the enterprise, absorbing profits, depreciation funds, and so on'.[107] Such councils are thought to exhibit only short-term and self-interested goals. Desperate circumstances convert the psychological *creed* into psychological *greed*?

As noted, Sachs places his confidence in the discretion of newly constituted corporate boards and managers appearing as a result of privatization. It is they, in the main, that should have power over and responsibility for creating the emergent economy. '[M]ass commercialization would also provide a system of enterprise governance, in a situation where no clear governance now exists. A supervisory board would be appointed for each enterprise, bound by the standard responsibilities defined in European and American corporate law.'[108] In addition, Sachs expects financial institutions to have supervisory influence over corporate boards.

More generally, it seems that when Sachs feels compelled to be more 'realistic', as mentioned above, the pursuit of institutional norms shifts from ideological neoclassicism (free markets, consumer sovereignty, free market pricing) to corporatist realpolitik (megacorp hegemony over production, private management of markets, private banking dominion over finance, minimal discretion for workers).[109] When the normative use of the model is awkward, a normative deference to achieved (or achievable) power will serve.

But the question of 'who watches the watchers' is not resolved in Sachs's proposals.[110] Are these loci of power (boards) to take responsibility for promoting the use of progressive rather than regressive criteria, as identified above? How is democratic accountability to be realized? Evidently for Sachs the comprehensive transfer of discretion to private corporate owners is not to be challenged, even if their individual behaviour may come under review.

In the short term, for Sachs, governments must be strong and tough-minded enough vigorously to push the privatization 'reforms' through to their conclusion (transfer of virtually all state property to mainly private holdings of various forms), even though opposition is substantial and the suffering demonstrably heavy. His political analysis suggests that

> The greatest risk in the region is that the populism, the confusion of property rights, and a splintering of political power in the parliaments, will lead to weak governments unable to take the remaining decisive steps to private ownership. ... The risk is heightened by the fact that each of the Eastern European countries has adopted proportional representation as the basis for parliamentary representation.[111]

One implication, for Sachs, is that really strong (and authoritarian?) governments are required if his privatization model is to be implemented rapidly and comprehensively. Indeed, one may well ask whether the model has been

fully introduced anywhere in the last half century without the use of autocratic power, as was evidently the case in Latin America?[112] Democratic
governance, as perceived by neoinstitutionalists, may not be well or fully
realized in the present political structure, but that is not his concern.

Criteria of Judgment

As argued above, all theories of institutional adjustment must encompass
value principles in terms of which choices may be made. The neoclassical
paradigm is, in my view, devoid of any credible theory of social value with
which to conduct inquiry, create institutional options and choose among
them.

Sachs and other neoclassicists quite obviously do make *normative use of
the competitive model* as a criterion in assessing progress in institutional
adjustment in Eastern Europe. But this tacitly accepted normative frame will
not generate credible judgments. A brief critique follows.

(a)   'The normative use of the competitive model has little, if any, historical warrant.'[113] The path-independency model in Sachs's hands is not based
on experience or rooted in warranted knowledge of past successful impositions, or emergent versions, of a competitive market model. Each major
contemporary industrial system – US, Japan, France, Great Britain, Germany
– has evolved its own distinctive array of economic institutions. Virtually all
major markets are managed but in quite different, if not unique, ways. For
example, management of product markets is generally slow and deliberate,
with stability induced by administered pricing, as observed in earlier chapters. Management of financial markets in contrast is often unstable, reflecting
rapid and sometimes cumulative consequences. Unfettered markets are hardly
dominant or characteristic, certainly not in the US, Western Europe or Japan.
Systems of direction and control vary. Managerial techniques, worker incentive systems, production flow patterns, technological innovation processes,
distribution systems – all are in considerable measure unique to each individual economy. Through reflective decisions, path-determinant institutional
adjustments build on the existing structural fabric of the culture. Thus, Poland, Russia, Hungary and the others will each find its own way to a mixed
economy, though the transformation of that *mixture* over time remains a
central concern. Resemblances, commonalities and similarities among economies exist, of course, but because cultural and national experiences are different, so also must be the structural characteristics of their economies.
Eastern European economies may wish to borrow and modify coordinating
patterns from other countries – East and West. But the neoclassical model per
se is (to repeat), 'a system which lives in the minds of economists but not on
earth'.[114]

(b)   The normative use of the competitive model retains archaic elements of eighteenth and nineteenth century natural law theory.'[115] Implicit in the neoclassical model, as Sachs seeks to introduce it, is an unreflective deference to the natural law of private ownership. 'Privatization' is evidently what he considers the major institutionally-defined End, although he has found it the most difficult to introduce.

The desire for property is presumed to be an inherent attribute of human nature; accordingly, to succeed, any Eastern European economy must grant the *right* to personal acquisition. The expectation is that once privatization is fully implemented, the system will operate as rational maximizing people and natural unfettered market institutions necessarily dictate.

But there is a naturalistic givenness about this premise. As Carl Becker observed more than a half century ago, the classical economists deified Nature: God created Nature; therefore, whatever was natural was 'good'[116] and in accordance with divine will. Their neoclassical descendants dropped references to the metaphysical source but not the substance of the natural order. What is natural remains nondiscretionary. It is an a priori analytical premise, not a product of processual warranted inquiry. Although privatization is a continuing goal for Sachs, even he acknowledges that some aspects of private discretion (asset stripping, price gouging) are not necessarily in the public interest. But this acknowledgment does not erode his basic anterior commitment to privatization.

Actually, of course, the evidence is all on the other side. *There are no natural institutions*; neither private property nor price competitive markets are uniquely natural. *All* institutions are created by human agents with brief or extensive reflection, to correlate and coordinate behaviour in perceived ways. Moreover, as any casual survey will confirm, ownership (conveying discretion) is not monotypic; forms of ownership vary widely across cultures, reflecting historical and cultural transformations, none of which is 'natural'. Accordingly, in its implicit deference to the natural order, his *normative* insistence on neoclassically warranted privatization fundamentally skews his value judgment deliberations.

(c)   'The normative use of the competitive model exhibits blatant, insensitive, and potentially dangerous ethnocentrism.'[117] A particular model, here Sachs's neoclassical design, is presumed to be as appropriate for Russia as for Poland, for Bulgaria as for the UK. The cross-cultural learning to which Sachs refers in his 'Privatization in Russia: Some Lessons from Eastern Europe',[118] concerns the techniques and timing of privatization efforts. It does not address the fundamental issues. For Sachs, the wisdom of establishing a 'private-ownership market economy' for Russia (or Hungary or Slovakia or Ukraine) is not at issue; it is a given and unarguable. A universally relevant system, refined especially by neoclassical/conservative economists in the US, is promoted as the ideal for any other economy regardless of its historical experience, cultural characteristics or popular support. To judge progress according to how closely one approaches or fails to approach this competitive model system is ethnocentric and an exercise in futility. Pragmatic, fact-driven recognition of unfulfilled promises and performance failures will eventually force an indigenous recasting of the coordinating structure. The longer it is delayed, the higher the cost in political disruption and deteriorating provisioning.

(d)   'The normative use of the competitive model does not, as the orthodox insist, expand economic discretion, the 'freedom to choose', generally. It *narrows* actual human choice.'[119] What is narrowed is the community's capacity to secure control over its own process of institutional innovation and implementation. The fundamental structure of Sachs's neoclassical model is not negotiable, even though some modest adjustments may be needed after privatization is complete. Even then, the predisposition is more fully to implement the neoclassical structure. Other institutional options are not generated out of this essentially sterile and barren resource. Institutional choice – creation and implementation – must always buck normative deference to the model and its structure.

Choices are also narrowed in the recognition that the change to alleged consumer-driven markets does not necessarily widen consumer choices generally. With the removal of price controls, there may be more goods on the shelves in Russian stores, but the fraction of the community that has the income to buy shrinks with inflated prices and increasing unemployment. Market participation is constrained by access to money income. Unfettered markets advantage the already pecuniarily advantaged!

Conditions affecting Institutional Adjustment

The comments concerning principles of institutional adjustment that follow may be appropriately characterized as democratic economic planning. In my view, it will be necessary, ultimately, for democratic governments to provide the primary, but not exclusive, initiative and leadership in the comprehensive transformation of Eastern European economies. But, as noted, it is *critical* to the whole transformation effort that governmental bodies be democratically constituted and have the means to hold decision makers accountable to the community at large. Neoinstitutionalists acknowledge that this is a difficult task in all economies, whatever the level of their development.

Moreover, governments must retain the capability of making institutional adjustments to respond to new issues and problems as experience informs because they are the only institutional resource available to the community as a community, through which to rewrite prescriptive rules.

The enormity of the present transition problems in Eastern Europe and the Commonwealth of Independent States must be candidly acknowledged. The effort required to transform an authoritarian past into a democratic present is unprecedented in scope and monumental in import. The dilemma is confounded to the extent that authoritarian means are being used coercively to impose a path-independent market model on an unfamiliar community in a post-collapse institutional vacuum. The creation (or recreation) of democratic institutions will demand maximum effort from the most committed and astute leadership available. Transformation compels institutional adjustment. Responsibility for initiating adjustments must generally rest with governments.

However difficult the present problematic circumstances may be, some reflection on both procedural and substantive limitations governing adjustments may prove useful. Again only generalities are possible. Much more detailed knowledge of individual Eastern European economies would be required if their recent 'reform' programmes were fully to be appraised with reference to the following three tenets that condition institutional adjustment. What is offered, then, is a partial research programme for further inquiry.

Technological determination

'[B]ring institutional structures into efficient correlation with technological aspects of the problem.' A sample agenda for policy consideration follows:

- Support pragmatic inquiry into determinants of structural breakdowns; identify causal determinants of impaired production and distribution.
- Draw extensively upon knowledge and skills of present managerial and professional cadres in rehabilitating production capacity.
- Establish coordinating and cooperative networks among production units and between relevant government agencies and production units to share knowledge, techniques and resources.
- Generate instrumental incentives to incorporate warranted knowledge and technological advances in organizations for enhanced production and distribution.
- Generate disincentives for retention of invidiously warranted coordinating patterns.
- Develop an extensive system of consultancies with non-ideologically oriented specialists, technicians, experienced managers *et al.*, not to mimic solutions elsewhere, but to broaden the information base for creating unique institutional solutions which are culturally compatible and instrumentally warranted.

In Sachs's model, the original three-part transformation (later five-part reform) does not correlate technological and institutional aspects of prob-

lems. The restructuring is not intended to be negotiable or significantly modified by an assessment of consequences. The institutionally defined goals are
given; only minor deviations en route to the goal merit discussion.

Recognized interdependence

'The immediate pattern of any institutional adjustment is specified by the
pattern of interdependencies recognized by members of the institution.' A
sample agenda for policy consideration follows:

- Undertake extensive and pragmatic deliberations on the substance and
  timing of all major adjustments proposed.
- Communicate directly and extensively with those whose behaviour
  will be modified, exploring the nature and extent of change. Why is it
  thought necessary? What improved consequences are anticipated? What
  will be the status of affected individuals after adjustment is completed?
  Their concurrence and support are critical to the actual achievement of
  reforms.
- Provide substantive, not pro forma, feedback mechanisms so that negative or invidious consequences can be foreseen and avoided, or dis-
  closed and removed, and so that positive and instrumental consequences can be enhanced and extended.

In the application of Sachs's model, there evidently was insufficient preparation for the introduction of 'reforms', hence 'market *shock*'; it was (is)
mainly a 'top down' adjustment process. Awareness of consequences develops only in ex post experience of deteriorating conditions. Was there sufficient warning that restructuring might mean falling employment, loss of
income, erosion of safety nets, loss of housing and inflationary destruction of
purchasing power? Continuing political instabilities suggest not.

Minimal dislocation

This 'discloses the limits of adjustment in terms of rate and in terms of
degree and area.' A partial agenda for policy consideration follows:

- An overall programme for reconstituting economies must set priorities
  (for example, as Britain did after World War II) with reference to
  urgency, magnitude and strategic impact.
- Stimulus, spread and linkage effects should be analytically anticipated
  and incorporated.
- Institutional structures of provisioning and distribution currently per-
  forming adequately in an instrumental sense should be continued and
  supported. Intrusions on non-problematic areas should be minimal.

- Since all significant change is dislocative and since people's ability to adapt to change is inversely proportional to its magnitude, institutional adjustment should be incremental, cumulative and processual. Where their rationale is communicated and accepted, scheduled, incremental adjustments will be less disruptive of existing instrumental patterns. Where communication and concurrence are vigorously pursued, change can be surprisingly rapid.
- Strategically, initiators of change (who are accountable) must at times 'seize the moment' and act to modify structure when conditions for adjustment appear most likely to generate instrumentally warranted outcomes that have community support.

In Sachs's approach, the neoclassical 'market shock' is not 'minimally dislocative'. It is maximally dislocative; it is convulsive. Few interim structures were established. Actual behaviour patterns therefore appear as erratic and, from the neoclassical view, irrational.

III   CONCLUDING OBSERVATIONS

Sachs's summary of the social and economic consequences of structural changes in Eastern Europe and the Commonwealth of Independent States in recent years suggests to me that the absence of a credible theory of institutional adjustment to guide the restructuring has contributed dramatically to substantial shortfalls and breakdowns in the provisioning and distribution of real income. His own review of consequences experienced includes: (a) elimination of chronic shortages but at sharply rising prices; (b) inflation in double digits, (c) cuts in budget deficits, (d) some increasing exports to the West, (e) falling living standards, (f) growth of small, especially service, enterprises, (g) a small increase in private industry and (h) substantial increases in unemployment.[120]

Sachs concedes that the foregoing have led to political instability in many countries. Somewhat contrary to his main design, he suggests that 'in a later stage, more structural policies involving the public investment budget and regional policies' may be needed, as well as a stronger 'safety net' to help the 'losers' in the transition.[121] But the second or later phase remains, evidently, undeveloped. For Sachs, currently, 'the Achilles Heel of the economic reforms in Eastern Europe is the state industrial sector'.[122] The privatization process has substantially bogged down. Sachs's main recommendations to address the foregoing poor levels of economic performance are to increase the pace of privatization and to finish the job of converting to a free market economy as rapidly as possible. Unfortunately, neither neoclassical theory nor recent experience suggests that these massive short-run dislocations will be followed by a more progressive and productive longer-turn outcome.

The inabilities of neoclassicists constructively to address institutional change, especially in Eastern Europe and the Commonwealth of Independent States, may be summarized as follows. Orthodoxy has (1) no relevant theory of institutional adjustment as such; (2) no theory of individual and communal discretion over institutional choices; (3) only an ideologically constrained and distorted theory of governmental initiative or participation in the economic process; and (4) no credible theory of social value to guide the design of institutional adjustments. From an neoinstitutionalist perspective, the neoclassicist direction of Eastern European economies from command systems to 'free-market economies' has not been a success. Even its proponents and advisers concur in this judgment. Happily, an alternative approach, much of which is compatible with the foregoing analysis, has recently been sketched out. The reform programme initiated by *The AGENDA-Group* is a promising approach on which to build.[123]

NOTES

1. Ericson (1991), p. 25.
2. Hutton (1993), p. 9.
3. Kregel, Matzner and Grabher (1992), p. 12.
4. Fischer (1993), p. 391.
5. Lipton and Sachs (1990a), p. 75.
6. Coase (1992), p. 714.
7. Sachs (1993), p. 2.
8. Ibid, pp. 4–5.
9. Ibid, p. 5.
10. Dopfer (1991), p. 535.
11. A neoclassical institutionalism, the so-called 'new institutionalism', is now being developed, though space constraints preclude consideration of that literature here. My reading indicates that although it does appear to mimic the 'old' institutionalism in discussing historical change, it founders on its incorporation of standard neoclassical rational choice assumptions. See North (1990).
12. The referential content of 'agency' and 'agent' in this chapter departs from neoclassical usages to some extent. Herein 'agency' connotes the ability to act, choose or execute; 'agent' means 'discretionary actor'. 'Agency' does *not* connote contracting between individuals wherein one serves in lieu of or represents another, nor is any principal-agent connection implied. On the latter, see *The New Palgrave: A Dictionary of Economics*.
13. Jensen (1988), pp. 89–123.
14. Lane (1991), p. 41 and ch. 5.
15. Dopfer (1991), p. 539.
16. Ibid, pp. 536.
17. Neale (1988), pp. 227–56.
18. Foster (1981a), p. 933.
19. Dopfer (1991), p. 540.
20. Ibid, pp. 537–9.

21. These comments apply generally to traditional neoclassicists, but not necessarily to neoclassical institutionalists, the so-called 'new institutionalists'.
22. Foster (1981b), p. 946.
23. For the US economy, see Munkirs (1985), Galbraith (1967), Galbraith (1973) and Reagan (1963).
24. Thompson (1991), p. 2.
25. Galbraith [1952] (1980).
26. Munkirs and Sturgeon (1985), pp. 899–922.
27. Beije and Groenewegen (1992), pp. 87–114; Groenewegen (1992), pp. 1–17.
28. Tool (1993a), pp. 325–49.
29. Ramstad (1993), pp. 173–233.
30. LeGrand (1982).
31. Tool, ch. 5 in this volume.
32. Hayden (1984), pp. 273–6.
33. Trebing (1988), pp. 289–319.
34. Tawney (1962), pp. 55–62.
35. Marx (1906), pp. 197–341.
36. Dugger (1989).
37. A particularly thoughtful discussion of this matter is provided by Wojtyna (1991).
38. Habermas (1975).
39. Hickerson (1988), pp. 167–93.
40. Bush (1988), pp. 125–66; Bush (1989), pp. 455–64.
41. Dewey in Ratner (1939), p. 400.
42. Ibid, p. 401.
43. Dewey; quoted by Westbrook (1991), p. 415.
44. Myers (1956), pp. 236–43.
45. Tool [1979] (1985), p. 293.
46. Tool (1994).
47. Sachs (1993), p. 5.
48. Tool [1979] (1985), pp. 300–306.
49. Tool (1993b), pp. 127–31.
50. Bush (1986), pp. 25–45.
51. Curry (1989), p. 1087; Streeten (1981).
52. Gough (1994), pp. 25–66.
53. Doyal and Gough (1991), p. 56.
54. Ibid, p. 60.
55. Gough (1994), p. 28. See also United Nations Development Programme (1993) for information on measuring and comparing national levels of provision of the material means of life.
56. Doyal and Gough (1991), p. 74.
57. Tool [1979] (1985), pp. 310–14.
58. Swaney and Olson (1992), pp. 1–25.
59. Brown (1993), p. 19.
60. Michels [1915] (1949).
61. Hobbes in Sabine (1937), p. 463.
62. Keynes (1936); Dillard (1980), pp. 255–74; Dillard (1987), pp. 1575–86.
63. Foster (1981a), pp. 929–35.
64. Ibid, p. 932.
65. Ibid, p. 933.
66. Ibid, pp. 933–4.
67. Ibid, pp. 934–5.
68. Girvetz (1963), pp. 27–47.
69. On the 'Costs of Rationality', see Lane (1991), pp. 43–57.
70. Sachs (1991a), p. 30; Sachs (1993), p. xiii.
71. Sachs (1991b), pp. 317–18.
72. Sachs (1991a), p. 29.

73. Dopfer (1991), p. 542.
74. Ibid.
75. On axiomatic preference theory, see Newman (1965).
76. Dietz (1975), pp. 93–127.
77. Hayek (1948), pp. 94–106.
78. Friedman (1962), p. 2.
79. Sachs (1992), pp. 43–54.
80. Lipton and Sachs (1990b), pp. 293–341.
81. Kregel and Matzner (1992), p. 35.
82. Lipton and Sachs (1990a), pp. 75–147; Lipton and Sachs (1990b), pp. 293–334; Sachs (1991a), pp. 26–34; and Sachs (1992), pp. 43–48.
83. Sachs (1991a), pp. 27–8.
84. Ibid, pp. 27–30.
85. Sachs (1993), p. 79 and passim.
86. Tool (1986), pp. 181–202.
87. Here again, I remind the reader that the work of the neoclassical 'new institutionalists' is not considered in this chapter.
88. Sachs (1993), pp. 26–34.
89. Polanyi [1944] (1957), pp. 130–50; Neale (1991), pp. 467–73.
90. Kregel and Matzner (1992), p. 34.
91. Sachs (1992), pp. 43–8.
92. Ibid, p. 45.
93. Rothschild (1994), pp. 175.
94. Klein (1980), pp. 871–3.
95. Spulber (1989), pp. 38–9.
96. Girvetz (1963), pp. 65–89.
97. Hayek (1944).
98. Typical in the Western European and Japanese economies in the 1950s and 1960s and in Pacific Rim economies in the 1970s and 1980s. Amsden (1989); Wade (1990).
99. Sachs (1992), pp. 43–6.
100. Sachs (1991a), p. 28.
101. Ostas (1992), pp. 513–23.
102. Sachs (1991a), p. 29.
103. Ibid.
104. Ibid, p. 26.
105. Lipton and Sachs (1990b), p. 293.
106. Arestis (1994), pp. 31–5.
107. Sachs (1992), p. 44.
108. Ibid, p. 47.
109. John Henry (1993), personal correspondence.
110. Lipton and Sachs, (1990b); comments by Lawrence H. Summers, pp. 334–8.
111. Sachs (1991a), p. 31.
112. Foxley (1983).
113. Tool (1986), pp. 113–14.
114. Coase (1992), p. 714.
115. Tool (1986), pp. 114–15.
116. Becker (1932).
117. Tool (1986), pp. 116–17.
118. Sachs (1992), pp. 43–54.
119. Tool (1986), pp. 117–22.
120. Sachs (1991a), pp. 27–8.
121. Ibid.
122. Ibid.
123. Kregel, Matzner and Grabher (1992).

REFERENCES

Amsden, Alice (1989), *Asia's Next Giant: South Korea and Late Industrialization*, New York: Oxford University Press.

Arestis, Philip (1994), 'Macroeconomic Policy II', in Geoffrey M. Hodgson, Warren J. Samuels and Marc R. Tool (eds), *The Elgar Companion to Institutional and Evolutionary Economics*, Aldershot: Edward Elgar. Hereafter cited as *The Elgar Companion*.

Becker, Carl (1932), *The Heavenly City of the 18th Century Philosophers*, New Haven: Yale University Press.

Beije, Paul R. and Groenewegen, John (1992), 'A network analysis of markets', *Journal of Economic Issues*, **26**, March.

Brown, Lester R. (1993), 'What on earth is the world coming to?', *Manchester Guardian Weekly*, 8 August.

Bush, Paul D. (1986), 'On the concept of ceremonial encapsulation', *Review of Institutional Thought*, **3**, December.

Bush, Paul D. (1988), 'The Theory of Institutional Change', in Marc R. Tool (ed.), *Evolutionary Economics I: Foundations of Institutional Thought*, Armonk, N.Y.: M.E. Sharpe.

Bush, Paul D. (1989), 'The concept of "progressive" institutional change and its implications for economic policy formation', *Journal of Economic Issues*, **23**, June.

Coase, R.H. (1992), 'The institutional structure of production', *American Economic Review*, **82**, September.

Curry, Robert L. Jr. (1989), 'The basic needs strategy, the Congressional mandate, and US foreign aid policy', *Journal of Economic Issues*, **23**, December.

Dewey, John (1939), 'The Democratic Form', in Joseph Ratner (ed.), *Intelligence in the Modern World: John Dewey's Philosophy*, New York: Modern Library.

Dietz, Gottfried (1975), *In Defense of Property*, Baltimore: Johns Hopkins University Press.

Dillard, Dudley (1980), 'A monetary theory of production: Keynes and the institutionalists', *Journal of Economic Issues*, **14**, June.

Dillard, Dudley (1987), 'The evolutionary economics of a monetary economy', *Journal of Economic Issues*, **21**, June.

Dopfer, Kurt (1991), 'Toward a theory of economic institutions', *Journal of Economic Issues*, **25**, June.

Doyal, Len and Gough, Ian (1991), *A Theory of Human Need*, New York: Guilford Press.

Dugger, William M. (1989), *Corporate Hegemony*, New York: Greenwood Press.

Eatwell, John, Milgate, Murray and Newman, Peter (1987) (eds), *The New Palgrave: A Dictionary of Economics*, New York: Stockton Press.

Ericson, Richard E. (1991), 'The classical soviet-type economy: nature of the system and implications for reform', *Journal of Economic Perspectives*, **5**, Fall.

Fischer, Stanley (1993), 'Socialist economy reform: lessons of the first three years', *American Economic Review*, **83**, May.

Foster, J. Fagg (1981a), 'The theory of institutional adjustment', *Journal of Economic Issues*, **15**, December.

Foster, J. Fagg (1981b), 'Current structure and future prospects of institutional economics', *Journal of Economic Issues*, **15**, December.

Foxley, Alejandro (1983), *Latin American Experiments in Neoconservative Economics*, Berkeley: University of California Press.

Friedman, Milton (1962), *Capitalism and Freedom*, Chicago: University of Chicago Press.

Galbraith, John Kenneth (1967), *The New Industrial State*, Boston: Houghton Mifflin.

Galbraith, John Kenneth (1973), *Economics and the Public Purpose*, Boston: Houghton Mifflin.

Galbraith, John Kenneth [1952] (1980), *A Theory of Price Control*, Cambridge: Harvard University Press.

Girvetz, Harry K. (1963), *The Evolution of Liberalism*, New York: Collier Books.

Gough, Ian (1994), 'Economic institutions and the satisfaction of human needs', *Journal of Economic Issues*, **28**, March.

Groenewegen, John (1992), 'The European answers to dilemmas of competition, cooperation and mergers', a paper presented at meetings of the Association for Evolutionary Economics, New Orleans, January.

Habermas, Jürgen (1975), *Legitimation Crisis*, Boston: Beacon Press.

Hayden, F. Gregory (1984), 'A Geobased National Agricultural Policy for Rural Community Enhancement, Environmental Vitality, and Income Stabilization', in Marc R. Tool (ed.), *An Institutionalist Guide to Economics and Public Policy*, Armonk, N.Y.: M.E. Sharpe.

Hayek, Friedrich A. (1944), *The Road to Serfdom*, Chicago: University of Chicago Press.

Hayek, Friedrich A. (1948), *Individualism and Economic Order*, Chicago: University of Chicago Press.

Hickerson, Steven R. (1988), 'Instrumental Valuation: The Normative Compass of Institutional Economics', in Marc R. Tool (ed.), *Evolutionary Economics I: Foundations of Institutional Thought*, Armonk, N.Y.: M.E. Sharpe.

Hobbes, Thomas; quoted by George H. Sabine (1937) in *A History of Political Theory*, New York: Henry Holt.

Hutton, Will (1993), 'Free marketeers ignore Russia's real needs', *Manchester Guardian Weekly*, 4 April.

Jensen, Hans E. (1988), 'The Theory of Human Nature', in Marc R. Tool (ed.), *Evolutionary Economics I: Foundations of Institutional Thought*, Armonk, N.Y.: M.E. Sharpe.

Keynes, John Maynard (1936), *The General Theory of Employment, Interest and Money*, New York: Harcourt Brace.

Klein, Philip A. (1980), 'Confronting power in economics: a pragmatic evaluation', *Journal of Economic Issues*, **14**, December. Reprinted in Philip A. Klein (1994), *Beyond Dissent: Essays in Institutional Economics*, Armonk, N.Y.: M.E. Sharpe.

Kregel, Jon A. and Matzner, Egon (1992), 'Agenda for the reconstruction of Central and Eastern Europe', *Challenge Magazine*, **35**, September/October.

Kregel, Jon A., Matzner, Egon and Grabher, Gernot (1992) (eds), *The Market Shock: An AGENDA for the Economic and Social Reconstruction of Central and Eastern Europe*, Vienna: Austrian Academy of Sciences; Research Unit for Socio-Economics.

Lane, Robert E. (1991), *The Market Experience*, Cambridge: Cambridge University Press.

LeGrand, Julian (1982), *The Strategy of Equality: Redistribution and the Social Services*, London: George Allen & Unwin.

Lipton, David and Sachs, Jeffrey (1990a), 'Creating a Market Economy in Eastern Europe: The Case of Poland', in William C. Brainard and George L. Perry (eds), *Brookings Papers on Economic Activity I*, Washington, D.C.: Brookings Institution.

Lipton, David and Sachs, Jeffrey (1990b), 'Privatization in Eastern Europe: The Case of Poland', in William C. Brainard and George L. Perry (eds), *Brookings Papers on Economic Activity II*, Washington, D.C.: Brookings Institution.

Marx, Karl (1906), *Capital*, New York: Charles H. Kerr (Modern Library reprint).

Michels, Roberto [1915] (1949), *Political Parties: A Sociological Study of the Oligarchical Tendencies of Modern Democracies*, trans. by Paul, Eden and Cedar, Glencoe, Ill.: Free Press.

Munkirs, John R. (1985), *The Transformation of American Capitalism*, Armonk, N.Y.: M.E. Sharpe.

Munkirs, John R. and Sturgeon, James I. (1985), 'Oligopolistic cooperation: conceptual and empirical evidence of market structure evolution', *Journal of Economic Issues*, **19**, December.

Myers, Francis M. (1956), *The Warfare of Democratic Ideals*, Yellow Springs, Ohio: Antioch Press.

Neale, Walter C. (1988), 'Institutions', in Marc R. Tool (ed.), *Evolutionary Economics I: Foundations of Institutional Thought*, Armonk, N.Y.: M.E. Sharpe.

Neale, Walter C. (1991), 'Society, state and market: a Polanyian view of current change and turmoil in Eastern Europe', *Journal of Economic Issues*, **25**, June.

Newman, Peter (1965), *The Theory of Exchange*, Englewood Cliffs, N.J.: Prentice-Hall.

North, Douglass C. (1990), *Institutions, Institutional Change and Economic Performance*, Cambridge: Cambridge University Press.

Ostas, Daniel T. (1992), 'Industrial reform in East-Central Europe: Hungarian and Polish contract law', *Journal of Economic Issues*, **26**, June.

Polanyi, Karl [1944] (1957), *The Great Transformation*, New York: Rinehart and Co.

Ramstad, Yngve (1993), 'Institutional Economics and the Dual Labor Market Theory', in Marc R. Tool (ed.), *Institutional Economics: Theory, Method, Policy*, Dordrecht: Kluwer Academic Publishers.

Ratner, Joseph (1939), *Intelligence in the Modern World: John Dewey's Philosophy*, New York: Random House (Modern Library reprint).

Reagan, Michael D. (1963), *The Managed Economy*, New York: Oxford University Press.

Rothschild, Kurt W., (1994), 'Power II', in Geoffrey M. Hodgson, Warren J. Samuels and Marc R. Tool (eds), *The Elgar Companion*, Aldershot: Edward Elgar.

Sabine, George H. (1937), *A History of Political Theory*, New York: Henry Holt and Co.

Sachs, Jeffrey (1991a), 'Crossing the valley of tears in East European reform', *Challenge Magazine*, **34**, September/October.

Sachs, Jeffrey (1991b), 'Spontaneous privatization: a comment', *Soviet Economy*, **7**, (4).

Sachs, Jeffrey (1992), 'Privatization in Russia: some lessons from Eastern Europe', *American Economic Review*, **82**, May.

Sachs, Jeffrey (1993), *Poland's Jump to the Market Economy*, Cambridge: MIT Press.

Spulber, Daniel F. (1989), *Regulation and Markets*, Cambridge: MIT Press.

Streeten, Paul *et al.* (1981), *First Things First: Meeting Basic Needs and Sustainable Growth*, London: Oxford University Press.

Swaney, James A. and Olson, Paulette I. (1992), 'The economics of biodiversity: lives and lifestyles', *Journal of Economics Issues*, **26**, March.

Tawney, R.H. [1926] (1962), *Religion and the Rise of Capitalism*, Gloucester, Mass.: Peter Smith.

Thompson, Grahame F. (1991), 'The evolution of the managed economy in Europe', a paper presented at meetings of the European Association for Evolutionary Political Economy, Vienna, November.

Tool, Marc R. [1979] (1985), *The Discretionary Economy: A Normative Theory of Political Economy*, Boulder: Westview Press.

Tool, Marc R. (1986), *Essays in Social Value Theory*, Armonk, N.Y.: M.E. Sharpe.

Tool, Marc R. (1993a), 'Pricing and valuation', *Journal of Economic Issues*, **27**, June (Chapter 4 in this volume).

Tool, Marc R. (1993b), 'The Theory of Instrumental Value: Extensions, Clarifications', in Marc R. Tool (ed.), *Institutional Economics: Theory, Method, Policy*, Dordrecht: Kluwer Academic Publishers.

Tool, Marc R. (1994), 'An Institutionalist Mode of Inquiry: Limitations of Orthodoxy', in Philip A. Klein (ed.), *The Role of Economic Theory*, Dordrecht: Kluwer Academic Publishers (Chapter 2 in this volume).

Trebing, Harry M. (1988), 'Regulation of Industry: An Institutionalist Approach', in Marc R. Tool (ed.), *Evolutionary Economics II: Institutional Theory and Policy*, Armonk, N.Y.: M.E. Sharpe.

United Nations Development Programme (1993), *Human Development Report*, New York: Oxford University Press.

Wade, Robert (1990), *Governing the Market: Economic Theory and the Role of Government in East Asian Industrialization*, Princeton: Princeton University Press.

Westbrook, Robert B. (1991), *John Dewey and American Democracy*, Ithaca: Cornell University Press.

Wojtyna, Andrzei (1991), 'In search of a new economic role of the state in the post-socialist countries', paper presented at meetings of the European Association for Evolutionary Political Economy, Vienna, November.

10. A synthetic analysis of economic systems*

This chapter, although not originally written as such, provides a useful summary and review for the volume as a whole. Many of the major concepts, constructs and themes of earlier chapters are here presented in more of an advocacy format.

My primary focus will be (1) on several areas of judgmental responsibility that discretionary agents in any economic system will necessarily confront in problem-solving endeavours, and (2) on neoinstitutionalist approaches to, and modes of inquiry for, investigating such areas of judgmental concern.

Most large modern communities are continuously trying to develop and sustain viable, well functioning economies. The task of formulating theory to guide the framing of policy to achieve such an outcome is, of course, omnipresent. Neoinstitutionalists believe that they can constructively contribute to this unending deliberative dialogue. Continuing questions are posed; provisional neoinstitutionalist responses are made. The topics addressed below include an economy's public purposes, structural character, resource creation, productive organization, market structure and price determination, income distribution, governmental roles and interest group involvement. The chapter concludes with some cautionary admonitions.

PROLOGUE FOR AN OVERVIEW

All economies are discretionary. All existing systems, although appearing as mainly customary complexes, necessarily exhibit an institutional structure determined by prior choices. Those earlier choices may have reflected an intention to follow traditional ways, to implement ideological recipes, to conform to an alleged natural design or to solve problems pragmatically. But all systems can be, and are, transformed through human agency. Most are constantly in a state of flux which can be directed to serve human purposes more adequately.

*Paper presented at meetings of the European Association for Evolutionary Political Economy, Vienna, November 1991.

All systems are in considerable measure idiosyncratic. While much can be learned or borrowed from other systems, people of each culture or social order must determine their own path to economic growth and development. What an economy has been and what it now is delimit in significant measure what it can become. All economies are discretionary, then, but that discretion is always constrained.

The analysis of discretionary economies is necessarily both normative and positive. Since the purpose of inquiry in economics has always been to help the community understand and resolve problems arising in the provisioning process, such inquiry is value laden. The identification of a problem requires that a distinction be made between 'what is' and 'what ought to be'. Analysis of economic systems is undertaken in an effort to improve their provisioning performance; that is, to come to know how they *ought* to change in order to enhance performance.

HOW SHALL PUBLIC PURPOSES BE DEFINED?

The following statements of public purposes reflect conceptions of 'oughtness'. All are necessary to the quest for enhanced and continuous well-being in a viable, functioning economy. They are neither hierarchical nor sequential in ordering. To pursue all purposes concurrently generates the most rapid and sustainable development of an economic system. These statements serve as criteria of achievement; they define the meaning of economic development; they identify what is meant herein by 'reform'.

- The generation of a technologically efficient, continuous and adequate flow of real income for the community generally is essential. Also implied are quality and variety in the provisioning of real products and services.
- The maximum development of each individual's potential to acquire knowledge and productive skills is essential. People are educable. A viable, functioning economy places very high priority on the educational development of community members. All individuals should be encouraged and empowered to develop fully their capabilities.
- The noninvidious treatment of people in all social, political and economic contexts is essential. Discrimination exists in all communities; it is grounded variously in race, gender, age, ancestry, ethnicity, caste, wealth and/or power; these are used as indices of relative merit or worth of individuals.[1] A viable, functioning economy will be enhanced by the continuing reduction of all such discriminatory determinants of participatory access in the economy and elsewhere.

- The aggressive pursuit of ecologically sensitive and environmentally supportive programmes by participants in the provisioning process is essential. Such pursuit is reflected, for example, in reduction of environmental hazards, reduced dependence on fossil fuels, preservation of life forms, conversion to organic agriculture, and recycling or safe disposal of wastes. What is required is coevolutionary (human and non-human) biotic development that in all important respects is sustainable. Ecological prudence and environmental stewardship are in no sense peripheral issues; they are at the heart of achieving and sustaining a viable, functioning economy.

- Increasing democratic determination of and control over productive and distributive activities are essential. Coercive organizational patterns are begrudged, resisted and inefficient. Participatory patterns encourage responsiveness, creativity and cooperation. With genuine choices, communities will continue pragmatically to insist upon policy revisions of productive and distributive arrangements until the incidences of flawed performance are diminished or removed. All those exercising discretion in redefining the character of the productive and distributive processes, then, must be held accountable by the community. For the exercise of power to be responsible, it must be insecure.[2]

- Reducing the degree and extent of inequality in income is essential. Access to money income in large measure defines the range of social choice available to individuals; it determines their economic freedom. While any quest for equal incomes would be utopian, a viable functioning economy should reduce the degree of inequality to what the general community regards as acceptable and fair. The negative impact on incentive and participation induced by wide inequality impairs productivity and adaptability in the economy.

HOW SHOULD THE STRUCTURAL TRANSFORMATION OF AN ECONOMY BE APPROACHED?

The causal determinants that generate pressure for economic change reflect substantive and pervasive failures to accomplish one or more of the foregoing public purposes. Recourse to reasoned discretion and feasible policies in pursuit of these public purposes has been absent, insufficient or deflected. In some general sense there is the recognition that the provisioning process has broken down; its operations have been impaired. There may be malfunctioning in significant sectors, disabling conflict among participant groups, mounting evidence of ecological assaults, lack of rapport among strategic institutions or internecine conflict between competing political cadres. The evidences of falling output, obstructed distribution, bread queues, underemployment and unemployment, deprivation of the young and old, environmental pollution, industrial conflict, etc, are all evidence of impairment.

At times, of course, natural disasters, destructive weather, or decimation of productive assets and people due to military conflict may cause significant impairment. While anticipatory and protective actions may reduce negative consequences, from the perspective of an economic policy analyst, these are largely non-discretionary.

More amenable to discretionary correction are such determinants as the ineptness of public and private leadership reflected, for example, in the mismanagement of resource creation and use; the pursuit of private goals of pecuniary aggrandizement and of increased authority at the expense of public purposes; and the attempted application of fatally flawed economic doctrine to problem areas for which it has little policy relevance.

Still another causative influence generating problems, ironically, can result from limited achievements in the provisioning process. Minor gains stimulate demands to accelerate the quest for major gains. Political unrest heightens when conditions are improving, but not fast enough. The growth of knowledge fosters awareness of the difference between what is and what might be. Demonstration effects (Galbraith) of differences between impressive achievements elsewhere and more modest ones at home may well fuel demands for domestic reform efforts.

Effectively to address the causal elements generating pressure for change requires that the *structural* character of the economic process be understood. Everywhere, institutions can be defined as socially prescribed and proscribed patterns of correlated behaviour and attitudes. They specify how individuals relate to one another in the performance of various productive activities. They organize and coordinate behaviour. They appear as laws, codes, rules, decrees, customs, contracts and agreements with which all are familiar. Problems take the form of structural breakdown, lack of rapport or disintegration in existing institutional arrangements.

Institutions become habitual. Most customary patterns are learned early and internalized, becoming part of an individual's ordinary behaviour patterns and attitudinal framework. Indeed, cultural conditioning (stipulated by the institutional structure) is a primary influence in the formation of personality and social identity. Existing structure tends, then, to be tradition-preserving, past-binding. Accordingly, policies purporting to change institutional structure will generally be resisted by those whose identities and power roles will thereby be threatened. Those introducing adjustments must be persistent in searching out feasible and humane, yet effective, ways of circumventing obstructive centres of non-accountable power.

The institutional fabric in any political economy is remarkably complex. Interrelations and interdependencies are everywhere. Analyses of institutional breakdowns or impairments, therefore, are never simple. A widening circle of consequences stems from virtually every significant alteration, for example, of the tax code, of property rights, of environmental regulations, of discretionary roles and the like. The nature of the change, the tracing of consequences, the implications of the shift and the assessment of outcomes become the primary objects of neoinstitutionalist inquiry. But how does one distinguish between progressive and regressive changes in the institutional fabric?

Neoinstitutionalists distinguish clearly between progressive and regressive change.[3] Progressive change is achieved with the use of reliable, warranted knowledge and technological innovations to fashion and implement institutional adjustments which serve or accomplish the public purposes identified above. Neoinstitutional economists refer to such choices as instrumental judgments.

Regressive change occurs when existing power systems, public and private, act to prevent or corrupt the growth of such knowledge and to prevent its use through intimidation or suppression on invidious grounds. Neoinstitutionalists refer to these choices of impairment as ceremonial judgments.

Institutional adjustments often occur in two stages.[4] In the first stage, power systems encapsulate new knowledge and technology, sequestering it sufficiently to prevent its use from becoming a threat to their own continuing ceremonial dominance. A second stage occurs when this ceremonial dominance is broken, usually through political reform, and when instrumental judgments in important areas begin to take precedence over and displace ceremonial judgments. Instrumental judgments are in effect liberated to permit achievement of public purposes.

It is important to recognize that progressive institutional change is not so much directional as it is conditional. It does not, for example, point to the realization of some previously assumed or designed capitalist or socialist model; rather it points to *conditions* conducive to enhanced and more frequent instrumental (in lieu of ceremonial) judgments. In addressing conditions, moreover, every problematic situation will have its own unique configuration of both ceremonially-warranted behaviour and instrumentally-warranted behaviour. Only extensive problem-focused inquiry, then, can identify the particular conditions of lack of rapport, disjunctions or impairments (rooted in ceremonially-warranted patterns) and recommend revisions that will be 'progressive' in the above sense.

Those framing policy alternatives as institutional adjustments to problematic conditions must recognize certain inherent limitations with which they must contend. These include the following.

First, available knowledge, broadly conceived, defines the range of options that may be considered. In a sense technology, defined as the growth and application of warranted knowledge, delimits what can be considered as feasible institutional change. Causal knowledge is never entirely adequate; consequences of actions can never be wholly anticipated beforehand. Nevertheless, the framing of proposed institutional adjustments must be based on the most comprehensive knowledge that can be mustered.

Second, those affected by proposed policy must be made cognizant of what changes are in store and what bearing they will have on their lives. They must be consulted and their participation solicited. Imposed reform from central authorities is often ineffectual and frequently resisted, especially if ceremonial indifference to the impact of consequences prevails.

Third, proposed institutional changes should be as 'minimally dislocative' as can be managed and still accomplish the instrumental function intended. In particular, disruption to areas of the political economy not considered problematic should be minimized. This implies that institutional reforms should generally be piecemeal and incremental rather than comprehensive. People can change some of their habitual economic ways of doing and thinking, often rapidly, if the second condition above is met. But because institutional arrangements become habitual and are internalized, demands for comprehensive or global recasting of habits and behaviours will generally prove impossible to implement.[5]

Fourth, the projected change must pass muster as environmentally and ecologically acceptable and must foster 'coevolutionary sustainability' (man and all other life forms) in the interdependent biotic community.[6] A failure to acknowledge this constraint over time seriously diminishes institutional options. Indeed, it can impede the realization of most other public purposes.

HOW CAN RESOURCE CREATION BE ENHANCED?

The contention that resources are discretionary, as are institutions, may still be novel for some. We are accustomed to thinking of resources as endowments and in analysis as being largely given. These views have long been outmoded. In fact, Zimmerman may have been the first to demonstrate that the premier resource in all cultures is the cumulative and usually accelerating growth of human knowledge.[7] Warranted knowledge and derivative technology *define* the resource base – physical, human and monetary. Expanding knowledge and technological breakthroughs can and do increase the resource base.

Elements of the earth's crust – oil sands, pitchblende, metallic ores, arable land, hardwood timber – are defined into the physical resource base by the technological demonstration of their physical character, properties and relevance for some productive purpose.[8] But without knowledge defining their pertinence and use, they are not economic resources. Material substances are constantly being defined into and out of the resource base. Economies will differ, obviously, on the presence or absence of currently defined resources. But given modern international interdependencies and capabilities, economic development is not necessarily precluded by the absence of 'endowed' resources.

Human resources are in large measure also discretionary. Although cultural and religious beliefs may be constraining, present knowledge permits significant increases (via public health measures) and decreases, or reductions in the rate of increase (via birth control) in the numbers of persons comprising a community. Discretionary judgments embodied in institutional forms may limit births, augment births or otherwise manipulate population levels. With the advent of the 'human capital theory', there is also wide understanding that productive skills and capabilities are created in people.[9] Lingual, manipulative, reflective, managerial and cognitive skills are all acquired, of course. Genetic endowments have a bearing on the potential direction and extent of human resource creation, noninvidiously conceived.

Finally, with regard to financial resources, discretionary agents in economic systems can formulate institutional ways of generating whatever monetary funding is required to accomplish the material provisioning activities the economy is otherwise equipped to undertake. At least since Keynes's *General Theory*,[10] the 'saving theory of progress' has been discredited; prior voluntary savings are not required to fund subsequent investment. An alternative *debt* theory of capital formation, contributed by institutionalists and Post Keynesians, explains how discretionary agents in endogenous institutional configurations generate the demand for and supply of monetary resources.[11] For a modern economy, scarcity of money funding need not be the defining constraint on development, although social control of debt-creating mechanisms is essential.

HOW SHOULD THE PRODUCTIVE PROCESS BE ORGANIZED?

To say that all major economies are now mixed economies is of course a cliché. The scholarly literature is replete with familiar distinctions between public and private enterprise, between corporate and non-corporate firms, among U, H and M forms of corporations, and between for-profit and not-for-profit organizations, among others.

But acknowledged diversity notwithstanding, major Western economies are, in differing ways, 'triadic':[12] each has (a) a public governmental sector with multiple autonomous functions and various regulatory roles; (b) a 'private' corporate sector comprised of cooperating megacorps, oligopolies and private central planning instruments that dominate most major extraction, production, communication, transport, distribution and financial functions; and (c) a very large number of smaller firms, variously constituted, mainly involved with final distributions and professional services. But the divisions are in no sense tidy or discrete. Overlaps, interdependencies, interpenetrations, intracoordinations, coercive connections and the like are legion. What needs emphasis, however, is that the modern political economy is a system of power.[13] Discretion over productive processes is held – and used – in all three sectors.

When one asks, then, how should the provisioning process be constituted institutionally, there is no simple or easy answer. Here especially, each community must accept the existing fabric as the starting point and, given its unique economic history, pursue alterations so as to achieve goals that serve or are at least compatible with public purposes. No recipes are available. Experience elsewhere can be instructive but not governing. Path-dependency habits cannot be permitted to stifle change; path-determining theory cannot provide a template; path-independency theory is largely irrelevant. No ism structure is relevant. Technology does not define needed structure, but it does transform the existential conditions that determine the range of choices as to which structural changes to introduce.

But here, as in much architecture, form should follow function. And the functions alluded to are the instrumental functions identified at the outset as public purposes. That is, revisions in the existing structure should alter conditions so as to enhance the provisioning process: increase its productive efficiency, provide educational infrastructure, generate environmental sensitivity, ensure noninvidious participatory involvement, provide mechanisms of control and accountability, and facilitate breadth and equity of distribution.

Incentives or motivations – all of which are acquired and patterned from the interaction of culture and individual – that undergird and stimulate initiatives for institutional change will necessarily be various. Some will be regressive; some progressive. The gamut will frequently include such mainly ceremonial motivations as singular maximization of pecuniary gains, establishment or restoration of status, rank or privilege, extension of discretion over others' behaviour, salvaging of tradition and/or the psychological 'high' of conflicts and contests. It may also include mainly instrumental motivations of active concern for the well-being of one's family and community, the pride of skilled workmanship, the growth of knowledge and capacity to manage and resolve problems, gratifications from providing leadership for the community's growth and development, facilitating the application of new knowledge to problem-solving responsibilities, and acquiring income to widen choices for constructive (instrumental) purposes.

Although these illustrative lists are, conceptually speaking, mutually exclusive, both sorts of motivations are routinely found in individual behaviour. Multiple motivations are almost certainly present in any given case. The practical recourse for those with discretion or influence is to seek ways to minimize the destructive consequences of ceremonial motivations and to encourage the substitution of instrumental ones. Since means chosen determine the character of consequences, ceremonial motivations are very likely to generate ceremonial consequences, not resolutions for real problems confronted.

WHAT ABOUT MARKETS AND PRICES?

In any viable, functioning economy, markets are essential. The fact that people live and mature only in social orders, in communities, in which conjoint provisioning is required for some major part of the flow of real income, requires commodity and service exchange among persons. As Hodgson has observed, 'markets … are organized and institutionalized exchange'. Markets are 'a set of social institutions in which a large number of commodity exchanges of a specific type regularly take place, and to some extent are facilitated and structured by those institutions'. Exchange, then, 'involves contractual agreement and the exchange of property rights, and the market consists in part of mechanisms to structure, organize, and legitimate these activities'.[14] Markets pattern exchange relationships; they coordinate exchange activity. They are institutional complexes amenable to analysis with regard to character, functioning and achievement, as with all other segments of the economy.

But what requires emphasis is that these organizing and institutionalized exchange arrangements are extraordinarily diverse and complex, perhaps involving prescriptive patterns from all three sectors in an economy. With exchange, discretion over the items involved is transferred. But that discretion will ordinarily be sanctioned and constrained by public authority, by corporate power, by labour laws, by customary rules, and the like.

Much of the observable exchange behaviour in markets is customary and habitual. So long as participants perceive no significant impairments to the provisioning process by such habitual exchange connections, they will continue. But markets are not isolated or insulated from ubiquitous change; they are the objects of legislation; they have an immediacy of impact on participants; they are significant structure everywhere in modern economies. Indeed, often the most obvious indicators of impairment or improvement in the provisioning process are rapid movements of market prices, however determined.

Markets, as institutional complexes, function in the pursuit of differing mixtures of ceremonial and instrumental warrant. Some exchange behaviour facilitates the provisioning process for participants, for example by providing warranted knowledge to inform purchasers concerning choices. Some impairs that provisioning process by false and misleading advertising and the promotion of carcinogenic products. The difference is often a reflection of where control over market exchange structure resides and on whose behalf and for what sorts of purposes it is being used.

A number of strident-sounding claims can be made: all major markets in modern economies are managed; market power is widely held at all levels and is used. The neoclassical free market model is an illusion; it does not describe reality. Indeed, its present role is not to describe what is, but to serve as a normative ideal for what ought to be. Progress for the orthodox is movement towards that which more exactly approximates this Platonic ideal. This quest is a rather malign distraction in the real world of provisioning and managed markets.

As explored in previous chapters, one of the major instruments of market management has been and remains the power to set prices, albeit with some constraints. As Eichner remarked: '[C]ertain firms, by virtue of their size and dominant market position, have considerable discretion in setting prices. These are the megacorps which, with their administered pricing policies for financing growth and expansion have become the locus of decisionmaking within the decentralized system of private planning that operates within the US economy and now, increasingly, on a world-wide scale.'[15] Virtually all significant prices are administered by identifiable discretionary agents.[16] These pricing judgments reflect achieved economic power, exhibiting both the motivations and the goals of the decision agents, as with Galbraith's 'technostructure'.[17]

Those with pricing power must be held accountable to the general community, whether that discretion resides with obscure figures in megacorps, public agencies, private trade associations, unions or wherever. In some sectors, specific instruments of accountability have been devised, as with regulatory commissions; in other sectors, indirect controls serve this function, as with supply management in agriculture. But the exercise of pricing power, wherever it occurs, should be judged with reference to its contribution to the public purposes herein identified.

HOW SHOULD INCOME BE DISTRIBUTED?

Economists confront no more difficult question of analysis, exposition or recommendation. The significance of focusing on income distribution cannot be overstated. The forms and magnitudes of income received define the range of choices available to members in any exchange economy. They determine at what level people may live. Income levels define status, determine access to participation in various roles and groups, specify opportunity sets relating to education, housing, occupation, family sizes, longevity and more.

How should a community determine what shares of money and real income should go to whom? The answer historically provided by neoclassicism is largely discredited. The construct of a natural law, specifying that free competitive factor markets (if left unfettered) will return to each participant an income share equivalent to the market measured value of his/her contribution, was developed by John Bates Clark. It supports the neoclassical marginal productivity theory of distribution. This 'law' of 'equational justice' (Foster) provided a convenient apologia, both for accepting that income inequality was 'natural' and for avoiding governmental redistributive policies that would inject market imperfections. Since unfettered markets do not exist, the theory has become largely anachronistic and therefore irrelevant for the 'fettered' real world of collective bargaining, salary negotiations, legislative wage levels and limits, and administered income transfers.

It is a necessary but not sufficient answer for neoinstitutionalists to counter with the observation that most income distribution reflects traditional and habitual patterns. The cake of (distributive) custom is heavy indeed. Differential money income shares received by teachers and plumbers, CEOs and physicians, lawyers and clergy, or bricklayers and truck drivers reflect prior estimates of relative status and contributions. Existing income shares thus sometimes reflect past judgments of actual or presumed significance, for instance of surgical proficiencies, productive efficiencies, intellectual creativity, instructional skills, nurturing commitments, critical services and technical capacities. Income levels are in large measure culturally determined. Observed divergencies in cross-cultural comparisons of income levels for comparable professions are instructive on this point.

But for neoinstitutionalists, this is only part of the explanation. What must be emphasized is that distributive markets, like commodity markets, are *managed*. Prices paid for 'factor' services that are not merely customary are mainly administered by those who have acquired discretion over their own and often others' income shares. Economic power – discretion – is sought, acquired and utilized in the setting of income shares. Where does this discretion, with corresponding constraints, reside? In governmental bodies, in regulatory bodies, in corporate managerial centres, with the trade union leadership, in professional associations, with trade associations, with conglomerate or megacorp planning bodies and the like.

Most significant non-traditional determinations of income are either specified through public policy or negotiated among participant individuals and agencies. As examples, interest rates are mostly administered by monetary authorities; many wage rates are set via collective bargaining; price leadership in wage setting is commonplace, with major agreements setting patterns for the industry and beyond; profit rates are mainly administered as an aspect of setting selling prices; cost structures in public utilities are appraised by regulatory bodies; legislative rules define minimum wage levels and transfer income entitlements; tax laws specify tax expenditure subsidies (tax avoidance deductions). More generally, government policy determines where discretion over pricing will actually lie. However, only persistent inquiry will disclose where factor pricing power is held in particular cases and how it is being used.

But here as elsewhere for neoinstitutionalists, achieved economic power must be held accountable. Just as the medieval canonists decried avarice, usury and engrossing, so contemporary appraisers must determine what is a fair wage, a reasonable profit, a legitimate tax expenditure or an adequate transfer income. Even current interest in 'rent-seeking' behaviour reflects a tacitly normative concern.

Choices made in setting 'factor' returns must be judged by specific criteria. Those choices produce consequences that are observable and judicable. Value theory which explains constructive choice making is required. For neoinstitutionalists, the public purposes enumerated above indicate criteria by which distributional structure and outcomes may constructively be assessed.

WHAT FUNCTIONS SHOULD GOVERNMENTS PROVIDE?

From a neoinstitutionalist and democratic perspective, governments exist to facilitate the political process of determining and administering public policy. They possess the continuing powers of mandamus and injunction; indeed they are normally the primary repository of power or discretion in any major community. The 200 year nostalgic quest for *laissez-faire* does not foreclose governmental 'intrusion' and 'intervention'. The historic debate is not really over whether governments should intervene but rather on whose behalf and for what purposes. Of special import, however, is the recognition that governmental institutions usually provide the *only* mechanisms through which a community, through 'interventions', can seek continuously to adjust its operative institutional structure to resolve problematic impediments in the provisioning process. In brief, it is the task of governments to pursue instrumentally identified public purposes.

Of course, during its historical development, any political economy will have generated a unique and diverse array of governance institutions.

Taxonomies of forms go back at least to Aristotle. But whatever the character of that historical experience, all contemporary systems, whether authoritarian, democratic or a mixture of both, must continuously define and redefine what the structure and functions of government shall be. The agenda for government must constantly be rewritten. John Maynard Keynes's observation (via Bentham) of decades ago is still pertinent: 'Perhaps the chief task of Economists at this hour is to distinguish afresh the *Agenda* of Government from the *Non-Agenda*; and the companion task of Politics is to devise forms of Government within a Democracy which shall be capable of accomplishing the Agenda [emphasis in original]'.[18]

The economic 'agendas' of major Western governments would include promotion of education and growth of knowledge and technology, provision of public goods and services, macroeconomic stabilization, income redistribution, resource creation, defining and redefining property rights, regulating private and public power centres, ensuring an ecologically viable and sustainable environment, and legal and nonviolent resolution of disputes, among others. In pursuit of these functions, the drafting of budgets, in general and in particular, serve as de facto planning instruments determining (well or poorly) to what ends and through what means the communal provisioning efforts will be directed.

Central also is the recognition that since governments possess preeminent power, the design and implementation of mechanisms for holding them accountable is a critical and unending responsibility. Holders of power, public and private, may well come to define themselves with reference to that power. They may well resist change for fear of losing their sense of who and what they are. *Holding power is a major conditioner of subsequent behaviour*; it provides status and identity. Concern with retention of power often overrides commitment to public purposes. Some political figures, who are invidiously motivated, will lie, misrepresent issues and proposals, sabotage deliberative processes, manipulate individuals and use their positions to support private interests and ceremonial goals. Other holders of power, with instrumental commitments, will perceive their responsibilities as those of imaginative initiators of reform proposals in pursuit of public purposes, as educators in public policy, as problem-solving analysts and technicians, as stewards of the public interest willing continuously to have their performance assessed through accountability instruments. Did they use power in creative and progressive ways? Some will exhibit elements of each pattern of behaviour. But only those behaviours directed to imaginative problem-solving can provide for the continuity and instrumental efficiency of the provisioning process.

WHAT ABOUT ECONOMIC INTEREST GROUPS?

Three clarifying disclaimers are in order in considering the significance of economic interest groups; all are to some extent critical of neoclassical positions. First, the possession and use of economic power is not as such a matter of pathology or abhorrence. The presumption that the zero-power, free price-competitive neoclassical market can serve as an analytical model for contemporary economies has long since been rejected by practicing policy-oriented economists. Power cannot by fiat be driven from the conceptual temple. Power is acquired, held and used in both private and public sectors.

Second, given the fact that markets imply power, accountability can never be enhanced by movements towards free competitive markets. Market participants seek and use power to reduce insecurity; they have no other way of generating sufficient predictability of outcomes and security of expectations which allow them to produce and distribute a product or service. Entrepreneurs have been among the chief saboteurs of a free market system; their behaviour does not follow ideological rhetoric.

Third, the somewhat imperialistic efforts of neoclassicists to explain the political process through the use of the microeconomic model – with its constructs of rationality, maximization and the like – reveals little about the actual deliberative political process. The political process is not the counterpart of a market; for one thing, motivations are much more complex. The legislative bodies are not simply or primarily brokerage houses in which private economic interests are traded and balanced off against each other.[19] There is no real balancing of interests in the search for some sort of equilibrium condition. Although political reform is often needed to restore or enhance the problem-solving contributions and accountability mechanisms of the political process, its substance is not addressed in the neoclassical approach. The market model is ill-adapted to this analytical challenge.

Are there organized economic interest groups seeking legislative relief and favours? Of course. There are many such 'vested interests'. In Veblen's usage, such interest groups have acquired a legal right to get something for nothing.[20] Representatives of such groups, often constituting a 'third house' of the legislatures, lobby legislators hard in pursuit of their private interests, claiming of course that these coincide with the public interest. Some buy access to legislators through political contributions. Some legislators, in turn, become their lackeys. But buying votes remains illegal and for instrumental reasons; it corrupts the deliberative process, making genuine problem solving more difficult and remote.

Government's role is neither to defer to nor appease the private use of economic power in political settings. Communities, through their governments, must find effective ways for holding the private use of economic power accountable. There is no other arena in which this task can be approached. It is done by public government or it is not done at all. So-called free markets do not provide accountability.

Governments are not without accountability instruments, four of which can be mentioned here. First is public exposure. Most private interests wish to withhold from public view their efforts to 'gain' at public expense, fearing repercussions. Second, governments can use their taxing powers to direct investment expenditures, to expose frauds, to aid and abet environmentally sound production measures and the like. Third, governments can directly mandate those behaviours it prefers, or enjoin those it does not, through legislative constraints and stipulations. Drug marketing is an example. Finally, governments can and have set up formal bodies, such as regulatory commissions, to supervise and constrain private productive performance, to administer prices, regulate technological expansion, and the like.

Will private economic interest groups find ways to evade or avoid regulatory measures? Of course. Part of the continuing agenda of government is to discern developments and to update and modify its tactics for the public control of private enterprise, as the occasion requires. That this issue has been significantly ignored in the US and some other countries in the last two decades does not erode its significance. It only suggests that ideologically oriented governmental performance is no more successful than ideologically 'designed' economies in supporting public purposes through the provisioning process.

WHAT PROCEDURAL COUNSEL IS OFFERED?

Among a larger number of recommendations that merit consideration, only three cautionary admonitions are offered as a provisional conclusion.

First, 'do not block the way of inquiry'.[21] It is absolutely essential to keep open the pursuit of warranted knowledge. Clearly implied at every point above is the recognition that only through continuing, instrumental and pragmatic inquiry can relevant questions be posed and answers be generated. Academic and intellectual freedom to think, propose, assess and recommend is quite simply a *sine qua non* of any credible transformation of an economic system. Those in governmental bodies or private power centres who withhold information, sequester technological breakthroughs, forestall research, suppress dissent, intimidate investigators, threaten severance of employment connections and authoritatively impose their own wills on inquiry, are primary saboteurs of the political economy. Through available and constructive means, the inquiry process must be kept open, 'unfettered' and productive.

Second, 'do not make normative use of any idealistic model'. The quest for, say, a capitalist or socialist model can only corrupt the factual and analytical scholarship required to address and resolve problems. The institutional adjustments needed in any particular context (place and time) can *only* be fashioned by fully confronting the actual determinants of the problems impairing the provisioning process. Nor can pre-packaged institutional prescriptions be devised now which will be relevant two, five or ten years hence. Structural change must be problem specific. This suggests that the Western so-called 'free market' system, with its a priori institutional structure, is not a ready-made substitute for the now failing comprehensive 'planning' systems. Friedman cannot replace Marx, however much one might wish it.

Third, 'do not seek reform through undemocratic means'. Only governance by consent can lay claim to legitimacy because it is demonstrably the only method through which the above-mentioned public purposes can be realized. As Foster observed: '[T]he idea of democracy already has won. No one now seriously dares to bid for active support from the rest of the world under any other banner. ... [D]emocracy must be the spelling on whatever banners are carried.'[22]

Where the democratic banner reflects reality – where political accountability exists – discretionary judgments concerning the adequacy of institutional adjustments are continuously available. Analysts of economic systems must be wary, then, of those who identify their own private interests as surrogates for the public interest. What is good for 'the rich, the wise and the well-born' may not be 'good' for the community. What is in the narrow interests of megacorps, of controlling political parties or ethnic majorities may not ensure an efficient and equitable provisioning process for the whole community. An emerging collective sense of the meaning and importance of serving the public interest, non-invidiously identified, in pursuit of identified public purposes is what waving the banner of democracy is all about.

NOTES

1. Veblen (1934), p. 34.
2. Nader (1971), p. F9.
3. Bush (1988), pp. 1437–59.
4. Ibid.
5. Foster (1981a), pp. 923–35.
6. Swaney (1988), pp. 321–34.
7. Zimmerman (1951), p. 10.
8. DeGregori (1985).
9. Briggs (1988), pp. 257–90.
10. Keynes (1936), pp. 372–7.
11. Ranson (1988), pp. 315–28; Wray (1991), pp. 951–75.
12. Munkirs (1990), pp. 347–54.
13. Tool and Samuels (1989); Peterson (1988).
14. Hodgson (1988), p. 174.

15. Eichner (1988), p. 138.
16. Means (1963), pp. 213–39.
17. Galbraith (1967).
18. Keynes (1926), pp. 40–41.
19. Livingston and Thompson (1971), pp. 103–51.
20. Veblen (1946).
21. Peirce (1955), p. 54.
22. Foster (1981b), p. 976.

REFERENCES

Briggs, Vernon M. Jr. (1988), 'Human Resources Development', in Marc R. Tool (ed.), *Evolutionary Economics I: Foundations of Institutional Thought*, Armonk, N.Y.: M.E. Sharpe.

Bush, Paul D. (1988), 'The Theory of Institutional Change', in Marc R. Tool (ed.), *Evolutionary Economics I: Foundations of Institutional Thought*, Armonk, N.Y.: M.E. Sharpe.

DeGregori, Thomas (1985), *A Theory of Technology*, Ames: Iowa State University Press.

Eichner, Alfred S. (1988), 'Prices and Pricing', in Marc R. Tool (ed.), *Evolutionary Economics II: Institutional Theory and Policy*, Armonk, N.Y.: M.E. Sharpe.

Foster, J. Fagg (1981a), 'The theory of institutional adjustment', *Journal of Economic Issues*, **15**, December.

Foster, J. Fagg (1981b), 'The United States, Russia, and democracy', *Journal of Economic Issues*, **15**, December.

Galbraith, John Kenneth (1967), *The New Industrial State*, Boston: Houghton Mifflin.

Hodgson, Geoffrey M. (1988), *Economics and Institutions*, Cambridge: Polity Press.

Keynes, John Maynard (1926), *The End of Laissez Faire*, London: Hogarth Press.

Keynes, John Maynard (1936), *The General Theory of Employment, Interest and Money*, New York: Harcourt Brace.

Livingston, John C. and Thompson, Robert G. (1971), *The Consent of the Governed*, 3rd ed., New York: Macmillan.

Means, Gardiner C. (1963), 'Pricing Power and the Public Interest', in US Senate, Committee on Judiciary, Subcommittee on Antitrust and Monopoly, *Administered Prices: A Compendium on Public Policy*, 88th Cong., 1st sess., Washington, D.C.: US Government Printing Office.

Munkirs, John R. (1990), 'The triadic economy', *Journal of Economic Issues*, **24**, June.

Nader, Ralph (1971), *The New York Times*, 24 January.

Peirce, Charles Sanders (1955), 'The Scientific Attitude and Fallibilism', in Justus Buchler (ed.), *Philosophic Writings of Peirce*, New York: Dover Publications.

Peterson, Wallace C. (ed.) (1988), *Market Power and the Economy*, Boston: Kluwer Academic Publishers.

Ranson, T. Baldwin (1988), 'The Institutionalist Theory of Capital Formation', in Marc R. Tool (ed.), *Evolutionary Economics I: Foundations of Institutional Thought*, Armonk, N.Y.: M.E. Sharpe.

Swaney, James A. (1988), 'Elements of a Neoinstitutional Environmental Economics', in Marc R. Tool (ed.), *Evolutionary Economics II: Institutional Theory and Policy*, Armonk, N.Y.: M.E. Sharpe.

Tool, Marc R. and Samuels, Warren J. (eds) (1989), *The Economy as a System of Power*, New Brunswick: Transaction Publishers.

Veblen, Thorstein B. [1899] (1934), *The Theory of the Leisure Class*, New York: Modern Library.

Veblen, Thorstein B. [1919] (1946), *The Vested Interest and the Common Man*, New York: Viking Press.

Wray, L. Randall (1991), 'Saving, profits and speculation in capitalist countries', *Journal of Economic Issues*, **25**, December.

Zimmerman, Erich (1951), *World Resources and Industries*, New York: Harper and Bros.

Author index

Subject index